Bhajanamritam

Devotional songs of
Sri Mata Amritanandamayi

Volume 3

Mata Amritanandamayi Center
San Ramon, California, United States

Bhajanamritam
Volume 3

Published by:
Mata Amritanandamayi Center
P.O. Box 613
San Ramon, CA 94583-0613
USA

In India:
www.amritapuri.org
inform@amritapuri.org

In USA:
www.amma.org

In Europe:
www.amma-europe.org

Contents

The Significance of Devotional Singing	III-5
About Pronunciation	III-6
Preface	III-7
Bhajans	III-8
English bhajans	III-286
Ślokas and mantras	III-303
Index of Bhajans Volume 3	III-310

The Significance of Devotional Singing

"Darling children, to gain concentration in this spiritually dark age (Kali Yuga), bhajan is better than meditation. By loud singing, other distracting sounds will be overcome and concentration will be achieved. Bhajan, concentration, meditation, this is the progression. Children, constant remembrance of God is meditation.

If bhajan is sung without concentration, it is a waste of -energy. If sung with one-pointedness, such songs will benefit the singer, the listener and also Mother Nature. Such songs will awaken the listeners' minds in due course.

Bhajan is a spiritual discipline aimed at concentrating the mind on one's Beloved Deity. Through that one-pointedness, one can merge in the Divine Being and experience the Bliss of one's True Self.

It matters not whether one believes in Krishna or Christ, Mother Kali or Mother Mary; a formless God or even a flame, a mountain or an ideal such as world peace can be meditated upon while singing. By letting the mind expand in the sound of the divine chanting, each one can enjoy the peace born of one's inherent divinity."

—Sri Mata Amritanandamayi

About Pronunciation

The following key is for the guidance of those who are unfamiliar with the Sanskrit and Malayalam transliteration codes which are used in this book:

A	-as	a	in America
AI	-as	ai	in aisle
AU	-as	ow	in how
E	-as	e	in they
I	-as	ea	in heat
O	-as	o	in or
U	-as	u	in suit
KH	-as	kh	in Eckhart
G	-as	g	in give
GH	-as	gh	in loghouse
PH	-as	ph	in shepherd
BH	-as	bh	in clubhouse
TH	-as	th	in lighthouse
DH	-as	dh	in redhead
C	-as	c	in cello
CH	-as	ch-h	in staunch-heart
JH	-as	dge	in hedgehog
Ñ	-as	ny	in canyon
Ś	-as	sh	in shine
Ṣ	-as	c	in efficient
Ṅ	-as	ng	in sing, (nasal sound)
V	-as	v	in valley, but closer to a "w"
ZH	-as	rh	in rhythm, is somewhat a mixture of la and ya sounds, but the tongue does not touch the roof of the mouth.
R	is rolled.		

Vowels which have a line on top of them are long vowels, they are pronounced like the vowels listed above but are held for twice the amount of time.

The letters with dots under them (ṭ, ṭh, ḍ, ḍh, ṇ, l, ṣ) are palatal consonants; the ṭ, sounds almost like d. They are pronounced with the tip of the tongue against the hard palate. Letters without such dots are dental consonants and are pronounced with the tongue against the base of the teeth.

Preface

The songs in this book originally appear in Malayalam, Hindi, Sanskrit, Tamil, and English. The Indian languages were transliterated into the Latin script using the internationally accepted Sanskrit transliteration guide, or its Malayalam correlatives for the letters that do not exist in Sanskrit. Most words with more than five syllables were also separated to simplify singing.

The songs are formatted thus:

- The first word of a call and response sequence is capitalized.
- If the line is to be called but not responded to, "(call only)" will be written next to the line beginning with the capitalized word of the call; so it applies to the line or lines beginning with the capitalized word until the next capitalized word.
- The first verse is usually the chorus and it is sung after every verse unless there are other instructions after the verse(s).
- When the verse/line is to be sung by both the leader and the chorus, "(unison)" will appear at the end of the verse/line.
- If the response is different than the "call", what is to be responded will be indicated after the "call" line(s).
- Some songs have the option of being mainly "call only" or sung in unison; this is indicated by, "(call only/unison)."
- Any other variations are given in parenthesis. Namavalis — songs of the different names and attributes of the Divine — are more spontaneous in nature, that is, they tend to break off from the format into a more improvisational mood, be alert!

Bhajans

ADHARAM MADHURAM

Adharam madhuram vadanam madhuram
nayanam madhuram hasitam madhuram
Hṛdayam madhuram gamanam madhuram
mathurā dhipatē akhilam madhuram

Sweet are Your lips, sweet is Your face, sweet are Your eyes, sweet is Your smile, sweet is Your heart, sweet is Your gait, O Lord of Mathura, everything about You is sweet.

Vacanam madhuram caritam madhuram
vasanam madhuram valitam madhuram
Calitam madhuram bhramitam madhuram
mathurā dhipatē akhilam madhuram

Sweet are Your words, sweet is Your story, sweet are Your garments, sweet is Your presence, sweet are Your movements, sweet are Your roamings, O Lord of Mathura, everything about You is sweet.

Vēṇur madhurō rēṇur madhuraḥ
pāṇir madhuraḥ pādau madhuraḥ
Nṛtyam madhuram sakhyam madhuram
mathurā dhipatē akhilam madhuram

Sweet is Your flute, sweet is the dust of Your feet, sweet are Your hands, sweet are Your feet, sweet is Your dance, sweet is Your friendship, O Lord of Mathura, everything about You is sweet.

Gītam madhuram pītam madhuram
bhuktam madhuram suptam madhuram

Rūpam madhuram tilakam madhuram
mathurā dhipatē akhilam madhuram

Sweet is Your song, what is drunk by Thee is sweet, what is eaten by You is sweet and sweet is your sleep, Sweet is Your form, sweet is the mark on Your forehead, O Lord of Mathura, everything about You is sweet.

Karaṇam madhuram taraṇam madhuram
haraṇam madhuram smaraṇam madhuram
Vamitam madhuram śamitam madhuram
mathurā dhipatē akhilam madhuram

Sweet are Your works, sweet is Your conquest, sweet is Your theft, sweet is Your remembrance, sweet are Your offerings, sweet is Your cure, O Lord of Mathura, everything about You is sweet.

Gumjā madhurā mālā madhurā
yamunā madhurā vīcī madhurā
Salilam madhuram kamalam madhuram
mathurā dhipatē akhilam madhuram

Sweet is Your murmuring, sweet is Your garland, sweet is the Yamuna River, sweet are the waves, sweet is the water, sweet is the lotus flower, O Lord of Mathura, everything about You is sweet.

Gōpī madhurā līlā madhurā
yuktam madhuram bhuktam madhuram
Dṛṣṭam madhuram śiṣṭam madhuram
mathurā dhipatē akhilam madhuram

Sweet are the Gopis, sweet is Your divine sporting, sweet is Your union, sweet are Your experiences, what You behold is sweet, sweet are Your left overs, O Lord of Mathura, everything about You is sweet.

Gōpā madhurā gāvō madhurā
yaṣṭir madhurā sṛṣṭir madhurā
Dalitam madhuram phalitam madhuram
mathurā dhipatē akhilam madhuram

Sweet are the Gopas, sweet are the cows, sweet are the pearls around Your neck, sweet is Your creation, sweet are Your victories, sweet are Your jokes, O Lord of Mathura, everything about You is sweet.

ĀDI DIVYA JYŌTI MAHĀ

Ādi divya jyōti mahā kāḷi mā namō
Madhu śumbha mahiṣa marddini
mahā śaktayē namō

Salutations to You, O great Mother Kali, the Primordial divine Light, salutations to the great power, destroyer of the demons Madhu, Sumbha and Mahisha.

Brahmā viṣṇu śiva svarūpa
tvamna anyathā
Carā carasya pālikā
namō namaḥ sadā (2x)
Kāli mā namō

You are the very form of Brahma, Vishnu and Shiva, not different from them. O Protector of the entire creation, animate and inanimate, I always bow to You, O Mother Kali, my salutations unto You!

ĀDIMŪLA PARAM JYŌTI

Ādimūla param jyōti āzhimātē ūzhimātē
ādiyantam ezhātuḷḷa samsṛti mātē samsṛti mātē

Vēdasāra pālkkaṭalil udicciṭum jñāna sūryan
andhakāram akattunna nāḷ varillennō nāḷ varillennō

O Primordial Light! O Mother of the universe! You have no beginning or end. Will the day ever arrive when the sun of Vedantic knowledge will dawn and remove the darkness of my ignorance?

Kaṇṇunīril kaṭal cuttum niśvāsa kanal vātam
maṅgunnī dīpam ammē viracīṭunnu
Cuzhalavum cuzhalikkā taṭikkunnu naṭuṅgunnu
aṇayumī jīva dīpam kāttiṭuk ammē kāttiṭuk ammē

O Mother, this little light (individual soul) is threatened by the gathering storms of life's bleak experiences. It gets dimmer and dimmer and is in danger of being put out at any moment. Please keep a watchful eye over it, O compassionate Mother.

Kaṭal tāṇṭi karapattān ōṭivaḷḷam mātram ammē
kūṭevannu tuṇaykkuvān ārumill ammē
Vīṭaṇayān piṭaykkumen ārtta nādam kēḷkuvānāy
entamāntam jaganmātē pettatāyallē pettatāyallē

All I have is a tiny canoe which seems hardly adequate to take me across the ocean (of worldly existence). I am desperately trying to reach the shore and the safety of home, but there is none to listen to my cries for help. You are my Mother, the One who gave birth to me. I rely on You to save me. Why the delay to come to my aid?

Kuññe rumbin kālsva navum śraviccīṭum kṛpārāśē
ninṭe kuññin viḷi keḷkkān maṭiykka yennō
Viḷippōre rakṣa ceyyum gāyatrī dēvī nīyē
ennennum bhajikunnen śrī parāśakti śrī parāśakti

You are the Ocean of Compassion, who never misses even the sound made by the tiniest moving creature. Are You reluctant to respond to the cries of this child of Yours? You are the goddess Gayatri, the guardian of all those in need of help. I adore You always, O Supreme Sakti!

ĀDYAMĀY AMMA DARŚANAM

Ādyamāy amma darśanam tannū
caitanya dhanyamām citra tilude
manassile nombaram tīrtutannū amma
amma tan vaśyamām drişti yilūde
ādhyāmāy amma darśanam tannū

Mother gave me Her darshan (vision) for the first time through Her picture, vibrant with Consciousness. All the pain and sorrow of my heart was removed by Her captivating glance.

Āpattil ninn enne mōcitanākkiya
anubhavam ōrmayil otukki nirti
Ōru nāl ñān śrī vallikkāviletti
śri ammaye nērittu kānuvān

I treasured that experience in my memory and it protected me from all danger. One day, I came to Vallickavu to see Mother in Her physical form.

Tribhuvanam kākkunna māyā mahēśvari
tirtthātanan galil āyirunnu
Dēha milleṅgiḷum dēhitan sānnidhyam
darśana tullia muṇṭāyir unnu

However, the Supreme Goddess, the Enchantress of the Universe and Protector of the three worlds, was away on tour. Yet, though She was physically absent, I could feel Her presence. It was as if She was physically there.

Kanivintē kalavara kaṇṭu mataṅgumbōl
karalil kulirma nirañu ninnu
Varunne rakṣaki nintē nāmam
vārttan kazhiyunna tetra punyam

When I returned, having beheld that storehouse of compassion, my mind was immersed in a deep, soothing coolness. Oh Protector, living Goddess! It is only because of great punya (merit) that one is able to praise Your Names.

AJAM NIRVIKALPAM

Ajam nirvikalpam nirākāra mēkam
nirānandam ānandām advaita pūrṇam
param nirguṇam nirviśēṣam nirīham
para brahma rūpam gaṇēśam bhajēma!

Lord Ganesha I worship thee, unborn unmodified formless One, bliss beyond bliss, nondual whole, supreme attributeless, unqualified, of the form of supreme Brahman.

Guṇātīta mānam cidānanda rūpam
cidābhāsakam sarvagam jñāna gamyam
muni dhyēyamākāśa rūpam parēśam
para bhrahma rūpam gaṇēśam bhajēma!

Lord Ganesha I worship thee, whose nature transcends all qualities, who is of the form of knowledge and bliss, "pure consciousness appearing as something else", all-pervading, that which can be attained through knowledge, the object of meditation by ascetics, of the form of the sky, the supreme Lord, of the form of supreme Brahman.

Jagad kāraṇam kāraṇa jñāna rūpam
surādim mukhādim guṇēśam gaṇēśam
jagadvyāpinam viśva vandyam surēśam
para bhrahma rūpam gaṇēśam bhajēma!

Lord Ganesha I worship thee, the cause of the world, of the knowledge which is the ultimate cause, who originated from the face of the Gods (Parvati), the lord of attributes, pervading the whole universe, worshipped by all the Lords of Gods, of the form of Supreme Brahman.

AKATĀRIL ARIVINTE

Akatāril aṛivinte
naṛukānti parattum
anupama guṇa sadanē
amṛtēśvari ammē

O Mother Amriteshwari! Who is of incomparable virtues, who radiates the brilliance of knowledge in the inner heart.

Prakṛtē kṛtasukṛtē
gatiyaruḷuka cira sukhadē
Avirāmam mama hṛdi nī
teḷiyuka manaḥ sukhadē

O Performer of great and holy acts! O Blessed One! Lead me to the eternal goal of Realisation. Shine in my heart always, O Giver of mental happiness!

Ānanda ttiratalli
ātmāvil nirayū
ātaṅkakkaṭal tāṇṭān
pāram tuṇayaruḷū

Fill my Self raising the waves of bliss. Help me to cross over the ocean of sorrow.

Anaghē mṛdu hasitē
nutapari pālana rasikē
Praṇavē tava śubha dāyaka
prabha yennil coriyū

O sinless One with a sweet smile, who rejoices in protecting those who surrender. O Mother, the embodiment of Om, please shower Your auspicious light on me.

AKHILA MĀṆAMMA

Akhila māṇamma ātma jñāmaṇamma
ānandam varṣikkum megha māṇamma
Āśīrvādam tarum ārdra yāṇamma
amari yāṇamma amṛtānandamayi yāṇamma

Mother is all, Mother is Self-knowledge, the bliss showering clouds, the one who bestows blessings. Mother is immortal, the embodiment of immortal bliss.

Manassu koṇṭamma tan pādattil sparśicāl
hṛdayattil darśanam nalkum
Urukunna karaḷumāy guru nāmam uruviṭṭāl
arikil vannāśvāsam aruḷum amma

If you mentally touch Mother's feet, you will get Her darshan in your heart. If you whisper the Guru's name with an aching heart, Amma will come and console you.

Duḥkhaṅgaḷ tirumumbil kāṇiykka veykkukil
dānamāy dhairyam pakarnnu tarum
Janmavum karmavum janmattin kaṭamayāy
muṭaṅgāte tuṭarān paṛaññutarū

If you offer your sorrows to Amma, She will instil courage in you. Amma, teach me how to lead this life and perform my duties without ceasing.

ĀLAYA MAṆIŌSAI KĒKKUDAMMĀ

Ālaya maṇiōsai kēkkudammā kēkkudammā
Āṇḍhavan kuṛaḷ nammai azhaikkutammā
azhaikutammā
Aruḷmiku jyōti onru tōntutammā ammā
Ārumukham atilē kāṇudammā kāṇudammā

O Mother, the sound of the temple bells are being heard, the voice of God is beckoning us. A Divine Effulgence is being seen and in that light, the six faced Lord Muruga is visible.

Ōrāru mukhamum īrāṛu karamum
maravātu tuṇai nintu kākkudammā
Uyirāki uṭalāki uyir jñāna pazhamāki
guruvāki āṭkoḷḷum daivam ammā daivam ammā

Lord Muruga, who has six faces and twelve arms is protecting us always without fail. He has become our life, our bodies, the eternal self-knowledge and the Guru who grants refuge.

Muttāna muttu kumarā murukayyā vā vā
cittāṭum selva kumarā sintai-makizha vā vā

O dearest child Muruga, pearl of pearls, do come fast. Play in my mind, dear child Muruga, come fast to make my mind blissful.

Nīyāṭum azhakai kaṇṭu vēlāṭi varuku tayyā
Vēlāṭum azhakai kaṇṭu mayilāṭi varuku tayyā
Mayilāṭum azhakai kaṇṭu manamāṭi varuku tayyā
Mana māṭum azhakai kaṇṭu makkaḷ kūṭṭam varuku tayyā

Seeing Your beautiful dance, O Muruga, Your divine spear starts dancing. Seeing Your spear dance, Your peacock starts dancing. Seeing the beauty of the dance of Your peacock, my mind also feels blissful. Feeling the blissful condition of my mind, devotees start gathering.

Pannīril kuḷikka vaittu paṭṭāṭai uṭukka vaittu
Candanattāl cānteṭuttu aṅkam ellām pūśivaiyttu
Nīrpūśi tilakam vaittu neñcattil unnaivaiyttu
Anpu pūtta malarā lunnai arccippēn varuvāy appā

After bathing You in rose scented water and adorning You in silk, I decorate You applying sandal paste all over Your body, applying sacred ash and tilak on Your forehead. Then installing You in my heart, I shall worship You with flowers which have just blossomed today. Please do come, O Lord Muruga!

AMBA BHAVĀNI NIN AMBHŌJA

Amba bhavāni nin ambhōja nētrattin
santatānanda prakāśa dhāra
Ennila harnniśam samddīptam ākuvān
nin kazhalttār tozhunn ennum ennum

O Mother Bhavani, I bow at Your Lotus Feet always, for the ever blissful stream of light of Your lotus eyes, to illumine me day and night.

Sanmantra divya dhvani kaḷil tiṅgiṭum
nin dhanya snēha pīyuṣa rēṇu
Jīva cētassil patikkunna nēratt—
aṅgāmayān artthaṅgaḷ māññu pōkum

When the drop of nectarine love, which resides in the divine notes of auspicious mantras, spills on my consciousness, the ills and sorrows of my life will be dispelled.

Amba nin pāda praṇamya hṛttil tellu
samsāra paṅkam puraṇṭī ṭumō?
Ānanda tundila nākaṭṭe innu ñān
nin prēma sindhuvil muṅgi muṅgi

Mother! Will the heart that is consecrated at Your feet be ever tainted in the least by the stain of worldliness? Let me become intoxicated with bliss today, immersing again and again in Your ocean of Love.

AMBĀṬI KAṆṆĀ

Ambāṭi kaṇṇā ambāṭi kaṇṇā
ponnambāṭi kaṇṇā vā

O Kanna who resides in Ambadi, O dear Kanna, come!

Marataka maṇiyaṇi kiṅgiṇi kaivaḷa
kālttaḷa māril pūttā liyumay **(Ambāṭi ,**
varikari kanpoṭu gōpika māruṭe
karava layattil amarnu mayaṅgum
ambāṭi kaṇṇā **(Ambāṭi)**

O Krishna, who wears the girdle studded with emerald stones, bracelets, anklets and a flower garland, kindly come near me, You, who sleeps in the arms of Gopis.

Varik arikil vanamāli vaikāte varik arikil vanamāli
Gōpa vadhu jana mānasa
yamunā tīra vihārī tīra vihārī

Come near me without delay, O Vanamali (One who wears the garland of forest flowers), who sports on the banks of the Yamuna in the minds of the Gopis.

Gōvardhana giridhari gōpāla kṛṣṇa murārī
Sapta svaramaya jatikaḷ viṭartum
nṛtta mutirkkān ettuka nīyen
hṛttil orukkiya vēdiyil vēgam
ambāṭi kaṇṇā (Ambāṭi)

O Gopala! O Krishna! O Murari, who lifted the Govardhana mountain. O Kanna of Ambadi! Come quickly to the stage set in my heart, dancing to the musical notes.

Ōṭi varu nanda bālā arikil
ōṭi varu gōpa bālā
Ōmkāra poruḷ pāṭi yuṇarttum
muraḷī gāna vilōlā muraḷī gāna vilōlā

Come running near to me, O son of Nanda, come running, O cowherd boy, who awakens the meaning of Omkara through the melody of the flute.

Rāsa līla lōla kaṇṇā varunī gōkula bālā
Māmaka jīvita sangītāmṛta dhārayil āṭi pāṭi
kaḷiccu rasiccu varū nī ambāṭi kaṇṇā
(Ambāṭi Marakata)

Come O Kanna, who delights in playing the rasalila, O darling of Gokula, come playing, laughing, bathing, dancing and enjoying, in the flow of a nectarine stream of the music of my life.

AMBĒ MĀ JAGADAMBĒ MĀ

Ambē mā jagadambē mā (2x)
Amṛtāmayī ānandamayī amṛtānandamayī mā
Śāntimayī suhāsamayī amṛtānandamayī

Immortal and blissful Mother of the world, Mother of peace, Mother of beautiful smiles, Amritanandamayi.

Me hum anāth tū hī mātā
Māyātītā sadguru mātā
Vēd purān tū hī gītā
Amṛtāmayi ambē mā
Ambē mā jagadambē mā

I am an orphan and You are the Mother. Mother is the true Master, beyond maya. You are the Vedas and the Puranas, You alone are the Gita.

Vānī vīṇā pāni brahmāni
Lakṣmī nārāyaṇi mā kalyānī
Triśūla pāṇi ambā bhavāni
Amṛtāmayi ambē mā
Ambē mā jagadambē mā

Goddess of speech (Sarasvati) holding the veena, Lord Brahma's consort. Goddess Lakshmi, consort of Narayana (Vishnu), who bestows auspiciousness, holding the trident (trishul), consort of Shiva.

AMBIKĒ JAGADĪŚVARĪ

Ambikē jagadīśvarī paramēśvarī karuṇamayī
ārttanādam itonnu kēḷkkuva tinnu nī kanivēṛumō
Ēntinī vidham entinī vidham entinī vidham ambikē
ninte kuññine niṣṭhuram kadanattil iṭṭu
valaykkaṇam

O Ambika! Sustainer of the Universe! the Supreme Ruler! Compassionate One! Won't You kindly deign to hear this desperate cry? Why Mother, why, why do You mercilessly drag this child of yours through endless sorrows?

Andhanā oru piñcu paitale andha bhūviler iññu nī
māṛi ninnu rasicciṭunn atin entu nyāyam itambikē
Onnum onnum ariññiṭā tati dīnanā yoru kuññite
krūrajīvika ḷērumī vanabhūvil entinu taḷḷi nī

How unfair of You, Mother, that having thrown this blind babe into this dark world, You stand apart and enjoy the game! Why did You push this innocent, artless, helpless child into this jungle, full of cruel beasts?

Atbhutā vaham āyikam tava sṛṣṭilīla naṭappatil
ēnne nī baliyākkiṭunn oru krūramām vidhiyentinō
Prēma rūpiṇi alivezhunn avaḷ ennu pēru
pukazhnna nī
ēnneyiṭṭu valacciṭunn atin entu kāraṇam īśvarī

That You made me the scapegoat for fulfilling your mysterious magical play, may be my callous fate. Are You not renowned as "love personified" and "supremely compassionate"? Then, why do You persecute me like this?

Ambikē jagadiśvarī paramēśvarī karuṇāmayī
ēnnu teṅguvatinnu mātrame innenikku kazhiññiṭū
Ñānorēzha janiccu pōy tava paitalāy jagadambikē
rakṣayō atō śikṣayō tava niścayattin adhīnamē

Now I can only cry, "Ambike, Jagadishwari, Parameshwari, Karunamayi." Destitute that I am, I had to be born as Thy child. O Mother of the Universe, to come to the rescue or to commit infanticide, is entirely up to Thy whim!

AMMĀVAI PĀRKKA PŌKALĀM

Ammāvai pārkka pōkalām
anta ānanda jyōtiyai kāṇalām
ellōrum śērntu pāṭalām
nām entrumē ānandam tēṭalām

Oh let us go to meet Amma, to see that Light of Joy. Let us sing together and seek that bliss everywhere.

Ēzhaikaḷkkum śelvarukkūm orē oru ammā
siru varukkum peri yavarkkum sonta inta ammā
Mētaikaḷkkum pētaikaḷkkum
bhēdam illa jagadamba, amma
evaraiyum kāppātti tuṇaiyi ruppāḷ jagadambā

To the poor and rich alike, there is only one Mother, who belongs to the young and the aged, who protects and supports everyone. For the one Universal Mother, there is no difference between scholars and illiterates.

Tāṅkāta sōkattāl taḷarum tan makkaḷai
tōḷil aṇaittu tazhuviṭuvāḷ ammā
Ōyātai kaṇṇīrum tuṭai

tiṭuvāḷ jagadamba, amma
oru nimiṭam āvatu calitti ṭāmal inta amma

Amma embraces, takes upon her shoulders, and counsels those who are faltering due to unbearable sorrow. Ceaselessly, without a moment's rest, and without the slightest aversion, the Universal Mother wipes away our tears.

Jāti enṭrum matam enṭrum ūrētum bhēda millai
kaṭavuḷ illā pōruḷai eṅkum kāṇavē muṭiya villai
Karuṇai enṭra nilaimai eṅkum
varavēṇṭum enna amma, amma
kaṭal kaṭantu pāṭi varuvāḷ ulakam
eṅkum paṛantu chenṭru

Without distinguishing between caste, religion or nature, without being able to see anything as being apart from God, Amma crosses the seas and travels the world, ever singing and spreading the message of Compassion.

AMMAYĒ KAṆḌU ÑĀN

Ammayē kaṇḍu ñān - ānandam koṇṭu ñān
unmayil ellām maṛannirunnu
Kaṇkaḷil nōkki ñān kāruṇya raśmitān
nirmala dīptiyil muṅgiyallō

I saw Mother and was immersed in bliss, I lost myself in pure existence. Looking into those compassionate eyes, I was immersed in pure brilliant radiance.

Attiruvāy mozhi muttuka ḷokkeyum
cittam kulir piccatāy irunnu
Duḥkhaṇgaḷ ellām maṛannen manassātma
satyattil appōḷ layicci runnu

Those sacred soothing words from Her lips were all so refreshing to the soul. Forgetting all sorrows, my mind merged into the Self.

Ōmana makkaḷē ennu viḷikkumbōḷ
kōḷmayir koḷḷātta makkaḷuṇṭō
Ā naṟum puñciri pāl nukkarnnī ṭavē
ānanda nirvṛti āraṭayā, ammē

Is there anyone who does not experience a thrill when Amma calls one "Darling Child?" When one drinks in that nectarine milk of Her smile, will not one lose oneself in ecstasy?

AMMĒ AGĀDHAMĀY

Ammē agādhamāy ennōṭu kāṭṭiya
prēma kāruṇyatte ōrttu tēṅgi
ōrkunpōḷ inneni kāśvāsam ēkuvān
mādhuryam ōlumā cinta mātram

O Mother, remembering the deep love and compassion You have showered on me, I shed tears. Your sweet memories are the only consolation for me today.

Ōnnenik ēkū nīyenne piriññetra
dūramō pōyālum vēṇṭatilla
nin prēma mādhurya māvōlam nalkiyā-
gōpiye pōleyā bhāvamēkū!

You may go far away, leaving me behind, I won't mind. But I ask one thing: make me like a gopi, giving me in abundance your sweet love.

Nin makkaḷ santatam cārē vasikkilum
iṅgum uṇṭennōrkor ēzha makkaḷ

ninne piriyuvān en vidhi yeṅkilum
nin cinta tannenne dhanya nākkū!

Though You have Your children always by your side, please remember that here, too, there is a forlorn child. Though it is my fate to be separated from You, may I be blessed ever thinking of You.

Viśvam maṟannu nin cintā saraṇiyil
vismariccī ṭaṭṭe sarvvavum ñān
oṭṭum paribhavam kāṭṭila nī pōyāl
gōpikā prēmam nī tannupōkil

Oblivious to the world, dwelling in Your thoughts, may I forget everything. Even if You leave me, I will not be disappointed, if You bestow on me the love of the Gopi.

AMMĒ AMMĒ AMṚTĀNANDAMAYĪ

Ammē ammē amṛtānandamayī
Ammatan sannidhiyil aruma kiṭāṅgaḷ tan
anantakōṭi namaskāram

Oh Mother Amritanandamayi, in Your divine presence, Your darling children offer You countless millions of prostrations.

Kūriruḷ cūzhunna pātakaḷil ñaṅgaḷ
nērvazhi ariyāt alayumbōḷ
Nal kuḷir anpiḷiyāy amma vann udikkunnu
nērāya mārgam teḷiyunnu (2x)

When we wander along unlit paths, enshrouded in darkness, groping for the right path, Mother arises like the cool, full moon and the right path lights up before us.

Duḥkhaṅgaḷ ākunna ghōra vanāntarattil
ēzhakaḷām makkaḷ karayumbōḷ
Karuṇatan iḷamkāttāy vannamma tazhukunnu
kadanaṅgaḷ ñaṅgaḷ maṛakkunnu (2x)

When we helpless children cry in the fearful forest of sorrows, Mother comes and caresses us as the Breeze of Compassion, and we forget all our sorrows.

AMME AMRITĀNANDAMAYĪ

Amme amṛtānandamayī āśrayam nīye jananī
vismaya rūpiṇī viśva vilāsinī omkāra porullalle nī?
prapañca nanmayum tinmayum ulkkonda
pratyakṣa caitanyam alle nī?

Mother Amritanandamayi, you are our refuge! Aren't you the essence of Omkara, the One who evokes our sense of wonder, the One who sports with the entire world as Her arena?

Manam urukumbol māyāvi āyettum
mānava rakṣakiyalle nī?
janmattin porul marttyanu pakarān
janicca oralbhutam alle nī?)

Aren't you that Manifest Reality that contains within Herself all the good and bad things of the world, the Savior who rushes in like a magician when the mind is in turmoil, the Marvel that has chosen to be born among us with the sole intention of teaching us the true meaning of life?

Kannanu kaliyātān karatalam ākkiya
kālattin tapasvini alle nī?
Karuṇā tan uravinum kaliyude varavinum

kāranam ariñavall alle nī?

Aren't you that embodiment of austerities, who enticed even Kannan (Lord Krishna) to appear as Her playmate, that spring of compassion, the One who knows the reason for the strange happenings of the Kali yuga?

Viśva trimūrtikal vīticu nalkia
vīryam nukarnnavall alle nī?
Śaktiyum lakṣmiyum ādiyum maruvunn
sparśana sāyūjyamalle nī?

Aren't you the One who has sipped the nectar that Brahma, Vishnu, Shiva concocted specially for you with equal portions of their own divinity?

Kailāsattile bhaktiyum muktiyum
kavarnna kāncanayalle nī?
Vaikunthattile vaśyata muzhuvan
vahicca mohini yalle nī?

Aren't you the One blessed by the gracious glance of Lakshmi and Sakti; the Supreme Devotee who has captured the essence of devotion, and liberation preserved in Kailasa; Mohini (enchantress) who personifies all the glories of Vaikuntha?

Sarva pradāyini śatru samhārini
rudira mahā kāliyalle nī?
Brahmānda nāyaki śri parameśwari
ādi parā śaktiyalle nī?)

Aren't you the great Goddess Kali, the Bestower of all boons, the Destroyer of enemies on the spiritual path, the Primordial Power, the Presiding Deity of the entire cosmos, the Supreme Goddess?

AMṚTA PADATTIL ANAYKKUKA

Amṛta padattil aṇaykkuka ñaṅgaḷe ammē snēhamayī
amṛtapurēśvari dēvī bhavānī amṛtānandamayī
amme amṛtānandamayī

O Mother Amritanandamayi, Goddess Bhavani, ever loving, dwelling in Amritapuri, please take us to the immortal state.

Amṛta padam tava pāda sarōjam tāyē praṇavamayī
Aṭi paṇiyun nī makkaḷ satatam
ammē priya jananī
Ammē priya jananī ammē
ammē priya jananī

O dear Mother, Embodiment of "OM", Your lotus feet are the seat of the state of immortality, Your children bow down to You eternally.

Nīla sarōruha ramyam nin mukham ānandābja vikāsam
Samsāra smṛti nīkkum nin madhu rūpam divya layam
Janma śataṅgaḷ arukkum nin
kṛpa tūkum nayana yugam
Prēma spandita vimala sukōmaḷa
hṛdayam madhura mayam

Your face, enchanting like a blue lotus, radiates bliss. Your sweet form, permeated with Divinity, erases all concerns with worldly problems. Your compassionate eyes can cut asunder the bonds developed over hundreds of lifetimes. Your pristine heart throbbing with divine love is ever so sweet.

Anava ratam jana durita vipāṭana muditē karuṇarase
Akhila janārchita vandita caraṇē durge guṇa nilayē
Niṛakatir aṛivām iruḷ inn
oḷiyām ammē jñānamayī
Nirvṛti dāyaka tava pada
kamaḷam abhayam mama jananī

O Compassionate One, ever engaged in removing the afflictions of Your devotees, O Durga, full of divine attributes, worshipped by all. Embodiment of supreme knowledge and universal love, like a light that eradicates darkness without a trace.

Śrī laḷitē lasitōjjvala vaibhava mahitē brahmamayī
Śrī paramēśvari pārvati bhairavi viśva prēma mayī
Śrī kari śri dhari pūrṇṇa
sanātani parama dayāmayi śakti
Śrī caraṇāmbu ruham mama
śaraṇam amṛtānandamayī

O Amritanandamayi, You are the playful Goddess, effulgent like millions of suns, the embodiment of the Supreme Absolute, the goddess Parvati, Bhairavi and Shakti, the primordial power, forever full and eternal, giver of auspiciousness, supremely compassionate. Your feet are my refuge!

AMṚTA RŪPIṆI

Amṛta rūpiṇi mṛdusu bhāṣini
abhaya dāyini vandanam
Abhaya dāyini vandanam
Amṛtē vandanam

Salutations to the one who protects, whose form is immortality and who speaks softly.

Janaka nandini jana nirañjini
jani vināśini vandanam
Sakala suramuni vidhini ṣēvini
sughana śyāmala mālini(2x)

Salutations to the Daughter of Janaka, who purifies all, destroyer of births. Sage of all the devas, who destroys fate, who is beautiful and pure.

Prakṛti kārini durita vārini
praṇata rakṣaki vandanam
Amṛita vāhini jaya maheśvari
śiva kuṭumbini vandanam (2x)

Salutations to She who is the cause of Nature and takes away all misery, who protects all those who surrender at Her feet, who dwells in immortality, the victorious Goddess, who belongs to the family of Shiva.

AMṚTAMAYĪ ĀNANDAMAYI

Amṛtamayī ānandamayi amṛtānandamayi
jai mā jai mā jai mā jai mā
Vēdamayi sudhāmayi amṛtānandamyi
amba śrīguru satcinmayi (2x)
Jai mā jai mā jai mā jai mā

amritamayi	Mother of immortality
anandamayi	Mother of bliss
amritanandamayi	Mother of Immortal Bliss
vedamayi,	Mother of the vedas
sudhamayi	Full embodiment of nectar
amba sriguru	Mother as well as Master
satcinmayi	Embodiment of truth and consciousness

Kṛpāmayi amba karuṇāmayi amṛtānandamayi mā
Amba tējōmayi jyōtirmayi
Prēmamayi dayāmayi amṛtānandamayi
amba dīṇā nukambā mayi (2x)
Jai mā jai mā jai mā jai mā

kripamayi	Graceful mother
karunamayi	Compassionate mother
tejomayi	Radiant mother
jyotirmayi	Effulgent Mother
premamayi	Mother of love
dayamayi	Mother of mercy
amba dina nukamba mayi	Mother who is compassionate to the downtrodden

AMṚTĀNANDAMAYI SADGURU MAMA JANANI

(VARUVĀN)

Amṛtānandamayi sadguru mama janani (2x)
Varuvān amāntam innentenn ambikē
paitalin rōdanam kelkkāttatō
piṭayunnu hṛdayam ninnuṭe vērpāṭil
takarunnu ñan taḷarunu

Oh, satguru Amritanandamayi, you are my Mother! Why delay to come today, Mother, can't you hear the crying of this child? My heart becomes dry because of the separation, and I become exhausted.

Ēkāntatayil ērunna cintayil
ēriyunnu nān piṭayunnu
Vingumen hṛttil nin
pratīkṣatan kiraṇaṅgaḷ
maṅgunnu ñān kēzhunnu

My mind is agitated by racing thoughts. I am burning and trembling because of this solitude. In my aching heart my hopes are diminishing, and I am weeping.

Vaikarutammē ī kuññine kāttiṭān
uḷḷil teḷiyukennammē
Ende ī janmattin
sāphalyam ennennum
nī tanne ammē nī tanne

Don't delay any further to come to Your child. O Mother, you are the goal, and by feeling Your presence in my heart, the fullfilment of my life.

AMṚTĒŚI DIŚATU SAUKHYAM

Amṛtēśi diśatu saukhyam
ānanda pūrṇa jananī
akhilēśi madhura vāṇi
vandanam pada paṅkajē

O Mother of Absolute Bliss, please show the way to happiness. O Goddess of the entire Universe, whose words are sweet, Prostrations unto Your Lotus Feet, Amritesi!

Paramēśi haratu śōkam
kailāsa nātha ramaṇī
sakalēśī lasatu hṛdayē
santatam hṛdi cintayē

O Parameshwari who delights the Lord of Kailasa, dispel my sorrows. O Goddess of all, please reside in my heart, which always thinks about You.

Kaḷavāṇī jayatu kāḷī
kāruṇya pūrṇṇa jananī
hṛdayēśī jayatu vāṇī
mangaḷam śubha mandirē

O Mother who is full of compassion! O Kali, whose voice is sweet, victory unto You! O Goddess who resides in my heart, who fills it with auspiciousness, O Saraswati, victory unto You!

AMṚTEŚVARI AMMĒ SUKṚTEŚVARI

Amṛteśvari ammē sukṛteśvari
akhilam niraññu nilkkum paramēśvari
tavanāda gamgayil aliyunnu ñan
tirumumbil sāyūjva mariyunnu ñan

Goddess Amriteshwari, You inspire holy deeds, You pervade all. O Supreme power, I merge in the stream of Thy melodies. In Thy presence, I find fulfillment.

Ātmāvin niramāya jagadīśvari
aviṭutte dayavāṇen jayamīśvari
kadanattin irul nīkkum karuṇāmayī
karalin karalāṇu nī cinmayī

Universal Mother, You are the shade of my soul. Your mercy is my success. Compassionate one, dispeller of the darkness of sorrow, pure consciousness, You are the heart of my heart.

Kārmēgha niramārnna kālīśvari
karppūra dīpamāṇen manamiśvari
tripurēśvari ammē sarveśvari
tṛppadam mātramāṇen gatiyīśvari

Mother Kali, You are the color of dark clouds. My mind burns like a camphor lamp. Mother, Goddess of all the worlds, Thy holy feet are my sole refuge.

AMṚTĒŚVARI JAGADĪŚVARI

Amṛtēśvari jagadīśvari
surapūjitē śaraṇam (3x)

O Amriteshwari, worshipped by the whole world and by the gods, I seek Your refuge.

Ati mōhanāmga rūpam
amṛtēśi divya rūpam
mati mōhanāmga rūpam
hṛdi jyōtirātma rūpam

Yours is an enchanting form that bewitches the intellect, divine like the effulgence of the Self in the heart.

Madhuram nirañña nāmam
amṛtēśvarī divya nāmam
Puḷakam vitacca nāmam
amṛtatva siddhi nāmam

Your name is full of sweetness. It bestows immortality. It is an enthralling name, a divine name.

Navarāga bhakti dharmam
amṛtēśvari prēma dharmam
sakalārtti nāśa dharmam
caturveda sāra dharmam

Amriteshwari's dharma of supreme love is the dharma of bhakti (devotion) consisting of all the nine rasas (nuances). It is also the dharma that destroys the proliferation of desires, and it contains the essence of the Vedas.

Jagadarttha mōcakārttham
amṛtēśi śaśvatārttham
Nara lakṣya dāya kārttham
puruṣārttha sādhyam arttham

The name 'Amriteshwari' bestows the goal of human life, namely, liberation from transmigratory existence. It grants that which is eternal.

Muni mānasāntya kāmam
paramārtma vastu kāmam
paripūṇṇa kāma kāmam
parituṣṭi puṣti kāmam

You are the final object of desire in the mind of ascetics, the desire for the ultimate truth, the desire which bestows all other desires, the desire which gives the supreme bliss as well as worldly achievements.

Laya mānasāpta mōkṣam
viṣayārtti jāla mōkṣam
paramātma dātumōkṣam
amṛtēśī jīva mōkśam

You are the liberation that comes to those whose minds are dissolved, the liberation from the hosts of worldly sorrows, the liberation which bestows the Supreme Self; O Amriteshi, you are the liberation of all the creation.

Bhuvana pradīpu jyōti
hṛdayān trastha jyōti
Laya sṛṣṭitatva jyōti
amṛtēśi brahma jyōti (Amṛtēśvari)

You are the light that illumines the world, the light which shines in the cave of the "heart", the light which is responsible for creation, preservation and destruction; O Amriteshi, You are the Light of the Supreme Brahman!

AMṚTĒŚVARI MĀ AMṚTĒŚVARI

(HE ŚĀRADE MĀ)

Amṛtēśvari mā amṛtēśvari mā (he śārade mā)
ajñanata se hamē par dē mā

O Mother Amriteshwari, please take us beyond the state of ignorance.

Tu swar kī devi ho sangīt tujh sē
har śabdh tērā hē har git tujh sē
Ham he akele ham hai adūre
tere śaran me hame pyār de mā

You are the deity of sound, all music emanates from You. All sounds originate from You. We are forlorn, we are incomplete. We have come to You seeking refuge. Please give us Your love.

Muniyon ne samajhe guniyon ne jāne
vedom ki bhāsha purānom ki vāni
Ham bhi kya samajhe ham bhi kya jāne
vidyā ka hamko adhikār de mā

The sages and seers have known this and conveyed it through the words of the Vedas and the scriptures. Please make us also worthy of receiving this knowledge.

Tu śvēt [śyām] varṇṇi dēvōm ki dēvī
hathōm mē vīṇā galē mē sumālā
Manasē hamārē miṭhā dē andhērā
Ham ko ijālom ka sansār dē mā

O Mother, You are white in complexion, the Goddess to all the devas. You hold the veena in your hands, a garland adorns your neck. Please remove the darkness from our minds. Give us a life filled with light.

AMṚTĒŚVARI SUSMITA

Amṛtēśvari susmita candra mukhī
aruṇābha sugātri jaga jananī
kamalō pama nētri kṛpāla harī
caraṇābhaya dātri sucārumatī

O Amriteshwari whose face shines like the full moon, with a radiant smile! O Universal Mother, whose form is resplendent like the rising Sun! O Lotus eyed One, the ocean of Grace, One who provides refuge at Her Feet, O virtuous One!

Karuṇāmṛta vāridhi kalpalatē
kavitāmṛta varṣiṇi kāvyakalē
Varadā bhaya dāyini vandyapadē
śaraṇāgata pālini pāpa harē

O wish-fulfilling tree, ocean of nectarine compassion! The One who showers the nectar of poetry, who is the very art of poetry, who bestows refuge, who protects those who surrender at Her adorable Lotus feet, who destroys their sins.

Svararūpi sarasvati nādamayī
śiva kāmini śaṅkari rāgavatī
Sukhadātri surēśvari sarvvamayī
śubha mūrtti śivaṅkari haimavatī

O Saraswati, the embodiment of words and sounds, beloved of Shiva, the auspicious One, the loving One, bestower of joy, the Goddess of the Devas, One who has become everything, the embodiment of purity, One who bestows auspiciousness, O Goddess Haimavati (daughter of Himavan)!

Śiva rūpiṇi śāmbhavi śaila sutē
śrutirūpi surārccita pādayugē
Śama dāyini śarvari viśvanutē
bhava bhañjani bhairavi bhāvaghanē

O Parvati, the consort of Shambu, One who has the form of Shiva, who is of the form of the Vedas, whose Holy Feet are worshipped by the Devas, bestower of mental poise, who is worshipped by the entire world, who destroys Samsara, O Bhairavi, whose moods are Divine.

AMṚTĒŚVARI VANDANAM

Amṛtēśvari vandanam
jagadīśvari vandanam
patitāvani vandanam
paramēśvari vandanam

Salutations to Amriteshwari, Goddess of Immortality! Salutations to the Goddess of the Universe! Salutations to the Uplifter of the Helpless! Salutations to the Supreme Goddess!

Caturānana nandinī
śaraṇāgata pālinī
bhavabhīti vibañjinī
muni mānasa rañjinī
Amma amma amma amma

O Daughter of He with four faces (Brahma)! Who protects all who take refuge in Her. Who demolishes all the fear arising out of bondage. Who gives enjoyment and happiness to the minds of sages.

Karuṇā rasa sāgarē
kavitāmṛta dāyikē
nigamāgama varṇṇitē
nikhilāmara pūjitē
Amma amma amma amma (Amṛtēśvari)

O Ocean of mercy! Bestower of immortal poetry (poetic genius), who is described in the Vedas and Tantras, worshipped by all the immortals.

Sakalāmaya hāriṇī
śaraṇāgata pālini
mṛtijanma vimōcini
śruti mantra vihāriṇi
Amma amma amma amma

O Destroyer of all sorrows! Protector of all who take refuge, Destroyer of the cycle of birth and death, Who pervades the Vedas and mantras.

Naḷinī daḷa lōcanē
nayanāmṛta vigrahē
mṛdu mōhana susmitē
jaya dēvī namōstutē
Amma amma amma amma (Amṛtēśvari)

O Lotus-eyed One! Whose form is like nectar to the eyes. With a soft and enchanting smile. Victory to You, Devi, salutations!

ĀNANDA RŪPIṆI AMMĒ ENIKKU

Ānanda rūpiṇi ammē enikku nī
ananda mentē vilakki
Ātma prakāśam nirañña nityānanda
nirvṛti entē muṭakki

O Blissful Mother! Why have You denied bliss to me? Why have You not granted me the fulfillment of eternal bliss, radiant with Self-effulgence?

Amme amme amme amṛtāndamayi
jagadambe amṛtānandamayi
Andhatamō laya lōkam viḷakkiṭum
candrika pōloḷiyālē
Enn aka kūriruḷ nin naṛum puñciri
māykkān maṭikkayō tāyē (2x)

O Mother! You are the moonlight which brightens the darkness of ignorance, why are You hesitating in dispelling the darkness of my mind with the illuminating rays of your radiant smile?

Ñān ñān ninaccu ñān ñānām kayaṅgaḷil
tāṇu maraññiṭum munpē
Ennuṇ mayāḷe kṛpāvaśam enne nī
ninnōṭu cērttu rakṣikku (2x)

Through my notions of "I", "I", I am drowning in the depths of the ego. O Mother, You who are my very Self! Please be compassionate and merge me in Thee before this happens.

Kōṭisūrya prabha onnāy viṭarnniṭum
prēma saundarya tiṭambē
Ātma harṣaṅgaḷ kananta raśmikkakam
ñān nin mṛdu smitamākām

O Ecstatic Beauty of Pure Love! Thy form radiates the effulgence of a billion suns! Let me be Thy soft smile, among the infinite rays of the bliss of the Self!

ANĀRĀ VINĀRĀ

Anārā vinārā (3x)
Veṅkata ramanūni cū cārā mīru
Veṅkata ramanūni cū cārā

Rādhā mōhana veṅkaṭaramaṇā
Gōpāla gōvinda veṅkaṭaramaṇā (2x)
Veṅkaṭaramaṇā sankata harana
Veṅkaṭaramanūni cū cārā mīru
Veṅkaṭaramanūni cū cārā

Anārā vinārā (2x)
Gōvinda gōvinda veṅkaṭaramaṇā
Gōvinda hari veṅkaṭaramaṇā
Gōvinda gōvinda veṅkaṭaramaṇā (2x)
Gōvinda hari veṅkaṭaramaṇā (3x)

Anātha nātha veṅkaṭaramaṇā (2x)
Āpat bhāndava veṅkataramaṇā
Gōpāla govinda veṅkaṭaramaṇā (2x)
Gōvinda hari veṅkaṭaramaṇā (3x)

Śrīnivāsa veṅkaṭaramaṇā
Seshādri nilayā veṅkaṭaramaṇā
Ādi nārāyaṇa veṅkaṭaramaṇā

Jaya govinda veṅkaṭaramaṇā
Hari gōvinda veṅkaṭaramaṇā
Veṅkaṭaramaṇā sankata harana
Veṅkaṭaramaṇūni cū cārā mīru
Veṅkaṭaramaṇūni cū cārā

ANNAIKKU NĪRĀṬṬA VĒṆṬUM

annaikku nīrāṭṭa vēṇṭum — nānum
ābhiṣēkam pala seyya vēṇṭum
tirumēni nān tuṭaikka vēṇṭum
tikazhāṭai uṭuttiṭavum vēṇṭum

I worship my beloved Amma by bathing Her and showering Her with sacred offerings, by wiping Amma's divine body and decorating it with pure, fragrant and beautiful clothes.

kaṇṇukku mai tīṭṭa vēṇṭum— nānum
kavin netri pōṭṭiṭavum vēṇṭum— vaṇ
malar mālai nān sūṭṭa vēṇṭum — nal
vaḷaiyaṇikaḷ nān pūṭṭa vēṇṭum

I paint Her eyes and put a beautiful bindi between Her eyebrows, garland Her with a colorful garland and decorate Her arms with shiny bangles.

annai tanai alaṅkarikka vēṇṭum
avaḷ pādam namaskarikka vēṇṭum
irupāda cilambaṇiya vēṇṭum
iruntazhakai nān rasikka vēṇṭum

After making up my dearest Amma, I prostrate at Her feet. I adore Her blessed Feet with ornamental anklets and sit and behold the beauty.

Ōm śakti ōm śakti ōm ōm
śiva śakti jaya śakti ōm
aṭimalarai arccikka vēṇṭum — nānum
āratti arppikka vēṇṭum
tiruppāda pūjai seyya vēṇṭum - dinam
pūttūvi vaṇaṅkiṭavum vēṇṭum

After worshipping Her sacred feet, I wave camphor lights in praise. Daily I will perform ritual worship to Her Holy Feet and shower flowers with devotion.

Ōm śakti ōm śakti ōm ōm
śiva śakti jaya śakti ōm
uṇṇanān uṇavūṭṭa vēṇṭum
uvappōṭu atai pārkka vēṇṭum
paṇiviṭaikaḷ nan seyya vēṇṭum
paruka nān nīr taravum vēṇṭum

With great joy I feed my lovely Amma and offer cool, sweet water. I serve Her by doing all that needs to be done.

pozhutellām arikirukka vēṇṭum
pon pōle pōtriṭavum vēṇṭum
uṭaniruntu viḷaiyāṭa vēṇṭum
oru kōṭi muttam tara vēṇṭum

I spend the whole day in Her company, playing with Her and giving Her endless kisses, cherishing Her as the invaluable golden treasure.

tāyavaḷin aruḷ pārvvai ventum
dharani tanil tuyarnīṅka ventum
tālāṭṭu pāṭiṭavum vēṇṭum
taṅkamavaḷ kaṇṇayara vēṇṭum

I long and beg for Her bewitching and gracious glance for my sorrows and sufferings to vanish forever. I will sing a lullaby and let the golden Mother rest for a while.

Ārāri rārāri rārō ārāri rārāri rārō

ANPIYANNAMBA

Anpiyann amba pūntēn mazhapōle
mandahāsam pozhicu
andhakāram tutacu akatāril ambā
nī tān vasikkū!

O loving Mother, pouring out Your smile like a rain of honey, wipe out the darkness in my heart and stay inside there.

Antaram gattil ammē nirantaram
cinta ceyyunnu ninne
santat ānanda dāyi dayāmayī
bandhurāmgi namastē!

I meditate on You constantly in my heart, O Mother! O embodiment of eternal bliss, of compassion, of beauty, salutations to You!

Uḷḷam malarkke-yennum turannu ñan-
uḷḷilotuṅgi nilkkē
uḷkaḷam śōbhayetti prakāśikkū
ulpala nīlanētrē!

Always opening my heart wide, as I wait inside, bring light into my heart, and shine there, O Mother with eyes like a blue lotus!

Snēhalābham tiraññu nirutsāha
bhāvamuḷḷil kaviññu!
dūradūram tiraññu taḷarnnu ñan
dīnadīnam karaññu

Searching to find love, my heart filled with despair, I searched far and wide and became weak and cried with deep pain.

Kaṇṇu nīrilla kaṇṇil karayuvān-
āvatill ētum ammē!
kanmaṣatīyil ente karaḷkānpu
katti yamarni-ṭūnnu

There are no tears left in my eyes; I am not able to cry. My inner core is burning down in the fire of my sins.

Kāruṇya māri tūki parādhīna
śoka bharaṅgaḷ nīkki
snēhāmritam pakarnnen hridayatte
śrīpāda pīthamākkū!

Mother, shed the rain of mercy and remove my sense of bondage and grief. Fill my heart with the nectar of love and make it a pedestal for Your holy feet.

Vēṇṭa svarlōkasaokhyam varānanē
vēṇṭa saobhāgya-lābham
vēṇṭatēkānta bhakti jaganmayi
vēṇṭatajñāna mukti

Oh beautiful faced One! I do not need the happiness of heaven. I do not need any fortune. What I need is one-pointed devotion to Thee. Oh, You who pervades all the worlds! What I need is liberation from ignorance.

Nāvil nin nāma mantram mahēśvari
kātil nin divya nādam
kaṇṇil ānanda bāṣpam kṛpāmayi
uḷḷil nin dhanya rūpam

Oh great Goddess! May your name be on my tongue, your voice in my ears, tears of bliss in my eyes, and your divine form within my heart, Oh compassionate One!

ANPUM ARUḶUM

Anpum aruḷum initē aḷittiṭum
amṛtānandamayī dēvī

O Amritanandamayi, bestower of love, grace, and all that is beneficial!

Amma untan tuṇai vēṇṭi
ēṅkiṭum ennai kaṇpārttu
Anpuṭtan jñāna pālūṭi amma
akattil iruḷai pōkkiṭuvāy

O Mother, please glance at me who beseeches Your help. Feed me the milk of knowledge with love, and eradicate the darkness within me.

Tumbaṅkaḷ tīrkkum tūmaṇiyē enṭrum
tūyavar uḷḷattil oḷirpavaḷē
Nanṭrum tītum ariyā ennai
kālam muzhutum kāttiṭuvāy

O destroyer of sorrows, who takes up a secret abode in the heart of devotees, please watch over me who does not know what is beneficial and what is harmful.

Idaya kōyilil uraipavaḷē
uyirāy uṇarvvāy iruppavaḷē
Imai pozhutum unnai maravā tirukka
pozhin tiṭuvāy untan pēraruḷai

O Dweller in the temple of my heart, You who are my very life, my innate vibrancy, please grant me Your grace so that I may never lose sight of Your presence.

ANUTĀPAM VAḶARUNNU

Anutāpam vaḷarunnu manamāke piṭayunnu
arutī-vidham agatikkoru gati yēkuka bhagavan

Sorrow is overpowering me, my mind is tiring. O Lord! Please do not give such a destiny to this orphan!

Mōhaṅgaḷ perukunnu dēhamitō taḷarunnu
āruṇṭivan avalambam nīyallāt ulakil

Delusions multiply, this body also tires, who else will shelter me save Thee?

Sukṛtattin balamilla prakṛtattin mikavilla
durita kaṭal nīntān nin kṛpa tūvuka śivane

O Shiva! My collection of merits is not big enough; my conduct is also poor. Please shower your grace for me to cross the ocean of suffering!

Paramārppaṇa bhāvattin ponkiraṇa prabhatūki
bhava rōga timirattinn iruḷ nīkkuka śivane

O Shiva! Please shower in me the radiant boon of total dedication. Please! May this blindness of transmigration be dispelled forever!

Hara śaṅkara śiva śaṅkara bhava śaṅkara bhagavan
śiva śaṅkara hara śaṅkara bhavanāśaka bhagavan

ARIVUKKUM ARIVĀNA

arivukkum arivāna ammā— eṅkaḷ
amṛtānandamayī ammā
ariyā piḷḷai kaḷai kāppāy nī— untan
anpālē onṭrāy cērppāy

You are the Supreme Knowledge, our Mother Amritanandamayi! Protect your ignorant children and unite them with your love.

pārkkinṭra iṭamellām nīyē!
pari pūrṇṇa ānandam nīyē
sērkkinṭra tōṇiyum nīyē!— dēvī
sintaiyil vanta marvāyē

Wherever we look, it is only You, Devi, which we see. You are the eternal bliss. Devi, You are the lifeboat that takes us ashore. You blossom in our mind.

onṭrēyānāy palavānāy
ovvoru uyirum nīyānāy
nanṭrēyānāy nalamānāy— dēvī
nallavarkk ēnṭrum uravānāy

You are the Supreme One as well as the many. You pervade in all life forms. You are always the relative of the righteous people.

kanṭrai pōla ōṭi vantāl
kanindaruḷ surakkum pasuvānāy
enṭrum unnai pōtrukinṭrōm
emakkaruḷ amṛtapuri tāyē

When we run like a calf seeking You, You shower your grace, like a cow feeding its calf. We praise You forever. Please shed your divine grace, O Mother of Amritapuri!

ARIVUM ABHAYAVUM

Arivum abhayavum aruḷunn ammē
amṛtānanda suramyē
teḷiyuka cemmē tikavezhum ammē!
Sukha sandāyini ammē!
sukha sandāyini ammē!

O Mother, the Beautiful One of Immortal Bliss! who bestows knowledge and protection, please manifest forth, O Mother, the Perfect One, the Giver of all joys!

Abhiruci bhēdam ariññ anuvāsaram-
anubhava bhēdam uṇartti
Maruvu naviṭunn amṛtamayi pala
bhāva rasaṅgaḷ uṇartti (2x)

Always awakening different experiences in people in accordance with their varied tastes. Shine, the blissful One of countless moods and expressions.

Nirayuka nīyenn akamalaril tū-
vamṛtāya nupadam ammē!
Paṭaruka nīyen sirakaḷi luṇarvvin
pulari katirā yammē! (2x)

O Mother, incessantly fill my heart with the Divine nectar, and as the animating rays of dawn, permeate each atom of my body.

Karaḷin kamala daḷaṅgaḷil ninmṛdu
pada tārūnnaṇam ammē!
Karuṇārdrā yata nayanam jīvanū
tuṇayāy tīraṇam ammē! (2x)

O Mother, Thy Lotus Feet should shine in the lotus petals of my heart, Your compassionate eyes should become the support of my life.

ĀRŌTU COLLITUM

Ārōtu collitum en manō vēdana
amma kēttitān maticītukil
Aśwāsam ēkuvan āruvann ītumen
amma anangāt irunnitukil

To whom else can I tell my mental pains, if Mother is unwilling to listen? Who else will come and comfort me, if Mother refuses to make a move?

Amritam koticilla amarā purikalum
ammatan vatsalya mē koticu
Innatin śikṣa ñān ēttuvāng ituvān
nīri pukañu dahicitunn en

I didn't wish either immortality or heavenly palaces. I desired only for Mother's affection. I am burning with unbearable pain as if I am being punished.

Nin prēmam ninnotu prēmam atonnilen
pūmanam vāsanta ramyam ammē
Samsāra grīshma maruvil kariññitān
pūmulla tallola pūm palike

The blossoms of Your love towards me and my love towards You, beautify my mental garden as if at the onset of spring. Don't let this jasmine flower burn in the summer heat of transmigratory existence (samsara).

Innu vannītume ippozh ettītume
ennamma ennu ñān kattiruppū
Nīrumī jīvante dīrga niśvāsattin
āśvāsam amma tan manda hāsam

I have been expecting and waiting every day for my Mother's arrival. My Mother's sweet smile is the only relief and comfort from the extreme unbearable pain of life.

ĀṬIṬUVŌM NĀMUM ĀṬIṬUVŌM

Āṭiṭuvōm nāmum āṭiṭuvōm
kaṇṇanuṭan sērntu āṭiṭuvōm
pāṭiṭuvōm nāmum pāṭiṭuvōm — anta
bālaka nin pukazh pāṭiṭuvōm

Let us dance and dance along with the Lord Krishna and sing gaily His glory for ever and ever.

Ānanada nin mukham kaṇṭiṭuvōm
ānanda kaṭalil mūzhkiṭuvōm
Anaittum maṛantu ninṭrīṭuvōm
abhyam nīyenṭre kūṛiṭuvōm

Seeing the face of the Blissful One, let us get ourselves immersed in the ocean of bliss, forgetting everything else, in seeking His refuge.

Vṛndāvanamām enṭran neñcil
pullāṅkuzhalisai purikinṭrāy
Cendāmarai kaṇ koṇṭavanē — un
Cevvitazh rādhai nān tānē

O Krishna! You are playing your pleasant music in the Vrindavan of my heart. O the One with lotus eyes! I am your Radha with reddish lips.

Kṛṣṇa harē jaya kṛṣṇa harē

ĀVŌ MĒRĒ NANDALĀL

Āvō mērē nandalāl āvō mērē nandalāl
Rādhā pukkārē tujhē
Āvō mērē nandalāl

Please come, O Nandalal (Krishna), I, Your Radha, am calling out to You.

Tērē sivā mē jīnahī pāvūm
suddh buddh man kī mē khō jāvūm
Kyā nahi rādhā śyām kī pyārī
ab tō lauṭṭāvō murārī

Without You, My Lord, I cannot survive, I lose my consciousness quite often. Am I not most dear to You, Krishna? Please do come back, O Murari!

Tērē yādhōmē pikalttī rahīhē
śyām kī rādhā rōttī rahīhē
Ōr vilamb nahō giridhārī
dūr karō duḥkh hamārī

I am melting, dwelling in Your thoughts. I have been crying continuously for You. Please do not delay any further, O Lord, Please put an end to all my sorrows.

BAHUT TARASĀ

Bahut tarasā tēri darśan kō
Āvōgi kab mēri mā mēri mā

How much I yearn for your darshan! My Mother when will You come?

Ōr nahi sahāra kōyi
dēdō śaraṇ mēri mā

There is no one to support me other than You, O Mother, take me into Your shelter.

Nahi tap dhyān nahi niṣṭhā
mē kyā jānū tēri mahimā
Dē kar bhakti mā mēri
cuḍhāvō bandhan is sansār kī

No austerities, no meditation, nor discipline do I have, What do I know about Your glory? Bestowing devotion, O Mother, release me from the bondage of samsara.

Rāh dēkhu har kṣaṇ tērī
andhērē man ke sāyē mē
Dēr na kar nā mā mēri
ghabarā huvā hē putr tērā

I am waiting for You every moment in the shadows of my mind. O Mother, please don't delay anymore; this son of Yours is in the grip of fear.

Kissekē kahumē duḥkh apni
kōn hē mērā tēre sivā
Mā ō mā pukārē mērā man
anāth ki vināti sunōgi kab

To whom shall I narrate my grief; whom do I have save Thee? "Mother! O Mother!" cries out my mind. Won't You ever pay attention to this orphan's cry?

BHAJŌ RĒ BHAJŌ

Bhajō rē bhajō kṛṣṇa harē rām
Gōvinda gōpāla kṛṣṇa harē rām
Mādhava mōhana kṛṣṇa harē rām

Chant, O man, chant the name — Krishna, Hare Ram, chant Govinda, Gopala, Krishna, Hare Ram.

Hē madhusūdana bhava bhaya bhañjana
harē prēm mantra bōlō kṛṣṇa harē rām

O slayer of Madhu, destroyer of fear of transmigratory existence, chant the mantra of Love— Krishna, Hare Ram.

Gōvinda gōpāla kṛṣṇa harē rām
mādhava mōhana kṛṣṇa harē rām

Govinda Gopala Krishna Hare Ram, Madhava, Mohana Krishna, Hare Ram.

BRAHMA MURARI

(LIṆGĀṢṬAKAM)

Brahmā murāri surārccita lingam
nirmmala bhāṣita śōbhita lingam
janmaja duḥkha vināśana lingam
tat praṇamāmi sadāśiva lingam

I prostrate to that eternal Shiva lingam[1] worshipped by Brahma, Vishnu and the "Shining Ones/gods" (devas), which shines by its own pure effulgence, destroyer of the sorrows that follows human birth.

Dēva muni pravarārccita lingam
kāma daham karuṇā kara lingam
rāvaṇa darppa vināśana lingam
tat praṇamāmi sadāśiva lingam

I prostrate to that eternal Shivalingam worshipped by the devas and sages, which is compassionate and eradicates lust/desires, which destroyed the pride of Ravana (wicked king who abducted Sita).

Sarvva sugandi sulēpita lingam
buddhi vivarddhana kāraṇa lingam
siddha surāsura vandita lingam
tat prāṇamāmi sadāśiva lingam

[1] The Shiva lingam, "symbol/mark of Shiva", is the simplest and most ancient symbol of Lord Shiva, as God beyond all attributes and forms. The lingam is a rounded, elliptical, an-iconic image, usually of stone.

I prostrate to that eternal Shivalingam well annointed by all perfumes, which helps to develop the intellect, worshipped by Perfected Ones, the Shining Ones, and asuras (mischievous second world beings).

Kanaka mahāmaṇi bhuṣita lingam
phaṇipati vēṣṭita śōbhita lingam
dakṣasu yajña vināśana lingam
tat praṇamāmi sadāśiva lingam

I prostrate to that eternal Shivalingam decorated by gold and jewels, wearing Vasuki (the king of snakes) as a garland, who destroyed Daksha's yagna (the sacrificial rite of his father in law).

Kumkuma candana lēpita lingam
paṅkaja hārasuā śobhita lingam
sañcita pāpa vināśana lingam
tat praṇamāmi sadāśiva lingam

I prostrate to that eternal Shivalingam decorated with vermillion (kumkum) and sandal, adorned with a shining garland of lotuses, destroyer of all accumulated karmas.

Dēva gaṇarccita sēvita lingam
bhāvair bhakṣi bhirēvaca lingam
dina karakōṭi prabhākara lingam
tat praṇamāmi sadāśiva lingam

I prostrate to that eternal Shivalingam served by the devas and other subtle beings, worshipped by the proper emotional attitudes (love and devotion), having the effulgence of a hundred million suns.

Aṣṭa dalōpari vēśṭita lingam
sarvva samud bhava kāraṇa lingam
aṣṭa daridra vināśaka lingam
tat praṇamāmi sadāśiva lingam

I prostrate to that eternal Shivalingam sitting in an eight-petaled lotus, from which everything arises, which destroys the eight types of poverty

Suragura suravara pūjita lingam
suravana puṣpa sadārccita lingam
parātparam paramātmaka lingam
tat praṇamāmi sadāśiva lingam

I prostrate to that eternal Shivalingam worshipped by the Guru of the devas (Indra) with flowers from heaven-realm gardens, which is the Supreme, beyond all, of the nature of the Self.

Lingāṣṭakamidam puṇyam
yaḥ paṭhētśiva sannidhao
śiva lōkam avāpnōti
śivēna saha mōdatē

The one who chants this sacred hymn in Shiva's presence (Shiva temple/Shiva lingam/one's Self), attains the abode of Shiva and revels along with Him.

CINNA CINNA

Cinna cinna padam vaiyttu
kaṇṇā nī vā vā vā
maṇi vaṇṇā nī vā vā vā

Oh dear One! Dark colored One! Come treading with Your little feet!

Vaṇṇa vaṇṇa uṭai uṭuttu
kaṇṇā nī vā vā vā
maṇi vaṇṇā nī vā vā vā

Oh dear One! Dark colored One! Come wearing Your colourful garments!

Mallikai mullai malarālē
arccanai śeyvōm vā vā vā
Mādhavanē Kēśavanē
Yadavanē nī vā vā vā

We shall offer prayers with jasmine flowers . O Madhava, come! Oh Yadava, come!

Draupadi mānam kāttavanē
aṭiyarkk aruḷiṭa vā vā vā
Kārazhakā Maṇivaṇṇā
Kaṇṇā nī vā vā vā

You who saved Draupadi's chastity, come and bless Your devotees. Come, come, come, Kanna! Dear, dark coloured One!

Kaṇṇil teriyum kāzhci yellām
kamala kaṇṇā un tōttram
Kālam ellām Un aruḷai
Vēṇṭukirōm nī vā vā vā

Oh lotus-eyed One! All that we behold is but Your form. We beckon You to come to us! We seek Your blessings for all time to come.

DARŚANAM AMBIKĒ MŌHANAM

Darśnam ambikē mōhanam
sparśanam kāḷikē pāvanam
Vigraham tāvakam śyāmaḷam
ugrasa tvōjvalam kōmaḷam
Darśnam ambikē mōhanam

Your darshan is enchanting, O Mother! O Kali! Your touch is purifying. Your dark form, though terrible, is resplendent and charming.

Ambikē tāvakam vīkṣaṇam
pāpa nirmōcakam bhāsuram
Indu manda smitam sundaram
santatānanda sandāyakam
Santatānanda sandāyakam

O Goddess Ambike! Your glance removes all sins and is auspicious. Your moon-like benign smile is beautiful and bestows everlasting happiness.

Kāmadam mōkṣadam tvatpadam
jñāna kalpa drumam śāntidam
Śuddha satyātmakam śāśvatam
saccidānanda mām daivatam
Saccidānanda mām daivatam

Your Holy Feet fulfill all desires and give emancipation. They are the wish-fulfilling tree and abode of peace, the eternal form of Truth, The Supreme Being, the Existence, Knowledge and Bliss.

Vāraṇam samsṛti māraṇam
kāraṇam dēvitē smāraṇam
Santatam kāḷikē vandanam
śaṅkari dēhimē mangaḷam
Śaṅkari dēhimē mangaḷam

O Devi! Your remembrance is the ultimate cause that destroys all temporal existence, O Kali! Prostrations unto Thee forever, O Shankari! Bestow on me all that is good and auspicious.

DĒ DARŚAN MĀ DĒVĪ

Dē darśan mā dēvī mā ambē mā bhavāni mā (2x)

O Divine Mother, bless me with Your vision.

Riśtenāte bhandhanu jhūṭe
saccā he bas pyar tērā
Sathān mān dhan yē bhi cūṭe
Saccā hē bas sāth tērā)

All relationships and bonds in this world are false. The only truth is Your Love, O Mother. All positions and wealth, too, will leave surely. Only the association with You is true (permanent).

Jai jai mā jai jai mā jai jai ma
Dē darśan mā dēvī mā ambē mā bhavāni mā
Bhavsāgar se ham ko bacālo
isa jīvan ko dhanya bānālo
Gōdh me tēre ham ko basālo
Param prēm mā ham me jagādo

Save me from the ocean of transmigration. Make this life blessed, O Mother. Always keep me seated on Your divine lap. Awaken the springs of Divine Love in me.

Jai jai mā, jai jai mā, jai jai ma
Dē darśan mā dēvī mā ambē mā bhavāni mā

DĒVĪ MĀTĒ

Dēvī mātē jai janani mā
dīna nāthe amṛtamayi mā

Victory to Mother, the Goddess, the Mother of immortality, who protects the grief-stricken.

Jai jai mā jai jai mā jai jai jai mā
Vānī rūpē mṛdu caraṇē mā
vīṇā hāstē śaśivadanē mā

In the form of Sarasvati, with soft feet, holding the veena, whose face is like the full moon.

Ādyā śaktē śivadaytē mā
ātmā rāmē kamala bhavē mā

Who is the primordial energy, giver of auspiciousness, who delights in Her Self, sitting on a lotus.

Kāḷi durge kali śamanē mā
kālātītē śiva caritē mā

Who is Kali and Durga, destroyer of the evils of the kali yuga, beyond time, who praises Shiva.

Līla mūrtē giri tanayē mā
śōbhā rūpē śubha varadē mā

Always playful, the daughter of the mountain, whose form is effulgent, giver of auspicious boons.

DĒVĪ NINNE KAṆI KAṆṬIṬṬU

Dēvī ninne kaṇi kaṇṭiṭṭu mānasam
puḷakitam ākaṇam ennum ennum
Nin tiru nāmam japiccu koṇṭunmatta
bhāvam uḷkoḷḷanam ente cittam

O Devi, my mind should always become ecstatic when I see Your blessed form. Chanting Your holy name, my mind should become intoxicated.

Nin kara vallitan sparśattāl ennamme
jīvitam puṣpitam ākiṭēnam
Nin maṭi taṭṭilāy enneyaṇ accamma
tazhukita lōṭiyura kiṭēṇam

By the touch from Your tender hands, O Mother, my life should blossom. Mother, put me on Your lap and while caressing me, put me to sleep (like a baby).

Duḥkham niraññiṭum laukika bhōgattil
āśakaḷ oṭṭum janikkarutē
Ānanda rūpiṇi ninne nirantara m
cintanam ceyyuvān śakti nalkū

Do not allow desires associated with misery and worldly indulgences to arise in my mind. Give me the strength to have the constant remembrance of Your blissful form!

DĪNATĀRIṆI DURITA VĀRIṆI

Dīnatāriṇi durita vāriṇi triguṇa sañcaya dhāriṇi
Sujana pālini nidhana kāriṇi saguṇa nirguṇa rūpiṇi
Dēvī nī bhava tāriṇi jaya śōka mōha vimōcini
pāhi pāhi bhavā nitāvaka pāda paṅkajam āśrayē

Thou art the protector of the helpless. Thou art the remover of sins. Thou wears the three gunas (qualities of nature) together. Thou art the protector of good people, the Supreme cause for dissolution, with and without form. O Devi, who protects people from transmigration, victory unto You, who removes sorrows and delusions. O Bhavani! Protect us, protect us. I take refuge at your lotus feet.

Matsya kūrma varāha narahari toṭṭupatta vatāravum
citsamē bhava damśamallayo pañca bhūta samastavum
Darśanaṅgaḷil ārilum tava dṛśyamalla svarūpavum
pāhi pāhi bhavā nitāvaka pāda paṅkajam āśrayē

O Mother! the embodiment of knowledge, are not the ten incarnations, like the fish, tortoise, pig, etc. (Matsya, Kurma, Varaka — avatars of Vishnu), all the creation made by the five elements (earth, fire, water, air, ether) a part of You? In the six chakras your real nature can't be seen. O Bhavani! Protect us, protect us. I take refuge at your lotus feet.

Ādiyum punarantavum tava dēvī nahi nahiyeṅkilum
pāda sēva karā yavarkkāy rūpabheda meṭuppu- nī
Kāla bhedam atiṅkalum sthiticeyvu nī jagadambikē
pāhi pāhi bhavā nitāvaka pāda paṅkajam āśrayē

O Devi! Though You have no beginning or end, You assume different forms for those who serve your feet. You are the unchanging truth even when the time changes, O Mother of the universe! O Bhavani! Protect us, protect us. I take refuge at your lotus feet.

Rūpamuḷḷil nin acciṭunn oru sādhakannu sarūpiṇi
rūpahīna matāyupā sitayākil dēvi yarūviṇi
Jyōti rūpa matāy lasipporu brahma rūpa sanātanī
pāhi pāhi bhavā nitāvaka pāda paṅkajam āśrayē

For the spiritual aspirant, who meditates on your form, You assume a form and those who worship You as the formless, You appear as formless. O eternal truth! the embodiment of Brahman (Supreme Absolute), You remain as the embodiment of supreme light. O Bhavani! Protect us, protect us. I take refuge at your lotus feet.

Svantam ākiyakazhi vezhunn avaruṇmay
yathakāṇkayāl
cinmayē atutānahō para brahmam ennu riyāṭuvōr
Ambadēvī turīya mennatu nirvvacikkuka
sāddhyamō?
pāhi pāhi bhavā nitāvaka pāda paṅkajam āśrayē

Those who are capable of seeing your real nature say, O embodiment of knowledge, that I am that Supreme Brahman! O Mother, Devi! Can anyone define the Turiya state (Pure Consciousness, which both transcends and pervades the three states of waking, dreaming, and deep sleep)? O Bhavani! Protect us, protect us. I take refuge at your lotus feet.

ĒKĀSRAYAMĀM AMMA

Ēkāsrayamām amma tan pādattil
ēkākini ñān aṇaññū
Ēzhakal kāśvāsam ēkumā pādatte
ēkāgramāy ñān bhajippū

Loner that I am, I surrender at the Feet of Mother who is my sole refuge. I worship single-mindedly the sacred Feet that give solace to the destitute.

Kālattin kaikal koruthoru vīthiyil
kāliṭarāte ennum naṭappān
Kātara cittayāy kāmita varadē
kālam enālum ñān bhajippū

To walk with unfaltering steps on the path woven by the hands of time, I, with a yearning heart, worship forever the Mother who fulfills all desires.

Aśaraṇar kāśvāsa mēkumā pādattil
aharnniśam aham arppippū
Amaratvam ēkum amṛtēśi pādaṅgaḷ
ātaṅka muktikkāy ñān bhajippū

Ever surrendering to You, O Mother who comforts the forlorn, I worship Your sacred Feet day and night. I surrender myself to You, O Amriteshi, who bestows immortality, to redeem me from all sorrows.

ELLAM ARIYUNNAR AMME

ellam ariyunnar amme - ente
vallāyma nīyaṛiyillē
vallāte ñān alayunnī ghōra
samsāramām sāgarattil

O Mother, who knows all, don't you know my misery? I wander much in this ghastly samsaric ocean.

illa mattārumī vāzhvil - ente
allal-akattuvān ammē
etranāḷ ī vidham ammē - ñān ī
duḥkha bandham cumakkēṇṭū

Nobody else have I in this world, to assuage my grief. How long do I have to bear this burden of sorrow, O Mother?

prēma svarūpiṇi ammē - ennil
kāruṇyam tūvukay illē
allum pakalum entammē - vannen
uḷḷil viḷaṅgaṇam ammē

O Love incarnate, Mother, won't You shower compassion on me? Please do come Mother, and reign in my heart day and night.

vēdānta vēdiyall ammē - avi-
vēkiyā yuḷḷoru paital
mātāvu nī amṛtānanda maya -
pālūṭṭi nirvṛtiyēkū

I am not a knower of Vedanta I am only an ignorant child, My Mother art Thou, feed me with Thy milk of immortal bliss.

ENTINU ŚŌKAM MANASSĒ

Entinu śōkam manassē
nin nija bhāvam atalla
Sāndra sukhāmṛta sāmrājyattin
ēkādhi patiyenn ōrkkū

Wherefore grieve, O mind ? Sorrow is not thy true nature! You are the sovereign monarch over the infinite empires of immortal bliss!

Māttam verumoru mārā niyamam
mārā poruḷine nī puṇarū
Maruvil salila bhrānti kaṇakke
māyā kṛtamī ulakellām

The constant change you see, that seemingly relentless law, is but a passing show. Like the mirage in the desert, all the world is a mirror game of Maya.

Āndhyam akattuka manassē
akhilavum ātmāvāṇ ennariyū
Aṛivin śrīmukha prabhā darśikkū
aṛivā 'ṇaha' mē nin rūpam

Seek the changeless Reality. Cast off your blindfold now, O mind! Realize all is the Atman alone. Behold the effulgent face of knowledge pure, which, O Self, is your pristine form.

GAJAMUKHA GAJAMUKHA

Gajamukha gajamukha gaṇanāthā (3x)
gaurī nandana gaṇanāthā
Pāśānkuśa dhara gaṇanāthā
Gaṇanāthā hē gaṇanāthā
Paśupati nandana gaṇanāthā
Gaurī nandana gaṇanāthā

O Lord of Ganas! The elephant-faced One, son of Gauri (Goddess Parvati), who wields the rope and goad, son of Pashupati (Lord Shiva).

GAM GAṆAPATAYĒ NAMŌ NAMAḤ

Gam gaṇapatayē namō namaḥ (4x)

Prostrations to Lord Ganapati.

Guruguha sōdara gaṇanātha
nata jana pālaka suravandya
Paritāpa harē paramēśa
mṛti bhaya nāśaka gaṇēśvara
Gam gaṇapatayē namō namaḥ (4x)

O brother of Lord Subramanya, the leader of Ganas, Protector of those who seek You, O Supreme Lord, dispeller of sorrows, O Ganesha, the destroyer of the fear of death.

Iha para sukhada guṇaśīla
sahṛdaya rasika bhavasāra
Budha jana sēvya matinātha
śubha gati dāyaka gaṇapāla (Guruguha; Gam)

Giver of both heavenly and worldly joys, abode of noble qualities, who delights the pure-hearted, who is the very essence of the world, who is worshipped by the intelligent, who is the Lord of the intellect, who is the bestower of Liberation, protector of Ganas.

Gajamukha sundara varadātaḥ
nijasukha kāraṇa nigamārttha
Praṇata janāmaya parihantaḥ
praṇava rūpa jaya gajānana (Guruguha; Gam)

O beautiful elephant faced Lord, bestower of boons, who is the cause of real happiness, who is the very essence of the Vedas, who completely destroys the sorrows of those who seek refuge, whose form is Pranava (the Primordial Sound), victory to You, O Lord Ganesha!

GANĒŚA NAMAḤ ŌM

Ganēśa namaḥ ōm ganēśa namaḥ ōm
ganēśa namaḥ śrī ganēśa namaḥ ōm
Ganēśa namaḥ ōm ganēśa namaḥ ōm
Ganēśa namaḥ śrī ganēśa namaḥ ōm
Hē gaṇanāyaka śūbha phala dāyaka
vighna vināśaka kāri
Vidyādāyak bhuḍḍhi pradāyaka
Siḍḍhi vināyaka svāmī

Salutations to You, O Lord Ganesha! O Leader of the Ganas, the bestower of the good, remover of all obstacles, bestower of knowledge and intelligence, O Lord Siddhivinayaka (another name of Lord Ganesha).

Lōg karē tēri pūjā pehlē
gāvē tērī mahīmā
Dūru karō prabhō sāri amangaḷ
Hō sukh śānti jag mēm

You are worshipped first by the devotees who sing Your glories, O Lord, remove all inauspiciousness from the world, Let peace and happiness prevail in the world.

GIRIJĀSUTA ṢAṆMUKHA

Girijāsuta ṣaṇmukhā
sujanārccita śubhamukha
Muruga duritāpahā
muruga bhavasāgarā

O Shanmukha, son of Parvati! You are worshipped by all good people. Your face is indeed auspicious, O handsome One (Muruga)! You destroy the difficulties of Your devotees, O Muruga! You take them across the ocean of mundane existence.

Kṛtadānava bhañjana
dhṛta kaṅkaṇa kuṇḍala
Sarasīruha lōcana
śaravaṇa bhava sundara

You destroyed the demons (Surapadma, Taraka and others). You are adorned with bracelets and earrings. Your eyes are as beautiful as lotuses, O handsome One who was born amongst the reeds in the Holy River Ganga.[2]

Bhuvanākhhila rakṣaka
mama mānasa rañjaka
Muruga ati pāvana
muruga paripāhi mām

You protect the whole universe. You enchant my mind, O handsome One! You are ever pure. Please protect me!

Tripurāntaka nandana
praṇavārttha subōdhaka
Hara hara hara ṣaṇmukha
harihara nara kīrttita

---

[2] Lord Subrahmanya was born from the effulgence which emanated from the third eye of Lord Shiva. The fire God carried the effulgence and deposited it in the Ganges River among some reeds. There appeared 6 beautiful babies. When mother Parvati saw the babies she hugged them all together. They combined and formed the six-headed baby Subrahmanya.

You are the son of Lord Shiva, who destroyed the three cities (Tripura). You taught Brahma the meaning of the sacred syllable OM. O six-headed one, You are none other than another manifestation of Shiva. You are adored by Vishnu, Shiva, and all beings.

GŌPA BĀLAKA GŌKULĒŚVARA

Gōpa bālaka gōkulēśvara
gōpikā hṛdaya nandanā (2x)
Devakī tanayā dīna pālana
dēva dēva danu jāntakā (2x)

O cowherd boy, Lord of Gokula, who delights the hearts of the Gopis. O Son of Devaki, protector of the poor, O Deva, destroyer of the demons.

Rāmasōdara ramēśa sundara
rādhikā sukha vivarddhanā
rāgalōla muraḷī manōhara
rāsakēḷi rāsa lōlupā (2x)

O brother of Balarama, enchanting Lord of Rema (Goddess Lakshmi), One who increases the joy of Radha, who plays sweet melodies on the flute, who delights in playing the Rasalila.

Mukunda mādhavā mañjulā nanā
makara kuṇḍala sumaṇḍitā
manda manda gamanā manōharā
manō ramaṇā muraḷi gāyakā (2x)

O Mukunda, Madhava, the One with a beautiful face, who is adorned with Makara (fish-shaped) earrings, and who has a slow graceful gait, O the enchanting One, the player of the flute, You are the enthraller of the hearts.

Vēṇu vādaka varābhaya pradā
śyāmaḷāṅga sarasī ruhekṣaṇa
cāruśīla sakalāgama samstuta
vāsudēva tava mangaḷam (2x)

O Divine Flute Player, the protector, and bestower of the boons, the dark complexioned One with Lotus eyes, One with sweet disposition, who is praised by all the Vedas, O Vasudeva, glory to You!

GŌPĀLA KṚṢṆĀ GIRIDHĀRI

Gōpāla kṛṣṇā giridhāri kṛṣṇā
gōlōka nandana kṛṣṇā
gōvinda kṛṣṇā ghana śyāma kṛṣṇā
gōpī janēśvara kṛṣṇā

O Krishna, the cowherd boy, who uplifted the Govardhana mountain! O Krishna, whose real abode is Goloka! O Govinda, dark-blue colored! O Krishna, the Lord of the Gopis!

Sukumāra kṛṣṇā surapūjya kṛṣṇā
sukhasāra vigraha kṛṣṇā
kamanīya kṛṣṇā karuṇādra kṛṣṇā
kalidōṣa nāśana kṛṣṇā

O Krishna! The perfectly beautiful, who is adored by all celestial beings, whose essence is happiness, You are the one who, full of compassion, destroys all sins in the dark age of materialism.

Navanīta kṛṣṇā naṭarāja kṛṣṇā
nalinī dalēkṣaṇā kṛṣṇā
yadunātha kṛṣṇā yatisēvya kṛṣṇā
yamunā taṭāśrita kṛṣṇā

O Krishna, the butter thief, the King of dance, O Lotus-eyed One, The Lord of Yadava's lineage who is served by all sages and saints.

Vrajavāsi kṛṣṇā vanamāli kṛṣṇā
vasudēva nandana kṛṣṇā
jayadēva kṛṣṇā jagadīśa kṛṣṇā
janamāna sēśvara kṛṣṇā

O Krishna, who lives in Vraja, adorned with a garland of wild flowers, son of Vasudeva, Jayadeva is a great devotee of Yours. O Krishna, You are the Lord of the Universe and of all souls.

GŌPĪ GŌPĀLA VĒṆU GŌPĀLA

Gōpī gōpāla vēṇu gōpāla
mukunda mādhava gōpī gōpāla
Kṛṣṇa harē jaya kṛṣṇa harē (4x)

Jaya hari bol jaya rām bol
Hari hari bol gōvinda bol
Hari aur śaṅkar sab he tera nām

Sab sukh le lō sab duḥkh le lō
Jaya hari bol jaya rām bol
Hari hari bol gōvinda bol
Hari aur śaṅkar sab he tera nām

Chant the names of Rama and Krishna! Victory to the Lord of the senses, the protector of the cows, the divine flute player, the bestower of liberation, the beloved of Lakshmi, the irresistible Lord. Hari (Vishnu) and Shankar (Shiva), they are all your names. Lord, take all my happiness and my sorrows.

GOVINDA DAMODARA

Gopāla nārāyaṇa
Govinda govinda nārāyaṇa
Govinda gopāla nārāyaṇa
Govinda ānanda nārāyaṇa

Govinda ānanda nārāyaṇa (4x)
Govinda govinda nārāyaṇa (6½x)

Śrī kṛṣṇa govinda nārāyaṇa (4x)
Śrī rāma rameti nārāyaṇa (5x)

Govinda ānanda nārāyaṇa
Nārāyaṇa nārāyaṇa lakṣmī nārāyaṇa (4x)
Nārāyaṇa nārāyaṇa sriman nārāyaṇa (5x)

Victory to the blissful Lord of the cows who had a pestle tied to his waist, who rests on the Primal Waters! Praises to Rama and Narayana, consort of Lakshmi, the Goddess of spiritual and material prosperity.

GŌVINDAM GŌPĀLA

Gōvindam gōpāla bhajamana kṛṣṇa harē (4x)
Hē prabhu dīna dayāla bhajamana kṛṣṇa harē

Worship Lord Krishna, the Lord and Protector of the cows, the All-attractive One, Praises to the Lord! The uplifter of the downtrodden!

GURU CARAṆAM SADGURU

Guru caraṇam sad guru caraṇam
amṛtānandamayī caraṇam

guru caraṇam bhavabhaya haraṇam
amṛtānandamayī caraṇam

The Guru's feet, the Satguru's feet, Amritanandamayi's feet - they annihilate the fear of transmigratory existence.

Akhila janārcchita satcaraṇam
jani mriti nāśaka śrī caraṇam
Samasta dēvī dēvamayam - sad
guru caraṇam praṇamāmi sadā

I offer my obeisance to the Satguru's feet which are worshipped by all the devotees, which are blessed by the presence of all the gods and goddesses, and which bring the cycle of births and deaths to an end.

Guru mahimā sad guru mahimā
avarṇṇanīya guru mahimā
Brahmātmaikya nidāna padam - sad
guru caraṇam praṇamāmi sadā

The Satguru's greatness is indescribable. I bow down to the Satguru's feet, which remind one of the unity of the individual soul and the Supreme.

GURU DĒVA

Guru dēva jaya dēva māhādeva dayā maya
Vibhuti sundara sasaṅka śekhara
Śiva śaṅkara dayā karō

Supreme Guru, victorious Lord, merciful One. O beautiful ash-covered Lord Shiva! Whose crest is adorned with the crescent moon. O merciful Lord Shiva, the doer of good!

Gōkula rañjana gōpī gōpāla
Raghukula bhuṣana sita rāma
Prēma janardhana dayā karō

O Gopala! The delight of the gopis in Gokula. O Rama, beloved of Sita, the ornament of the Raghu dynasty, uplifter of humanity with love and grace, be merciful.

GURUKṚPĀ AÑJAN PĀYŌ

Gurukṛpā añjan pāyō mōre bhāyi
Rāmabhinā kac jānat nāhi
Gurukṛpā añjan pāyō

O my brother! I received some collyrium that I put on my eyes - it is called Guru's grace. As a result, I don't know anything that exists that is not Rama.

Antar rām bāhir rām
Jahām dēkhē vahām rām hi rām **(2x)**
Gurukṛpā añjan pāyō

Everything within me is Rama, so is everything outside of me. In fact, wherever I look, I see nothing but Rama. All this is Rama, all this is Rama!

Jāgat rām sōvat rām
Sapnē mē dēkhat rām hi rām
Rām hi rām rām hi rām
Gurukṛpā añjan pāyō

When I am sleeping, it is Rama that is sleeping. When I am awake, it is Rama that is awake. In my dreams, it is Rama that appears in various forms. All this is Rama, all this is Rama!

Kahatē kabīr anubhav nīkhā
Jahām dēkhē vahām rām hi rām (2x)
Rāma sarīkā rāma sarīkā
Gurukr̥pā añjan pāyō

Kabir says "It is my experience - wherever I look, (I see) Rama and Rama alone".

GURUVAṬIVĀNAVAḶĒ

Guruvaṭiv ānavaḷē amr̥tānandamayi
Tiruvaṭi paṇinṭēn varam onṭru taruvāy
Amr̥ta purēśvari ānanda vaṭivē
Aruḷoṭu enaiyum padamalar sērppāy
Guruvaṭivān avaḷē ammā ammā ammā

O Mother Amritanandamayi! You are the form of the Guru. I prostrate at your lotus feet; please grant me a boon. O Mother of Amritapuri! Who is the embodiment of bliss, unite me to your lotus feet through your grace.

Dayai vaṭiv ānavaḷē śiva śakti pārvati
Tanayan azhaittēn ezhund aruḷvāyē
Dinam unai nāṭi varum bhaktarkaḷ kūṭṭam
Manam tanil tōnṭrumē dēvī nin rūpam

O Mother! The embodiment of compassion, the unmanifest Being and the manifest (generative) power, Parvati, your son is calling You, please come! The crowd of devotees rushes daily to have your darshan. Your form will be revealed in our mind.

Aruḷ vaṭiv ānavaḷe ādi parāśakti
Anpuṭan tutittēn [azhaitten] ādarippāyē
Vēdattin sārattai tarum nin upadēśam
Pāpattai pōkkiṭum tāyē un dariśanam

O Mother of Grace! The primordial power! I salute you with love. Protect me. Your teaching gives us the essence of the Vedas. Your vision will vanish all our sins, O Devi!

Tiṅkaḷai cūṭukinṭra śivanin tiru nāmam
Eṅkaḷai kāttiṭavē anu dinam kūrukirā
Kavitayil ezhutiṭavē
Enakkum iyala villai
Puviyāḷum un perumai ezhuttinil aṭaṅka villai

You chant the divine name of Lord Shiva, who wears the crescent moon as an ornament on his head. I am unable to write your greatness in poems. O ruler of the earth! Your glory can't be written or expressed in words.

GURUVĀYŪR APPĀ TUṆA NĪYĒ

Guruvāyūr appā tuṇa nīyē
ennu karuti ñān kai tozhunnēn
Kai tozhunnēn kaṇṇā kai tozhunnēn (2x)

O Lord of Guruvayur, considering You as my refuge, I join my palms in salutations. I fold my palms in salutation, O Kanna!

Perukiya śōkaṅgaḷ nīkkiṭēṇam
ente manassiluḷḷa tāpam nī akattiṭēṇam
Kai tozhunnēn kaṇṇā kai tozhunnēn (2x)

Quell my mounting sorrows, dispel the agony of my heart, I join my palms in salutation, O Kanna, I join my palms in salutation.

Āśriṭa vatsalā abhayam tarunn avane
āśritarām ñaṅgaḷe kāttu koḷḷaṇē
Kai tozhunnēn kaṇṇā kai tozhunnēn (2x)

You are affectionate to those who seek refuge in You. Protect us, O Lord. I join my palms in salutation, O Kanna.

Ninpāda paṅkajam ennun namicciṭunnēn
aravinda nētranē abhayam nalkēṇamē
Kai tozhunnēn kaṇṇā kai tozhunnēn (2x)

Ever I bow at Your Lotus Feet, O lotus-eyed One, give me refuge, I join my palms in salutation, O Kanna, I join my palms in salutation.

HAR HAR MAHĀDĒV ŚIVA ŚIVA

Har har mahādēv śiva śiva mahādev (2x)
Kāl kāl mahādēv muṇḍamāl mahādēv
muṇḍamāl mahādēv
Lōknāth mahādēv ēkanāth mahādēv

Tāṇḍav narttan bhuta gaṇēśvar
sūry candrānal nētrā
Sury candrānal nētrā
Hē praḷayaṅkar dēv śivaṅkar śaṅkar rudr mahēśā

Har har mahādēv śiva śiva mahādev (2x)
Tāṇḍav narttan bhuta gaṇēśvar
sūry candrānal nētrā
Sury candrānal nētrā
Hē praḷayaṅkar dēv śivaṅkar śaṅkar rudr mahēśā

har mahadev	O Destroyer, Great God
kal mahadev	Lord of time/death
mundamal	Who wears a garland of skulls
loknāth	Lord of the universe
eknāth	The One and only Lord

tāṇḍav narttan	The One who dances the tandava dance
bhuta gaṇeśvar	Lord of the Bhutas
sūry canranal nētrā	Who has three eyes
pralayankar	Creator of the deluge
śiva śankara	Bestower of welfare and auspiciousness
rudr	Ferocious One

HARĀYA JAYA

Harāya jaya madhu sūdanāya nama om
Mādhavāya keśavāya yādavāya nama om

Salutations to that captivating, victorious Madhusudana, the One who exudes sweetness like nectar! Prostrations to the Lord of Lakshmi, who has long and handsome hair, the Lord of the Yadu clan.

Hari om hari om hari om hari om
Bōlō rādhe rādhe bōlō rādhe rādhe
Bōlē rādhe rādhe bōlō rādhe rādhe bōlō
Man mōhana kṛṣṇa māyā vibhanjaka
mathura nātha mangala dhāma

Krishna, the enchanter of the mind and destroyer of illusion. Who is the Lord of the city Mathura and the source of all auspiciousness.

Mērē nandalālā pyāre gōpi lola
Govardhana dhāri gōkula vasi

My Nandalala, the beloved of the gopis. Who held up the mountain of govardhana and lives in Gokula.

Vṛndāvana kē kuñja vihāri
kanmaṣa nāsak kāmita dāyaka

He who sports in the forests of Vrindavana, who destroys all evil and fulfills all desires.

Mērē pyāre bālā muraḷī gāna vilōla
Rādhā mānasa cōrā hṛdaya vihāra

My darling child Krishna, player of the flute, stealer of Radha's mind, who resides in my heart.

HARĒ KṚṢṆA KṚṢṆĀ

Harē kṛṣṇa kṛṣṇā kṛpā pūrṇṇa kṛṣṇā
harē kṛṣṇa kṛṣṇā namōbāla kṛṣṇā

O Krishna Krishna, full of compassion, salutations to the child Krishna!

Calat pimcha kēśā taḍit pītavāsā
vrajastrī parītā namastē mukundā

Salutations to the Giver of Liberation, with hair waving about, dressed in lightning yellow robes, surrounded by the women of Vrindavan.

Ghana śyāma varṇṇā manō mōhanāmgā
ramākānta ramyā namastu bhyamīśa (Harē kṛṣṇa)

Salutations to Thee, O God, dark cloud-colored, with mind enchanting and captivating form, beloved of Sita, beautiful One!

Harē vāsudēvā prabhō prēma rūpā
yaśōdā tanūjā śubham dēhidēvā

Son of Vasudeva, Lord in the form of love. Son of Yashoda, giver of auspiciousness.

Jagat vandya murttē surōd gīta kīrttē
sadānanda śaurē dayānanda vandē

The whole world salutes Thee, the Gods praise You, singing your fame. Salutations to the mercifully blissful One, always happy and brave!

Dayārūpa dēvā jarā janmanāśā
mahādēva sēvya namō dēva dēva (Harē kṛṣṇa)

Shining One, embodiment of compassion, Destroyer of birth and death, served by the great Gods.

HARI OM NAMO NĀRĀYAṆAYA

Hari om namo nārāyaṇaya om namo nārāyaṇa
hari om namo nārāyaṇa
Hari om namo nārāyaṇaya om namo nārāyaṇa
Hari om namo nārāyaṇa
Hari om namaḥ śivāya (7x)
Hari om namo nārāyaṇaya

HĒ GŌVIND HĒ GŌPĀL UDDHARA

Hē gōvind hē gōpāl
uddhara mām dīnam ati dīnam bala hīnam

O Govinda! O Gopala! Please redeem me, forsaken as I am, most distressed am I, and powerless.

Vihita vihīnam viparyaya jñānam
sañchita sarva kaluṣa kalāpam (Hē Gōvind)

I have no good fortune in my fate, my knowledge also brings me ill-fate; my past deeds are all a confused mass of dirt.

Vēdam na jānē vēdyam na jānē
dhyānam na jānē dhyēyam na jānē

I have no knowledge of the Vedas, nor of the essential things to be known. I don't know how to meditate, nor what to meditate upon.

Mantram na jānē tantram na jānē
arkhyam na jānē pādyam na jānē (Hē Gōvind)

I do not know the proper mantras, nor Tantras to worship Thee, I do not know how to offer Thee water, to wash Thy holy hands and feet.

HE PRABHŪ TŪ ĀNANDA DĀTĀ

He prabhū tū ānanda dātā
jñān ham ko dījiyē (2x)
Śīghra sāre durgunom ko
dūr ham se kījiye

O Lord, Bestower of bliss, please give us true knowledge. Please eradicate all our undesirable tendencies without delay.

Līјiye ham ko śaran me
ham sadācāri bane (2x)
Śanti cahak dharma rakṣaka
dhīra vrata dhāri bane (2x)

Please accept us as refuge-seekers at Your feet. Make us followers of the path of virtue. Please make us desirous of peace, protectors of righteousness, determined observers of the vows (to be true devotees).

Prēm se ham gurujanom ki
nitya hī seva kare (2x)
Satya bōle jhūtu tyage
mel āpas me kare (2x)

May we serve our Guru with love and devotion forever, that we will ever be truthful in our speech and deeds, relinquishing falsehood, and may we cooperate with one another.

Nindā kisi kī ham kisīse
bhūl kar bhī nā kare (2x)
Divya jīvana ho hamārā
tere yaśa kā rāha kare (2x)

Even in a moment of forgetfulness, (we hope), we may not speak ill of others. Let our life be divine; let our lives be spent spreading Your glory.

HṚDAYA MANDĀKINI

Hṛdaya mandākini ozhiki varū śuddha
prēma pravāhame tazhuki varū
Āyira dala padma pītasta ennamma
puñciri cādum prabhāsa tīrtha prabhē

Let the flow of pure love flow forever from the heart, like the Mandakini river. The glow of the enchanting smile from my Mother, seated on a thousand petal lotus, is like the brightness from the surface of the holy Prabhasa lake.

Vāsanakal nīri bandhangal kattiṭum
kāśi mahēsa śmaśāna bhasmānkitē
Vairāgya jvāla vivēka samīranan
ōḷam ilakkum vicitra nī sarittu

You are smeared, like Lord Shiva at the funeral pyres in Kasi, with the ashes left behind after the vasanas (innate tendencies) and all human bonds have been burnt away. You are like a picturesque lake agitated violently by the storms of dispassion and discrimination.

Bhaktiyum muktiyum mugdha svar gangalum
nin pāda pūjakku kāttu kidakkave
Pūrṇattil pūrṇayām ātmatriptē varū
śāntitan śītala nāma taranga māi

Devotion, liberation and all heavenly attributes are waiting for a chance to worship Your lotus feet. You are the fullness of the full, always enjoying the bliss of the Eternal Self. Please come to me like waves of Divine Names bringing in their wake ineffable peace to my heart.

ĪŚVARA LĪLA YITELLĀM

Īśvara līla yitellām ulakil
amma tan līla yitellām
Ādiyu mantavum āzhavum kāṇātta
nitya nigūḍha tayellam

Everything is a divine play. The whole universe is a divine play of Mother's. This is all an unfathomable mystery,without beginning, end, or depth.

Ēkātma vastu atōnne ulakāy
nānātva veṣam aṇiññu
Amma tan ā mandahāsam oḷiyāy
puvana māyi viṭarnu

Everything is one absolute reality manifesting in this universe as different forms. The beautiful smile of Amma became the flower garden of the Universe.

Ādima niścala nidrā vaśam
nīyōru svapnam menaññu
Ā svapna līlayil oḷam ñangaḷ
eṅgane nin katha yōtūm

In the beginning, You had a dream. In that dream, we are all waves. How can we tell your story?

Etine ninticu tallum ñaṅgaḷ
ētine vāzhtti stutikkum
Ī viśva līlakal āṭum satte
eṅgane ninne parayum

How can I defame or praise something, everything being Your divine play. How can I talk about You?

JAI JAGADAMBĒ DURGĒ MĀ

Jai jagadambē durgē mā
jai mana mōhini bhadrē mā
Janma vināśini jai jai mā
jagadō dhāriṇi śrīkari mā
Jai mā jai mā jai mā jai mā

Victory to the Mother of the Universe, Mother Durga! Victory to the Enchantress of the mind, Auspicious One! Victory to the destroyer of births, Redeemer of the world, Bestower of auspiciousness! Victory to the Mother, Victory to the Mother!

Viṣṇu vilāsini lakṣmī mā
viśva vimōhini pārvati mā
Vidyā dāyini sarasvatī mā
vimala suhāsini jai jai mā **(Jai mā)**

O Mother Lakshmi, delight of Vishnu. O Mother Parvati, Enchantress of the Universe. O Mother Saraswati, bestower of knowledge. Victory to the Mother, the pure smiling One!

Kāmida dāyini dēvī mā
kāma vināśini kāḷi mā
Kāla svarūpiṇi bhairavi mā
karuṇā mayi jagadambē mā (Jai mā)

O Mother Devi, the wish-fulfilling One. O Mother Kali, the destroyer of desire. O Mother Bhairavi, of the form of Time. O Mother of the Universe, embodiment of compassion!

JAI MĀ AMBE JAI MĀ AMBE

Jai mā ambē jai mā ambē
jai mā ambē jai jai mā (4x)

Dīnajanā vani dēvī dayākari
dānava bhañjani mātē
durita vināśini duḥkha vimōcini
jaya jagadambē mātē

O Devi! Who is compassionate towards the poor, O Mother, the destroyer of Asuras (demons), who removes all troubles and liberates us from sorrows, Victory to You, O Universal Mother!

Karuṇā vāridhi kamala vilōcini
kavitā mṛtamayi mātē
Kalīmala nāśini kanmaṣa mōcini
jaya jagadambē mātē

O Ocean of compassion, the lotus-eyed One, who is the very embodiment of nectarine poetry, who is the destroyer of the evils of this Kali Yuga, who liberates us from sins, Victory to You, O Universal Mother!

Pāvana rūpiṇi pālana kāriṇi
pāpa nivāriṇi mātē
Pūrṇṇa sanātani parvata nandini
jaya jagadambē mātē

O Mother whose form is sacred, who sustains the creation, who removes all sins, who is whole and eternal, O daughter of the Himalayas (Goddess Parvati), Victory to You, O Universal Mother!

Sanmayi cinmayi sakala jaganmayi
sarva janēśvari mātē
Suramuni sēvita caraṇa sarōjē
jaya jagadambe mātē

O Mother whose form is existence and knowledge, who has become the entire universe, the Goddess of the entire humanity, whose Lotus Feet are worshipped by the Gods and the sages, Victory to the Universal Mother!

JAI MĀ JAI JAI MĀ

Jai mā jai jai mā
Lē lō karakamalōm mē mā
Jai mā jai jai mā

O Mother, victory to Thee, victory! Take me in Your arms, O Mother.

Jananī tērē caraṇa yugōm mē
jīvan arppit karttā hum mē

Janam janam mē mērāyē man
Prēm bharā hō mā
Lē lō karakamalōm mē mā

O Mother, I surrender this life at Your feet. Please fill my heart with devotion lifetime after lifetime, O Mother.

Karuṇāsē mujh kō tum dēkhō
śaraṇāgat kō apnāvō mā
Bhav bādhā har lō hē mātē
Bhakti dī jō mā
Lē lō karakamalōm mē mā

Please glance at me with compassion, accept this supplicant as Your own, take away this disease of worldliness that I have, and grant me devotion.

Tērī yād sadākar pāvūm
tērē arccan mēm lag jāvūm
Tērā hī guṇ gāvūm nisadina
Dījō var varadāyi mā
Lē lō karakamalōm mē mā

It is my fervent desire that Your memory will always be fresh in my mind, that my mind will always be engrossed in Your worship, and that I shall always be singing Your praises. Please grant this boon, O Mother who is ever ready to bestow boons.

Kar kamalōm mē mujhē uṭhālō
amṛt pilākar amar banā dō
Avikal bhakti mujhē tum dē dō
Ab apnālō mā
Lē lō karakamalōm mē mā

Sweep me into Your arms, nourish me with the nectar of immortality. Please bless me with unshakable devotion and make me Your own.

JANANĪ TAVA PADA MALARUKALIL

Jananī tava pada malarukalil
praṇamippū tava makkalitā
Karuṇayoṭ ennum kākkaṇamē
arivill āttavarī makkaḷ

O Mother, at Your Lotus Feet, Your children offer salutations. Kindly look after these ignorant children.

Dharmā dharma mariññīṭān
tāyē kaniv arulīṭa ṇamē
Atināy ñānita tirumumbil
añjali kūppi yirikunnu

O Mother, please shower Your mercy on me so that I can discriminate between dharma (righteousness) and adharma (unrighteousness). For that, I am waiting before You with folded hands.

Ariv illātatu kond adhikam
arutāt ullatu ceytēkkām
Alivārnn aruli koṇṭippōl
ammē māpparulīṭa ṇamē

Ignorant as I am, I may do a lot of forbidden acts. O Mother, please forgive me, showering Your merciful Grace now.

Nī kaniññu koṇṭēkaṇam ammē
ninnil nirmaḷa bhaktiye mātram
Vēṇda puṇyavum pāpavum vēṇda
vēṇdat ullatu bhakti yāṇallō

O Mother, graciously grant me pure devotion, which alone I seek. I do not want any merits or demerits; it is devotion alone that I seek.

Ajñānam vēṇdā vijñānam vēṇdā
vēṇdat ullatu bhakti yāṇallō
Vēṇda śuddhi aśuddhiyum vēṇdā
vēṇda tullatu bhakti yāṇallō

Ignorance I do not seek, wisdom I do not seek; it is devotion that I seek. I am unconcerned about purity or impurity. What I seek is devotion alone.

Vēṇda dharmam adharmavum vēṇdā
vēṇdat ullatu bhakti yāṇallō
Vēṇda kalatravum sambattum vēṇdā
vēṇdat ullatu bhakti yāṇallō

Neither righteous nor unrighteous action I seek, it is devotion that I seek. I neither want spouse nor wealth, it is devotion that I seek.

JAPA JAPA AMMĀ AMMĀ

Japa japa ammā ammā ambā nāma japa rē
Iśṭanām satyanām muktinām japa rē

Chant Amma, chant Amma, chant the name of the Divine Mother, chant the beloved, truthful and liberating Name!

Akhilandeśvari jagadamba japa rē
Iśṭanām satyanām muktinām japa rē

Chant the Name of the Mother of the Universe, the Goddess of Amritapuri. Chant the beloved, truthful and liberating Name!

Sadguru jagadguru jagadamba japa rē
Iśṭanām satyanām muktinām japa rē

Chant the name of the Mother of the Universe, our Satguru, Jagatguru (Universal Guru). Chant the beloved, truthful and liberating Name!

Amba nāma karma dhāma yoga dhāma japa rē
Iśṭanām satyanām muktinām japa rē

Chant the Name of Amba which is the abode of karma (action) and yoga (union). Chant the beloved, the truthful and liberating Name!

Amba nāma bhakti dhāma jñana dhāma japa rē
Iśṭanām satyanām muktinām japa rē

Chant the Name of Amma which is the abode of devotion and knowledge. Chant the beloved, truthful and liberating Name!

Amba nāma brahman nāma divya nāma japa rē
Iśṭanām satyanām muktinām japa rē

Chant the Name of Amma, the Name of the Absolute, the Divine Name, Chant the beloved, truthful and liberating Name!

JAYA JAGADAMBĒ JAYA JAYA MĀ

Jaya jagadambe jaya jaya mā
Jaya durga mā jaya kāli mā
Jaya mā jaya mā jaya jaya mā
Jaya durga mā jaya kāli mā

Amṛtānandamayī jaya jaya mā
Brahmānandamayī jaya jaya mā

Sītā rādha rukmini mā
Ūmā ramā brahmānī jaya jaya
Sītā rādha rukmini mā
Jaya mā jaya mā jaya mā jaya jaya mā
Jaya durga mā jaya kāli mā

Victory to the Goddess of the Universe! Victory to Durga, the protectress from worldly affliction! Victory to Kali, the dark One! Victory to the Mother of Immortal Bliss, the Supreme Absolute!

JAYA JAYA BHAYA BHAÑJINI

Jaya jaya bhaya bhañjini
janani bhuvana rañjini
Sakala hṛdaya hāriṇi
abhayam kuru mālini

Victory, victory to the Goddess, who diminishes fear, the Mother, who makes the world happy, attractor of everyone's heart! Do protect me!

Jayatu jayatu śaṅkarī jayatu jayatu śubhakarī

Victory, victory to the doer of auspiciousness.

Malayā cala vāsini mamatā mada śūlini
Janana maraṇa vāriṇi jaya jaya bhava tāriṇi
(Jayatu)

Victory to She who dwells on the Malaya mountain (full of sandalwoods), remover of my-ness and egoism, remover of birth and death, the Goddess Kali, who helps to cross the worldly ocean.

Śvētāmbara dhāriṇī śyāmā mṛdu gāmini
Śrīśaila vihāriṇi śōkārtti vināśini (Jayatu)

Dressed in white clothes, dark blue complexion, who walks gracefully, who moves freely on the mountain, dispeller of sadness and greed.

Ōmkāra svarūpiṇi hrīmkāra nivāsini
Kāmēśa vilāsini kāḷi kuḷa yōgini (Jayatu)

Having the form of (the sound) "OM", who dwells in (the sound) "Hreem", consort of Shiva, yogini, Goddess Kali.

JAYA JAYA DĒVĪ DAYĀLA HARI

Jaya jaya dēvī dayāla hari
Jananī sarasvati pālaya mām

Victory to the Goddess, Beloved of Vishnu, Mother Saraswati protect me!

Amalē kamālā sana sahite
Albhuta carite palaya mām

Protect me! You who are seated on a lotus, having a wonderful history.

Catur mukha bhāryē mām pahi
Vāṇi sarasvati vāg dēvī

O Daughter of Lord Brahma, protect me, O Goddess of speech!

Mātā mangaḷa guṇa śīlē
Manogña śīlē pālaya mām

To the Mother with all the auspicious qualities and with lovely form, I seek protection.

Sarasvatī pūrṇa kadākṣa vīkṣaṇi
Varapradāyini pālaya mām

O Saraswati! Who bestows all that is whole and full, who plays the veena, protect me!

Vīṇapāṇi kalay vāṇi
Janani sarsvatī pālaya mām

O She who plays the veena, Mother Saraswati, protect me!

JAYA MURALĪDHARA MĀDHAVĀ

Jaya muralīdhara mādhavā mukundā
vraja lalanārccita vēṇuvāda lōlā
Yadukula nāyaka rāsakēḷi ramyā
mṛdupada narttana rādhikā samētā

Victory to Muralidhara, Madhava, Mukunda (different names of Sri Krishna), the flute player worshipped by the maidens of Vraja. O Lord of the family of Yadavas, the beautiful One who dances the rasa-lila with tender feet, along with Radhika.

Surajana sēvita śōbhanātma rūpā
munijana mōhana mañjuḷ āvatārā
Janimṛti mōcana dēvakī tanūjā
bhava bhaya bhañjana bhavya divya līlā

O beauty incarnate, served by the Gods, who is the embodiment of the effulgent Self, enchanter of the minds of sages. O son of Devaki, the liberator from the cycle of birth and death, who engages Himself in the auspicious divine play of destroying the fear of worldliness.

Śaśimukha sundara gōpa vēṣa dhāri
paśupati pūjita pāpanā śakārī
Dṛtamaṇi nūpura vaijayanti mālī
śubhapada pallava pītavāsa dhārī

O beautiful One with the moon-like face, clad in the attire of a cowherd, worshipped by Pashupati (Shiva), destroyer of sins. O Lord, who wears anklets with bells and a garland of Vyjanti flowers, who has tender feet, who is clad in yellow clothes.

Kuvalaya lōcana kumkum āṅkitāngā
mṛduhasi tānana nīlamēgha dēhā
Āśaraṇa pālana pāvanā murārē
vraja jana jīvana vāsudēva śaurē

O Lord, who has long beautiful lotus-like eyes, whose body is smeared with vermillion, who sports a sweet smile, whose body is of the hue of the blue cloud. Protector of those who have no other refuge, O Murari! O Sacred One, who is the very life of the people of Vraja, O Vasudeva, Saure (Krishna)!

JAYA PARAMĒŚVARI JAGADAMBĒ

Jaya paramēśvari jagadambē
amṛtānandamayī ambē
Janimṛti nāśini karuṇābdhē
śubha matidāyini daya rūpē

Victory to the Supreme Mother, the Mother Goddess of the Universe! O Mata Amritanandamayi! Goddess of my heart, Destroyer of birth and death, Ocean of Compassion, Bestower of an auspicious intellect, Personification of Kindness.

Śritajana pālini mṛdulāngī
jana mana hāriṇi jayadātri
Kalimala mōcini kamalākṣī
tribhuvana mōhini tripurēśī

Victory to the Protector of those who take refuge in Her, whose body is very soft, the Stealer of hearts, the One who bestows victory, who destroys the stains of the Kaliyuga, who is lotus-eyed, the Charmer of the three worlds, Goddess of the three cities.

Nija sukha dāyini nikhilēśī
bhava bhaya hāriṇi bhuvanēśī
Manalaya kāriṇi hṛdayēśi
mṛdu pāda narttana paramēśi

Victory to You, O Mother, Giver of the joy of the Self, who is the Goddess of all, who destroys the fears of worldliness, who is the Goddess of the Universe, in whom the mind gets dissolved, who is the Goddess of the heart, the Supreme Goddess, who dances with small soft steps.

Karuṇā vāridhi kanakāmgi
kavitā kāriṇi kaḷabhāṣi
Vibudha rādhita varadātrī
jagadō dhāriṇi varavāṇi

Victory to the Ocean of Compassion, who is golden colored, who is of the Source of poetry and the Bestower of talent, who speaks exquisitely, whose words are sweet, who is adored by the gods (devas), who bestows boons and uplifts the world.

Surajana pūjitā sukharūpē
munijana sēvitā bhavanāśē
Śrutipāda varṇṇitā śubhamūrttē
śivavidhi vanditā caraṇābjē (Jaya paramēśvari)

Victory to the One who is the embodiment of happiness, who is worshipped by the gods, who is the Destroyer of transmigratory existence, who is adored by ascetics, the One of auspicious form, extolled in the scriptures, the One whose Lotus Feet are worshipped by Shiva and Brahma.

JAYATU JAYATU SADGURU

Jayatu jayatu sadguru śrī caraṇam
amṛtānandamayī śubha caraṇam

Victory to the Holy Feet of the Satguru! O Mother Amritanandamayi, blessed are Your Holy Feet.

Ātma prakāśaka sadguru caraṇam
mārga pradīpaka śrī caraṇam
Yōga sapōṣaka sadguru caraṇam
bhōga vipāṭana śrī caraṇam
āmṛtānandamayī śubha caraṇam

The Feet of the Satguru which enlighten the soul, those Holy Feet which light the path, those Feet of the Satguru which promote yoga (merging of the individual soul with the Supreme Self), those Holy Feet which eliminate sensuality.

Andhatam ōlaya sadguru caraṇam
bandhuram āyālaya caraṇam
Prēma rasāmṛta sadguru caraṇam
tyāga nidarśana śrī caraṇam
āmṛtānandamayī śubha caraṇam

The Feet of the Satguru which cause the dissolution of blinding darkness, those Holy Feet which remove the delusion of attachment, those Feet of the Satguru which are the essence of nectarine Love, those Holy Feet which show us the path of renunciation.

Satya sanātana sadguru caraṇam
nitya nirañjana śrī caraṇam
Guṇa nirguṇa maya dvandva viśālam
advaitātmaka parama padam
amṛtānandamayī śubha caraṇam

The Holy Feet of the Satguru which are the Eternal Truth, those Holy Feet which are eternally immaculate, which embrace the pairs of opposites, which are both with attributes and attributeless, the ultimate state of non-duality.

JHILAM JHILAM

Jhilam jhilam cilaṅkakal padam padam kiluṅgavē
ulaññu raññu lāsya mārnnu nṛttamāṭi kāḷikā
Kṣaṇam kṣaṇam kulu kiyaṭi vāḷ ilakki bhairavi
en manas sariññu taḷḷi aṭṭahāsam iṭṭavaḷ

Kali danced vigorously, the sounds 'jhilam, jhilam' of Her anklets resounding everywhere. Then Bhairavi shook Her body; She brandished Her sword, and then with a roar, She cut away the last vestiges of my mind.

Śūlam iṭṭiḷakki ente ñanine pilarnnaval
nisva nākki enne ātma vīthiyil eriññavaḷ
Naṣṭa māyoriṣṭa vastu keṭṭi yaññu pulkuvān
pāṭu peṭṭorenne nōkki durga hāsyam ārnnahō

She waved Her trident in front of me, then exorcised the "me" in me; She made me selfless and catapulted me onto the path of the Self. What I had been holding onto as something dear was lost forever. Durga laughed at me, who was totally nonplussed!

Teḷiññu maññiṭunna chitra jālamāya sriṣṭiyil
amba ninne ñan maranna tente kuttam ākkōlā
Devakaḷ trimūrttikaḷ maharṣikaḷ samastarum
dēvī ninte māyayil bhramiccuṭinna tillayō

O Mother, is it my fault that I forgot You, lost as I was in the kaleidoscopically ever-changing world of Your creation? Even the gods, the Trinity (Brahma, Vishnu and Siva), and the sages get enraptured by Your maya!

Kaṇṇuruṭṭi nāvu nīṭṭī ugra rūpa mārnniṭūm
ammaye namiccu kuttamēttu cōlli ñan mudā
Nirañña pū nilāvu pōle puñciriccu kāḷikā
teḷiññoren manassil āke śānti cinti ambikā

I bowed down, confessed all to this ferocious form of the Divine Mother, who was standing in front of me eyes rolling, tongue sticking out. Kalika smiled at me; it was like the full moon flooding me with its cool refreshing light. Ambika filled my mind with clarity, with ineffable peace.

Amba ninne visma riccha tettu ceytiṭ illini
ninṭe prēma bhakti mātram āśrayam kṛpāmayī
Smariccu ninne eppozhum marikkilum smariccitān
labhicci ṭāvu viśramam mahēśi nin padaṅgaḷil

Mother, I will never forget You and commit mistakes again. My only refuge from now on will be my love and devotion for You. I will always remember You, even at the time of my death. The only rest I will ever know will be when I am at Your feet.

JIS HĀL MĒ

Jis hāl mē jis deś mē jis veṣ mē rahō
rādhā ramaṇa rādhā ramaṇa rādhā ramaṇa bōlō
(3x)

In whatever condition, in whichever country, or in whatever form you might be, sing "radha ramana."

Jis kām mē jis dām mē jis gāv mē rahō
rādhā ramaṇa rādhā ramaṇa rādhā ramaṇa bōlō
(3x)

In whatever work, in whatever profession and in whatever village you may be, sing "radha ramana."

Jis sang mē jis rang mē jis dhang mē rahō
rādhā ramaṇa rādhā ramaṇa rādhā ramaṇa bōlō
(3x)

In whatever company, in whatever color or whatever state of emotion you may be, sing "radha ramana."

Jis yōg mē jis bhōg mē jis rōg mē rahō
rādhā ramaṇa rādhā ramaṇa rādhā ramaṇa bōlō
(3x)

In whichever path of yoga, in whichever state of sense pleasure or in whichever condition of disease you might be, sing "radha ramana."

JYŌTIR MĀYI MĀ

Jyōtir māyi mā muttumāri mā
Hē śiva śaṅkari dēvī bhagavati jyōtir māyi mā
Dīna dayālō tējōvati śrī jyōtir māyi mā

Kālī! Śūla dhāriṇi jyōtir māyi mā
Bhavāni jyōtir māyi mā muttumāri mā

Akhilāṇḍeśvari sundari bhagavati jyōtir māyi mā
Parāśakti jyōtir māyi mā muttumāri mā

Effulgent Mother, showerer of pearls! O beloved of Shiva-Shankara, Divine Mother, effulgent Mother! Protector of the down-trodden, who radiates the glow of divinity. Kali! Wielder of the trident, effulgent Mother! Bhavani, Goddess of the Universe, embodiment of light, beautiful one, effulgent Mother, the Supreme energy.

KAHĀ HŌ KANHĀ

Kahā hō kanhā mērē pyārē ghanaśyām
nandalālā nandalālā kṛṣṇa gōpālā
Bōlō nandalālā nandalālā kṛṣṇa gōpālā

Where are You, Kanha (Krishna), my darling Ghana Shyam? O Nandalala, Krishna Gopala!

Dahi makhan rakhē mēnē tērē hī svāgat mē
āyēngē āyēngē kanhā cāhā mē nē man mē
Āyō nahī nandalālā mākhan nahīm khāyō
nandalālā nandalālā kṛṣṇa gōpālā
Bōlō nandalālā nandalālā kṛṣṇa gōpālā

I have saved up butter and curds just for You. I have cherished this hope in my mind, that You will surely come. But You have not come yet, O Nandalala. You have not tasted the butter. Where are You?

Rādhā gōpiyōm kī bhakti dās nahī jānē
kahā hē nandalālā kōyi tō batāyē
ṭhukrānā dēnā kṛṣṇa phūl na jānā
nandalālā nandalālā kṛṣṇa gōpālā
Bōlō nandalālā nandalālā kṛṣṇa gōpālā

This servant does not know the devotion like Radha and the Gopis have. Will anybody tell him where Nandalala is? Please do not forsake me, Krishna. Please do not forget me.

KĀḶI MĀ JAI JAI MĀ

Kāḷi mā jai jai mā
Kāḷi mā

Śyāma sundarī bhairavī mā
Prēma sāgarī madhuri mā
Ōmkārēśvarī kāli mā
Hrīmkārēśvari kāli mā, Kāḷi mā

You are beautifully dark, Mother, You are indeed Bhairavi (a form of the Divine Mother). You are an ocean of love, You are indeed sweet. You are of the form OM (pranava mantra). You are of the form hreem (bija mantra), O Mother Kali!

Trilōka pālinī kāli mā
Triguṇa vināśini kāli mā
Virakta bhaktōn mādini mā
Nirasta māyā rakṣakī mā
Rakṣakī mā

You protect the three worlds, Mother Kali. You destroy the three gunas, O Mother Kali. You are very enthusiastic about Your devotees who have attained total detachment. O Mother! You protect us from delusion.

Parama dayāmayī śivadē mā
Karuṇārṇṇava madhu laharī mā
Jai jagavandinī varadē mā
Jai jagadīśvari śubhadē mā
śubhadē mā

You are of the form of Supreme compassion, O Mother, giver of all good things. You are the sweet wave on the ocean of compassion. Victory to You who is worshipped by the whole world, and who is the boon giver to all. Victory to the Mother, the Queen of the universe!

KĀḶIKĒ DĒVĪ AMṚTEŚVARI

Kāḷikē dēvī amṛteśvari lalitambikē pahi mam
Śyāme śive sundari sarveśvari pahi mam
Jaya durga bhavani ambikē pahi mam
Śakti śrī paraśakti hṛdayeśvari pahi mam

O Mother Amriteshwari, Goddess Kali, Mother Lalita, protect me! O dark-complexioned Consort of Shiva, beautiful One, Goddess ruling over all, protect me! Victorious Durga, Consort of Bhava (Shiva), Mother, protect me! O Luminous Power, Supreme Power, Goddess who resides in the heart, protect me!

KĀḶIKĒ ŚYĀMA CANDRIKĒ

Kāḷikē śyāma candrikē
kōmaḷāmgi nī sundarāmbikē
Mōhinī mōha nāśinī
nitya vandinī prēma rūpiṇī

O Kalike! the One like the blue moon, with beautiful limbs, enchantress and remover of desires, embodiment of divine love, who is always worshipped

Ammayāy amṛtēśvarī
śanta bhāvamāy kṛpāmayī (2x)
Bhōgavum bhakti muktiyum
nalkum ambanī prēma rūpiṇī (2x)

O Amriteshwari! the Mother of grace and love, You are the bestower of desires, devotion and liberation, with an outward expression of peace.

Karuṇā rasam tūkumā mukham
duḥkha mōcakam śanti dāyakam (2x)
Bhāṣaṇam laḷitōttamam
vaśya sundaram madhurāmṛtam (2x)

Your face, overflowing with compassion, is the cause for peace and the removal of sorrows. Your speech is simple and supreme, O Beautiful ambrosia of nectar!

Narttanam etra sundaram
nētrōtsavam prēma pūritam (2x)
Mandamay nṛtta māṭiyen
hṛttilēkiṭū divya darśanam (2x)

How beautiful is your dance! It is full of love and a festival for our eyes. Slowly dance, come within my heart and give me your vision.

KALYĀNA KṚṢṆA KAMINĪYA

Kalyāna kṛṣṇa kaminīya kṛṣṇa
Kāliya mardana śrī kṛṣṇa
Govardhana giridhārī murārī, gōpī mana sañcāri
Vṛdāvana ki tulasi mālā
Pitāmbhara dhārī murārī

O Krishna! Bestower of auspiciousness, Handsome One, subduer of the serpent Kaliya, who lifted the Govardhana mountain, destroyer of the demon Mura, who lives in the minds of the gopis, wearing a garland of tulasi from Vrindavan, who wears yellow robes.

KAMALĒ KARUṆĀRDRA MĀNASĒ

Kamalē karuṇārdra mānasē
śubhadē śaraṇā gatāśrayē
girijē guru rūpa vigrahē
varadē caturā nanapriyē

kamalē	One who is seated on a lotus
karuṇārdramanase	Whose mind is full of compassion
śubhade	One who bestows auspiciousness
śaraṇāgatāśrayē	Who is the refuge of those who seek Her
girijē guru rūpa vigrahē	Daughter of the mountain in the form of the guru
varadē	Bestower of boons
caturānanapriyē	Who is the beloved of the fourfaced Brahma

Sukhadē svararūpi śaradē
mahitē madhubhāṣi mañjulē

Lalitē layadātrī nanditē
rasikē mṛdugātri mōhanē

sukhadē	Giver of happiness
svararūpi śaradē	Sarasvati, the presiding deity of musical notes
mahitē madhubāṣi	Who is great, whose words are as sweet as nectar
mañjule	Who is beautiful
lalite laya dātri	Who is guileless and the cause of melody in music
nanditē	One who revels in Her own being
rasikē	One who delights in everything
mṛdugātri mōhanē	Who has lovely and tender limbs

Sarasī ruha sundar ānanē
nalinī dala nīla lōcanē
Gaja gāmini gāna lōlulpē
jani mōcini dīna vatsalē

sarasī ruha sundar ānanē	Whose face is as beautiful as a lotus
nālinidala nīlalōcanē	Whose eyes are like the petals of a blue lotus
gaja gāmini	Whose gait is as majestic as that of an elephant
gāna lōlupē	Who is immersed in music
jani mōcini	Who rescues (devotees) from the cycle of birth and death
dīna vatsalē	Who loves and helps the downtrodden

Amṛtēśvari viśva nāyakī
mana hāriṇi manda hāsinī
Kali mōcini sāma gāyakī
śama dāyini śaila nandinī

viśva nāyakī	Who is the empress of the universe
manahāriṇi manda hāsinī	Who steals the mind and smiles gently
kalimōcini	Who rescues one from the rigors of the age of kali
sāma gāyakī	Who singing reminds one of the beauty of the sama veda
śama dāyini	Who bestows patience
śaila nandinī	Daughter of the mountain

KANḌRUKAL MĒYTIṬA VANTĀY

Kanḍrukal mēytiṭa vantāy kaṇṇā
kārmukil nigarttiṭum kaṇṇā
Kudriṇai kuṭayāy piṭittavanē
kōvala en maṇivaṇṇā

O Kanna! The cowherd who lovingly took care of the grazing of his cattle and whose complexion reminds one of the dark blue clouds, who lifted up the hill Govardhana as an umbrella; my beloved of bewitching form!

Śiruviral kuzhalinai taṭava
sēvaṭi kiṅkiṇi muzhaṅga
Karavaigaḷ kūṭṭam naṭuvē
kanivuṭan uṭane varuvāy
Kaṇṇā maṇivaṇṇā
kuzhal mannā ezhil vaṇṇā

You lovingly come in the midst of the cows, while your lovely little fingers play the flute and the ornamental anklets adorning the feet give rise to music notes. Kanna. who plays the flute. of bewitching form.

Mizhikaḷil niraintiṭa vārāy
vinaikaḷai pōkkiṭa vārāy
Vazhikaḷai kāṭṭiṭa vārāy
vāzhvinil nalam tara vārāy
Kaṇṇā maṇivaṇṇā
kuzhal mannā ezhil vaṇṇā

Fill my eyes by blessing me with Thy beatific vision. Remove all my un- desirable qualities, lead me in the right path bestowing fullfilment of my life.

Māyavan unnai paṇivōm
mādhava manatil oḷirvāy
Tūyadōr ulakam kāṭṭi
tūmaṇi viḷakkāy aruḷvāy
Kaṇṇā maṇivaṇṇā
kuzhal mannā ezhil vaṇṇā

We supplicate ourselves to thee, master magician, who shines in our hearts. Show us a world of purity by guiding us with an incomparable leading light.

KANIVIN KAṬĀKṢAM

Kanivin kaṭākṣam coriyān nī varumō?
varadāna sunayanā śrī bhagavan murārē
Karaḷāke piṭayunnū paritāpam perukunnū
kaḷiyāyi tukarutātu ṭanarikil varumō?

O Lord Murari (Krishna), will You come to cast a glance of compassion? My heart is quivering and my grief is mounting. Do not take this lightly; will You come near me without delay?

Bhava bandhana mazhiyān manaḥ
sukham innu ivan aṇayān
taraṇē ceru tuṇa ninnuṭe kanivin mizhi munayāl
Naru puñciri vazhiyum mukha kamalam manataḷirin
kaṇi kāṇmatina aṭiyaniṭa yaruḷīṭuka bhagavan!

To loosen my worldly ties, to attain some mental peace, kindly give a little help with a compassionate glance from the corner of Your eye. O Lord, kindly grant me a vision of Your smiling lotus face.

Pala janmani pativāy kazhivi yalātuzha rukayāy
bhava nāśana bhagavan! tava pādatāratil aṇayān
Taḷarunnu ṭalatupōl mati balavum poy sakalam
ini yennuṭe gati ninnuṭe hitameṅgan eyatupōl

O Lord, I have been constantly searching through many births, unable to reach Your feet. My body is getting weak now, so is my mind; whatever You decide will be my fate now.

KANIVUṬAYŌN KAṆṆAN

Kanivuṭayōn kaṇṇan kaniviyann akatāril
varum ennu karuti ñān kāttirunnu

O Kanna, You are the embodiment of compassion. Hoping that You would kindly shower compassion and come to my heart.

Karayuvān kaṇṇunīr illātta kaṇṇukaḷ
kamanīya vigraham kāttirunnu kaṇṇā
kamanīya vigraham kāttirunnu

I waited to see Your beautiful form with eyes emptied of tears.

Karuṇatan kara kāṇa kaṭalāṇu nī nēril
ariyuvōr karivinte uravāṇu nī
Narajanma sukṛtattin phalamāṇu nī
Cuṭu vyathapūṇṭa hṛdayattin taṇalāṇu nī

You are the boundless sea of compassion. For those who have known Your true nature, You are the source of all knowledge, You are the fruit of the virtuous actions performed in many human births, You are a soothing shade to a burning grief-stricken heart.

Nirantara dhyānattin layamāṇu nī bhakti
paravaśa hṛdayattin amṛtāṇu nī
Agatikaḷkka viratam avalambam nī
Bhāva layahṛttil anubhūti dhanamāṇu nī

You are the blissful absorption arising from constant meditation. You are the nectar of the heart ecstatic with devotion, You are the constant refuge to those who have no other support, You are the wealth of experience of the heart absorbed in divine bliss.

KAÑJALŌCANĒ

Kañjalōcanē amba kamra vigrahē
kanma ṣāpahē amba kavini ṣēvitē

O Mother! The lotus-eyed One, the One with a beauteous form, the One who removes sins and impurities, the One who is worshipped by the sages (Rishis).

Sarva saukhyadē amba sadgati pradē
sarva siddhidē amba pāhimām śivē

O bestower of happiness, enlightenment and all powers, O Mother, the auspicious One, please save me!

Hari harārcitē amba mada vivarjjitē
harihara priyē amba sura supūjitē
O Mother! Who is worshipped by Krishna and Shiva, who is devoid of pride, favorite of Vishnu and Shiva, who is worshipped by the devas
Hamsa vāhanē amba hamsa lakṣitē
simha vāhanē amba sundarānanē

O Mother who rides on a swan (Saraswati), who is the goal of the mantra "Ham Sa", who rides on a lion (Durga), who has a beautiful face.

KAṆṆĀ TĀMARA KAṆṆĀ

Kaṇṇā tāmara kaṇṇā
kaṇṇā kārmēgha varṇṇā
Nīlōlpala mizhi nirupama lāvaṇya
nitānta ramaṇā kaṇṇā kaṇṇā
nitānta ramaṇā kaṇṇā

Kanna (child Krishna) Lotus eyed! Kanna, dark cloud-hued! Your eyes, like blue lotuses, shed heavenly grace. You are my eternal beloved.

Vṛndāvanattile rādhikaye pōle
indranī laprabha tēṭi

Iravum pakalum ariyāt uzhaḷum
iniyī manassil teḷiyū kaṇṇā

Like Radha of Vrindavan, I seek Thy dark-blue glow. Unaware of days and nights, I pine for Thee. Do manifest in this mind, O Kanna!

Kāḷiya mardanam gaurava bhāvam
kaikkoṇṭa nandana bālā
Karuṇā mayanē śaraṇā gatanē
kāṇān gatiyaruḷū kaṇṇā ninne

Son of Nanda, You took a fierce form to quell the dreaded snake Kaliya. O compassionate One, refuge of the destitutes, Do bless me with Thy vision.

KAṆṆUNĪR VĀRNNU

Kaṇṇunīr vārnnu vārnnammaye kāṇāte
nnuḷḷile paital taḷarnnu
Snēhō ṣmaḷaṅgaḷām tēn mozhi tīrtthatte
yennini ñān ācamippū

The child inside me is tired of crying without seeing Mother. When can I sip the drops of holy water of Her loving sweet words?

Kāttinte kaikaḷāl taṭṭi terippicca
kāṭṭumulla pūvu pōle
Innī vazhiyil anāthanāy tīrnnoren
ātma duḥkham ārarivū

Just like a jasmine flower blown astray at the way side by the wind, I am an orphan. Who knows the depth of my sorrow?

Otta kirunnu ñān tēṅgunnu jīvitam
duḥsvapnauttamāy māri
Āḷunna ti nānpilūṭen manam
nīri veṇṇīrāyi māri

I have been crying alone so long. My life is just like an unpleasant dream. My mind is turned into ashes in the flame of sorrow.

Nerāṇu nīyakannāl pinne ātmāvu
śūnyamāy tīrunnu tāne
Ērum nissāratā bōdham manassine
hā sadā nir vīryamākki

It is true that when You are gone, all I experience is a limitless void. I feel forlorn and my mind loses all its enthusiasm.

KARTTURĀÑJAYĀ PRĀPY

Kartturāñjayā prāpyate phalam
karma kim param karma tajjaḍam
kṛti mahodadhau patana kāraṇam
phalam aśasvatam gati nirodhakam

By the laws of the Lord, the fruits of an action are gained. How can that inert action be limitless? In the vast ocean of actions, impermanent result is the cause for fall (of man) and is a barrier to progress.

Īsvarār pitam neccayā kṛtam
citta śodhakam mukti sādhakam
kāya vāṅmanaḥ kārya muttamam
pūjanam japaścinnam kramāt

Actions done with an attitude of dedication to the Lord, without attachment to the result, purify the mind and are a means to attain liberation. The mental, oral, and physical actions viz. meditation, chanting, and ritualistic worship, are all most beneficial in that order.

Jagata īśvadhi yukta sevanam
aṣṭamūrti dṛdeva pūjanam
uttamastavā ducca mandataḥ
cittajam japa dhyāna muttamam

Serving the world with the attitude of serving the Lord is the (true) worship of the Lord, who is the wielder of the eightfold forms. To chant or sing (the glories of the Lord) is good. But superior to that is the loud japa. (Superior to that is japa done with the lips). Superior to that is japa done by the mind. Mental japa is the best (subtlest).

Ājyadhāraya strota sāsamam
sarala cintanam viralataḥ param
bheda bhāvana tse ha mityasau
bhāvanā bhidā pāvanī matā

Uninterrupted contemplation (on the Lord), which is like a stream of ghee (and) the flow of a river, is superior to interrupted contemplation. Instead of meditating with an attitude of duality (I am different from the Lord), the non-dual vision 'He am I' is purifying as it leads the jiva to the essential nature — this is the view of the Sruti.

KARUNA SINDHO BHAIRAVI

Karuna sindho bhairavi
amṛtānandamayī devī
Karuna sindho bhairavi

karuna sindho	ocean of compassion
sindho bhairavi	name of a particularly beautiful raga
bhairavi	Goddess

Pūṛṇa brahma svarūpiṇyai
saccidānanda mūrttaye
ātmā rāmāgra gaṇyāyai
amṛteśvaryai namo namaḥ

Adorations to Amma, the immortal Goddess, who is the complete manifestation of the absolute Truth, who is existence, knowledge, and bliss embodied, who is supreme among those who revel in the inner Self.

Sarva mangaḷa māngalye
śive sarvartha sādhike
sarṇye trayambake gauri
nārāyaṇi namostu te
Amṛteśvari namostu te

Salutations to You, Narayani, Amriteshwari, who is the good of all good, O auspicious Devī, who accomplishes everything, the giver of refuge, O three eyed Gauri.

Tvameva mata ca pītā tvameva
tvameva bandhus ca sakhā tvameva
Tvameva vidyā dravinam tvameva
tvameva sarvam amṛteśvari mā (2x)

You are my mother and father. You are my relative and friend. You are my learning and wealth. You are my All, mother Amriteshwari!

Śaraṇāgata dīnārtha paritrāṇa parayaṇē
sarvasyārthi hare devī

nārāyani namostu te
Amṛteśvari namostu te

Salutations to You, Narayani, Amriteshwari, who is intent on saving the dejected and distressed that take refuge under you; O Devi, who removes the suffering of all!

Śrīmātā śrī mahārājñī śrīmat simhāsan'eśvari
cidagni kuṇḍa sambhūtā deva kārya samudyatā
Amṛteṣvariyai namo namaḥ

Adorations to Amma, the immortal Goddess, who is the auspicious Mother, the empress of the universe, the queen of the most glorious throne, who was born in the fire pit of Pure Consciousness, who is intent on fulfilling the wishes of the gods.

Karuna sindho bhairavi amṛtānandamayī devī
Karuna sindho karuna sindho karuna sindho bhairavi

O Goddess Amritanandamayi, Ocean of compassion, Embodiment of the ocean of compassion (of the compassionate and beautiful raga)!

KARUṆĀMAYĪ HṚDAYEŚVARĪ

Karuṇāmayī hṛdayeśvarī amṛteśvarī sarveśvarī
Dayāmayī jagadambe mātā
Śaktī mayī ammā kāḷi maheśvarī
Ammē ādī parāśaktī

O Mother Amriteshwari, the supreme Goddess, full of compassion, the Queen of our hearts, You are our Mother. O Mother, You are all powerful, the Supreme Goddess Kali, the primordial supreme energy.

KARUṆĀMAYĪ KANIVU TŪKAṆĒ

Karuṇāmayi kanivu tūkaṇē
karaḷ uruki karayum ivanil kanivu tūkanē
Avaniyil ñān verum anāthan
aruḷaṇē hṛdi abhayam

O compassionate Mother, please shower grace upon me. Be kind to me who has been crying so long with a broken heart. I am an orphan in this unverse. Please give me refuge.

Akale yakaleyum arikil arikilum
hṛdaya malarilum niravu nī
Aṇuvil aṇuvum nī mahatil mahatum nī
praṇava svara layanil ayavum

You are farther than the farthest and nearer than the nearest.You are also in the lotus of my heart. You are smaller than the smallest and bigger than the biggest. You are the place where the sound of Om merges into itself.

Calavuma calavum calana hētuvum
calana mattati gamanavum,
Paravum aparavum parama śāntiyum
samayavum sthala makhilam nī

You are the movable and the immovable. You are the cause of all movements. You are everything in this univese and beyond. You are eternal peace. You are time and space.

Tikavil tikavu nī mikavil mikavu nī
sakala bhuvanaika kāriṇi
Arivin arivu nī arivin nuravu nī
nikhila nigamānta sāravum

You are the fullness of the full and the best of all that is splendid. You are the cause of the universe. You are the essence of wisdom. Wisdom springs forth from You. You are the source of all knowledge.

Arivil uṇaruvān amṛtu nuṇayuvān
abhayam aṇayuvān kaniyaṇē!
Bhava mahārṇṇava bhay nivāriṇi
taraṇamē sucir āśrayam

Oh, Divine Mother bless me with knowledge and wisdom. Protect me from all calamities and fear. Provide me with shelter and refuge.

KĀRUṆYA DHĀMAMĒ AMMĒ

Kāruṇya dhāmamē ammē
kattu koḷḷēṇamē ammē
Nin prēma monnināy kezhunno-renne nī
nin padam cērkkente tāyē dēvī
śrī lalitē viśvamātē

O Mother of compassion, protect me. I am crying for Your love. O Lalita! Mother of the universe, please make me merge into Your lotus feet.

Tārukaḷ tāzhattu kūmbī
tārakaḷ mānattu maṅgī
Andhata tiṅgiyoren vazhi tārayil
innumenn-amma vannīllā dēvī
en manam tēṅgi taḷarnnu

The stars in the sky bowed down and dimmed. Mother still did not come into my dark alley. O Devi, my mind is tired of crying.

Ī pakalum itā pōyī
ī rāvum ippōḷ kazhiyum
Vēdana tinnu tinnammaye kāṇāte
tōratta kaṇṇukaḷ mazhki— ammē
ī kuññu vāṭi ttaḷarnnu

This day also just went away like that. This night also will soon go away. My eyes have been shedding tears without seeing Amma. O Mother! I am exhausted after suffering through these pains for so long.

Innu vannīṭum ennamma
ippōzh ettīṭum ennamma
Ennumī cintayil ellā nimēṣavum
kātt irikkunnu nin paital— ammē
kaṇṇu cimmāt irikkunnu

Amma, this child of Yours has been waiting for You even without blinking the eyes, thinking that You will come just now, today itself.

Onu cintiykku-kennammē
entinī krūra vinōdam
Ikkoṭum kāṭṭil nī enne veṭiññīṭān
entu ñān ceytente tāyē—vekkam
enne nī vanne ṭukkeṇē

Mother, why this cruel play? Think for a moment; why are You leaving me alone in this thick fearful jungle? What did I do to deserve this? Please, Mother, come and carry me back.

KĀRVARṆṆANE KARUṆĀMAYANE

Kārvarṇṇane karuṇā mayane - kaṇṭō
kāyām pūkkaḷē niṅgaḷ?
Pūkkaṇi konnakaḷ pītāmbaravumāy
kāttu ninnīṭunnat āre? (2x)

O Kayambu flowers, have you seen the dark all-merciful Krishna, dressed in sparkling yellow, for whom these bunches of kanikkonna flowers are waiting?

Ōrmmayil eppozhum ōḷam tuḷumbumā-
vēṇu gānāmṛta rāga dhāra
Ōmkāra nāda taramgam uṇarttumī
ālila tennalin ārunalki?

The enchanting music of his flute is constantly ringing in my memory. Who is it, that imparted the music to the playful breeze which arouses the Om sound?

Nīla kaṭambukaḷ pūkkunn iṭaṅgaḷil
nīlā ravindam viṭarunn iṭaṅgaḷil
Tēṭittiraññ ente niṣphala nētraṅgaḷ
vāṭittaḷarnnu maṭaṅgi

My eyes are tired of searching for Him everywhere, in all places where the kadamba flowers bloom, in all places where the blue lotuses bloom.

Kaṇṇaṭaccātmāvil tiṅgum viṣādattāl
kaṇṇane yōrttu ñān etra tēṅgi
Kaṇṭill itēvare kaṇṇīru mātramen
kaṇṇan enikkentin ēki?

Closing my eyes and thinking of Krishna, I cried in anguish which filled my soul. Alas, I could not find him even now. Why has Kanna given me tears only?

KAṬALŌRAM TAVAM

kaṭalōram tavam ceyyum kāḷiyammā
kanilōṭu emāi kākkum śaktiyammā
maṭal viriykkum tāzhai ena bhakti veḷḷam
maṇpatayil pāyccu kintra śaktiyamma

O Mother Kali! Who does penance by the sea shore, who compassionately protects me, who irrigates the hearts of devotees with the floods of devotion, like a fully blossomed flower spreading its fragrance.

piravi yenum kaṭal kaṭakka tōṇi āvāḷ
pirpaṭṭōr nalam peravē ēṇi āvāḷ
marati enum mayakkatte pōkkiṭuvāḷ
manatil ire cintanaiyai vaḷar tiṭuvāḷ

She is the ocean liner who helps us to go across the ocean of worldly existence. She is the ladder by which the upliftment of the helpless takes place. She removes the delusion of forgetfulness and inspires divine thoughts.

uravu solli tiruvaṭiyai patti nirppōr
uyarvaṭaya varam taruvāḷ entrum avaḷ
turavi yerum pōṭṭru kintra tūyavaḷē
teviṭṭāte pērinpam taru pavaḷē

She bestows boons for the welfare of those who have taken refuge at Her feet. She is even glorified by renunciates. She is the bestower of eternal bliss.

KATTĪṬUKAMMĒ Ī KŌMAḶA

Kattīṭukammē ī kōmaḷa vigraham
kāruṇya pūrvvamī makkaḷkkāyī

pāvamī makkaḷkku vērillor āśrayam
prēma svarūpamī ammamātram (2x)

Amma, please protect your delicate body compassionately for these children. These poor children do not have any refuge other than Amma, this embodiment of Love.

Bhakta janaṅgaḷkku kiṭṭīṭumoṭṭere
mūrtti kaḷum guru bhutan mārum
Ennālīma kaḷkku vērillor āśrayam
ammayallāteyī pāriṭattil (2x)

The devotees can get a lot of Gods and Masters, but these children have none other than Amma as refuge in this world.

Ñaṅgaḷ tan śvāsani śvāsavum prāṇanum
ammayilennō layyiccupōyi
Amma yillāttorī lōkattil alpavum
vāzhuka yillayī makkaḷ ammē (2x)

Our very breath, the vital force, everything was dissolved in Amma a long time ago. These children can't live further in a world bereft of You.

Mattoru cintaykkum iṭamilla ñaṅgaḷil
muktiykkum illammē tellumāśa
Vēṇṭatī prēma svarupam atumātram
kāttīṭukammē ī vigrahatte (2x)

There is no place for any other thoughts in us. We don't even long for liberation. What we want is this embodiment of love. Therefore, please preserve your beautiful body.

KĒḶKKĀTTA BHĀVAM

Kēḷkkātta bhāvam naṭipatentē
ariyātta bhāvam naṭipatentē
Ammē ī kuññin ī piṭayunna hṛdayattin
tēṅgaḷ dhvanikaḷ aṅgettāttatō (2x)

Why pretend You do not hear my sobs? Why pretend as if You do not know my sorrows? O Mother, is it that the sobs of this throbbing heart have not reached Your ears?

Ēzhayām en vili kēḷkkā tirikkān
kāraṇam entennu colliṭāmō
Prēmam illāññatō jñānam illāññatō
kāruṇya tīrttham nī cori yāññatō (2x)

Could You tell me the reason for not responding to the call of this helpless child? Is it because Your child lacks love, or is it Your child's lack of wisdom, or is it because You do not wish to shower the sacred water of compassion?

Ārōrum illā torēzha ñān ammē nin
prēma lābhattināy entu ceyvū
Lōkam marakkām ñān enne marakkām ñān
ammē ninakkāy innellām marakkām ñān (2x)

Helpless and forlorn I am, what am I to do to gain Your Love, O Mother? I shall forget the world, I shall forget myself. For Your sake, I shall forget everything.

KṢAṆAM ENNU VANNIṬUM

Kṣaṇam ennu vanniṭum jagadamba vanniṭum
mama mānasam sadā eriyunnu kāḷikē

Urukunnu nencakam poriyunnu jīvanum
iruḷunnu cintakaḷ takarunnu śāntiyum

O Mother of the universe, Kalike, please come soon! My mind has been aching to see You. My heart is melting, my life is getting scorched, destroying every bit of peace from my mind.

Vazhi pārttu pārtumē mizhiyō kuzhi ykkakam
mizhinīr pozhiññitil vazhi pāzhilō śivē
Hṛdi āttu nōttu ñān tiru darśanārttiyil
teḷiyēṇam uḷḷil nī varum ennu kāḷikē

With tears in my eyes and gazing at the grave, I moved forward along the path very carefully. Oh, was it all a waste, Divine Mother? My heart longed for Your darshan (vision). O Kalike, when are You going to give me that vision?

Japamilla tellumē tapamilla collumē
arivētu millamē tuṇa āke nī umē
Kazhi vattor ēzha ñān mizhi vatta dīnanē
kuzhayum kuzhan taye tazhukān maṭikkolā

O Uma! You are my sole companion, no one else. I do not chant, I do not do austerities, I am a totally ignorant person. I am just useless and incompetent. But, please do not hesitate to protect and comfort me.

Murayiṭṭu kēṇiṭum ceru kuññin ambikē
tuṇayē kiṭānini maṭi kāṭṭolā śivē
Kuzhi ettiṭum pōzhum mozhi nāma jāpanam
ozhiyā tirunniṭān kazhiv ēkaṇē śivē

O Shive! Please don't hesitate to provide refuge to me! I have been crying for so long. Let me be able to chant Your name even at the time of death.

Śiva ganga nī śivē hima bindu ñānumē
orumi ciṭānini samayam eṭukkolā
Karuṇāmayī satī mṛudu hāsinī umē
oḷi cinti ettiṭān ini vaikolā śivē

O Shive! You are the Ganges and I a tiny snow flake ready to merge into You soon. O merciful Mother with a beautiful smiling countenance, Uma, come out of Your hiding place. Don't delay anymore.

Jaya dēvī pārvatī jagadamba śaṅkarī
jaya viśva nāyakī paramēśvari namaḥ
Śiva śakti kāḷikē lalitambikē namaḥ
hṛdayēśvarī namaḥ jagadīśvarī namaḥ

Praises to the Goddess, the Daughter of the Mountain, the Mother of the Universe, Shiva's Consort, the Supreme Mother Goddess, the Unmanifest and Manifest Power, the Black one, the Beautiful and Playful one, the Goddess of the heart.

KŪRIRUḶ PŌLE

Kūriruḷ pōle karutti ruṇṭuḷḷorī
bhīkara rūpiṇiyārāṇu
Śōṇita poykayil ōḷattil āṭiṭum
nīla malar kula yennōṇam

Who can that be with such a terrible form Dark as the darkest night?

Yuddham utirttoru rakta kaḷattiṅkal
nṛttam caviṭṭuva tārāṇu
Pratyamga kānti maraccuḷḷorī
dig vastra dhāriṇi ārāṇu

Who is that One dancing wildly in this battlefield, splashed with blood, like a bouquet of blue flowers twirling in a crimson lake?

Tīkkanal pōle yuruṭṭi mizhikkunna
tṛkkaṇṇu mūnuḷḷōḷ ārāṇu
Kārkoṇṭal pōle yazhiññu laññīṭina
kāṛkkūntalāḷi vaḷārāṇu

Who is that One with three eyes flashing like fireballs? Who is that One with thick, black, unfettered locks flowing like dark rain clouds?

Tannuṭe kālccuvaṭēttu muppāriṭam
ninnu kuluṅguva tentāṇu
Ī lasal kāmini tannuṭe kāntanā
śūlam dharicca śivan āṇu

Why do the three worlds tremble as Her dancing steps strike the earth? Oh, that resplendent damsel is the sweetheart of Shiva, the Bearer of the trident!

MĀ NĀM BŌLĒ DIL SĒ

Mā nām bōlē dil sē
madhura madhura nām hē yē
Mā nām sun lē man mē
amṛt madhur nām hē yē

Let's chant the name of the Divine Mother with all our heart, it is sweet as nectar, sweetest among all names. Let's hear the name 'Ma' in our mind.

Mā mā pukārē dil sē
prēm kā paryāy hē yē
Mā nām jap lē mukh sē
mōd sē pari pūrṇṇa hē yē
Mōd sē pari pūrṇṇa hē yē
Mā tūhī tō hē tērē sivā - kōyī nahī

Let us call 'Ma, Ma' whole-heartedly, it is the epitome of Love. Let our lips chant the Mother's name, it is full of divine bliss. O Mother, You alone are my true refuge, without You, I have nobody as my own.

Mā kahē mati mōh har lē
mā kahē hṛdi mōd bhar lē
Mā kahē sab śōk har lē
mā kahē sansār tar lē
Mā kahē sansār tar lē
Mā tūhī tō hē tērē sivā - kōyī nahī

Chanting the name 'Ma', annihilate all desires in the mind. Chanting the name 'Ma', fill your heart with divine bliss. Chanting the name 'Ma', remove all sorrows. Chanting the name 'Ma', cross over the ocean of samsara. O Mother, You alone are my true refuge, without You, I have nobody as my own.

Mā nām gūnje manmē
mā āke baiṭhē dil mē
Mā nām bōlō muh sē
mā kō hi pā lē ham rē!
Mā kō hi pā lē ham rē!
Mā tūhī tō hē tērē sivā - kōyī nahī

When the name 'Ma' echoes in the mind, Amma will enshrine Herself in our heart. Chanting the name 'Ma', let us merge in Amma. O Mother, You alone are my true refuge, without You, I have nobody as my own.

Mā jai jai mā jai jai mā jai jai mā

MĀ OH MERI MĀ

Mā oh meri mā sun le sara
choṭṭi si meri bath sun le sara
Tu antaryami, sab janti hai
Phir bhi tu mujhko keh ne de
keh ke ye man se miṭ ne de

Mother, my Divine Mother! Please listen to these simple things which I have to say. Even though You are Omniscient, knowing everything about me, allow me to tell you what I have to say so that everything will be cleansed from my mind.

Rahom me ham to bhattakthe rahe hein
Rahom me ham to bhattakthe
rahe hein kaise tere pās āvum
Tujhe man mein basavum dil
mein samavum yehi he duva āj meri
taki sadā ban jayein tu hamari

Being completely lost in this material world, how will I come towards You and be near You? Because of this, I am praying that you should live in my mind and dwell in my heart, so that you will become mine forever.

Kabhi dūr he tu kabhi pās he tu
Kabhi dūr he tu kabhi pās he tu kaisi yeh khel khelti he
Hum to akele hein besahare
tu hi he sab kucc hamari
aur manzil bhi tu he hamari

Sometimes You are so close to me and sometimes so far away. Why do you play all these games and tricks with me? I am alone, with no companion; You are my one in all. Don't You know that You are my ultimate goal in life?

Din bhar din teri aur shraddha hamari
Din bhar din teri aur shraddha
hamari badta hi calā jayein
Teri puja karu mein sajda karum
teri yād sadā satā satāyein
hamrahi ban jaein tu hamari

Let my faith and concentration in You increase day by day and forever. also, let divine thoughts of You come and disturb all my other thoughts. Let me decorate You and always worship You in my mind. Hence, by all this You will be my partner and companion forever in this and coming lifetimes!

MĀHEŚVARĪ RĀJA RĀJĒŚVARĪ

Māheśvarī rāja rājēśvarī
nikhila bhuvanēśvarī
patita jana rakṣakī

Great Goddess, Queen of Goddesses whole world's Goddess, fallen people's protector.

Jagadambikē dēvi laḷitāmbikē
amṛtavara dāyikē madana madanā śakē
Paripāhi mām bhakta paripālini
sakala guṇa śālini sujana hṛdivāsini

Mother of the Universe, Lalita, the playful One, who bestows the boon of immortality, diminishes the ego, who looks after devotees, having all good virtues, dweller in the heart of good people, protect and save me!

Mati mōhanam dēvī tava darśanam
kaluṣa kali nāśanam bhavati tava pūjanam
Muktipradē parama bhakta priyē
surasa mārādhitē sughana śyāmāmbikē

Devi, Your darshan is enchanting to the devotees' mind, Your worship dispels the bad features of this dark age, You bestow liberation, lover of supreme devotees, properly respected by the devas, dark blue complexioned.

Śrī rañjini śiva mano rañjini
duḥkha bhaya bhañjini janani priya darśini
Kāmēśvari sarva hṛdayeśvari sarasa
mṛdu bhāsiṇi triguṇa layakāriṇi

Who makes all the gods and Shiva's mind happy, who dispels sorrows and fear, Mother of beautiful form, Goddess of all desires, Goddess of Shiva's heart, who talks sweetly and softly, the merging cause of the three qualities of Nature.

MANAMŌHANA KṚṢṆA

Manamōhana Kṛṣṇa
dīna dayāla harē
gōvinda harē gopāla harē
Gōvinda hari gōvinda hari gōvinda hari gopāla (2x)

O enchanter of minds, You are the refuge to the grief stricken!

Jagadiśvara dēva kṛpāla harē
gōvinda harē gopāla harē (Gōvinda)
Paramēśvara pāvana rūpa harē
gōvinda harē gopāla harē (Gōvinda)
Yōgēśvarā yādava nātha harē
gōvinda harē gopāla harē (Gōvinda)

Lord of the world, You are compassionate. Supreme Lord, You are the embodiment of purity. Lord of the yogis, You are the leader of the yadava clan.

MĀNASA MALARIL

Mānasa malaril maṇi varṇṇan enttunna
sudinattin āyiram abhivādanam
hṛdayattil anavadya sukhadānam coriyunna
sudinattin āyiram abhivādanam

Welcome to that auspicious day when charming Krishna comes into the blossom of my heart. Greetings to that day when my heart will fill with an abundance of happiness.

Iḷam cuṇṭu mukarunna muḷantaṇṭil ozhukunna
kaḷagāna yamunayil ozhukaṭṭe ñān
Yadu kula kāmbōji rāga sudhārasa

dhārayen hṛdayatte tazhukiṭaṭṭe

I wish to flow through the Yamuna River of sweet melodious music, coming through the bamboo flute, played by the tender lips of Krishna. Let my heart overflow with that sweet nectar of the kamboji raga.[3]

Kṛṣṇa nāmam japicchum tapta bāṣpam pozhiccum
bhakti bhavōnmāda cittanāyum
Darśana saubhāgya tṛptanāy sādaram
viṣṇu caitanyattil ñān layikkum

Chanting the holy name of Krishna, shedding tears, intoxicated with divine love and having the vision of the Lord, I will merge into that all-pervasive Consciousness.

MANDAHĀSA VADANĒ

Mandahāsa vadanē manōnmani mangaḷa dāyini
mṛdu madhura bhāṣiṇi mṛdu madhura bhāṣiṇi

O Smiling One, the bestower of auspiciousness, who speaks softly and sweetly!

Bhava tāpa hāriṇi bhavāni
abhaya pradāyini
bhava bhaya vimōcini bhava bhaya vimōcini

O Mother Parvati, who allays the sorrows of existence, the bestower of protection, who liberates one from the great fear of transmigration.

Sumadhurā varṣiṇi suhāsini
kusuma bāṇahastā

[3] Ragas are traditional melodic patterns in Indian music, different patterns are given different names.

Who showers sweetness, who smiles beautifully, who holds flowers and arrows in Her hand.

Śrīchakra rāja nilayē śiva manōhari
Bindu maṇḍalā vāsini śrīkari
Līlā mānuṣa dhāriṇi
jaya ambikē jagadambikē

Victory to You, O Mother! The Mother of the world who resides in the Sri Chakra, the auspicious, who captivates the heart of Lord Shiva, who resides in the bindu mandala (the centre of the Sri Chakra), the embodiment of auspiciousness, who has assumed a human body by way of sport.

MĀṆIKKYACILAIYĒ

Māṇikkya cilaiyē marataka koṭiyē
tālē tālē lō
mādhavan taṅkāy mīn mizhi naṅkāy
tālē tālē lō
māṇikkya cilaiyē marataka koṭiyē
tālē tālē lō

Hail! Hail! Hail! O Mother of indescribable beauty like a sculpture made of emerald, like a flag bedecked with sapphires! O Consort of Mahadeva, O Minakshi!

Pāṇḍiyan kulattil tōntriya kiḷiyē
tālē tālē lō
Āṇṭavan maṭiyil āṭiṭum kaniyē
tālē tālē lō
Nāttrisai oḷiyai ēttriya viḷakkē
tālē tālē lō
Pōttriya pērkku pukaḷ tarum nilaivē

tālē tālē lō

Hail! O Divine Being born in the southern regions, who revels on the very lap of the Supreme. You are a lamp that has lit the way for all; You are one who provides sustenance to those who take refuge in You.

Mekhalai cūṭum melliya iṭaiyē
tālē tālē lō
Siṅkattin ulavum sītaḷa nilayē
tālē tālē lō
Pāvala ryārum pāṭiya azhakē
tālē tālē lō
Mūvulak āḷum mōhana poruḷē
tālē tālē lō

Hail! O Enchanting One, the three worlds are enamored by Your gorgeous form, Your melodious singing, strength like that of a lion, and Your calm disposition.

MĀTĀ MĀHEŚVARI

Mātā māheśvari bhairavi
śakti priye manōhari hṛdayeśvari
Ātma svarūpiṇi ānanda dāyini
śyamala sundara mana mōhini
Jai mā jai mā īśvari kālī mā
Prēma mayi amṛtēśvari satccidānanda rūpiṇi
Jai mā jai mā īśvari kālī mā

O Mother, Great Goddess, Consort of Shiva, who revels in Herself, Enchanting One, Goddess residing in the heart, of the nature of the Self, who bestows bliss, who is dark-complexioned and beautiful, captivating the mind, victory to You! Victory to the Goddess Mother Kali, Mother of Love Amriteshwari, of the nature of existence-consciousness-bliss!

MĀTṚ VĀTSALYA

Mātṛ vātsalya tōṭenne jagadamba samrakṣikke
nētraṅgaḷe cimmāte ñān uṇarnnirikke
vīṭṭinuḷḷil palapala mōṣaṇaṅgaḷ naṭakkunnu
ārttiyēttam vaḷarunnu manassil ammē

When the Mother of the Universe looks after me with Motherly Love, when I keep myself awake without winking my eyes; inside the house so many thefts take place. In my mind, grief is ever growing.

Prārtthanakaḷ pativāyi naṭattuvān pratijñakaḷ
ārttināśinī ñān palavaṭṭam ceykilum
Samayam vannaṭukkumbōl marakkunnuveṅkil atu
bhavadīya tantra menninn ariyunnu ñān

O destroyer of grief, even though I vow many times to pray regularly, when the time comes, I forget about it; I realise that it is all Your play.

Kuttakkāran ennākolle ivane nī yonnu koṇṭum
kuttamentu ñāniviṭe ceytumātāvē
Ikkāṇunna samsāram-aṅgāke tava līlayāṇe
nuḷkāmbil ñān ariyunnu jagadambikē

Don't blame me in any way. O Mother of the universe, what wrong have I done here? I know it in my heart that this samsara is all Your divine play.

Manassine yenikkāyi sammāniccha śeṣam amma
kaṭakkaṇṇin samjñā koṇṭonn aruḷiyallō
Cittamē ninakku pōkām samsārattil cennu vēṇṭum
uttama sukhaṅgaḷe nī bhujiccukoḷka

O Mother, after giving me the mind as a present, You conveyed to me the knowledge with a side glance, "O Mind, go to the samsara and enjoy the great worldly pleasures."

Akkāraṇam koṇṭaṭiyan alaññu tiriyunnu nin
sṛṣti jālaṅgaḷil kūṭi tuṇayillāte
Amṛtine viṭṭaṭiyan viṣam uṇṇukayāṇ ippōḷ
asatyatte satyamāyum dharikkayallō

For that very reason I am helplessly wandering in the world. Neglecting the ambrosia, I am consuming poison now, mistaking the untruth for the truth.

Amma tanna vāsanakaḷ ammaceyta karmajālam
avayuṭe phalaṅgaḷum enteyennōti
Entinammē enneyiṭṭī māyayil nī valaykkunnu
bhaktitannu rakṣikkillē jagadambikē

The vasanas that Mother instilled in me, the jugglery of actions which Mother performed, and the fruits of those were attributed to me. O Mother of the Universe, why do You confound me in this illusion? Will You not save me by granting devotion?

Maṇṇil vīṇāl uṭayumī maṇcirātil vāsana tan
eṇṇayum karmaṅgaḷṭe tiriyumiṭṭu
Janimṛti koḷuttiyum ericcuketṭ uttiyum nī
rasikkunnat entin ammē jagadīśvarī

Pouring the oil of vasanas and placing the wicks of actions in this earthen lamp, which will be shattered if it falls to the ground, and lighting the flame of birth and death and extinguishing it, why do you revel in this manner, O Mother of the Universe?

Entin enne pazhikkum nī entinenne śikṣikkum nī
ninteyallō vāsanakaḷ karma phalaṅgaḷ
Kaṇ turakkū jagadambē bhakti nalkū jagadambē
ennu mennum nin pādaṅgaḷ enikkāśrayam

For what will You blame me, for what will You punish me? Yours are the vasanas, yours are the fruits of actions. Open Your eyes, O Mother of the Universe; grant me devotion! O Mother of the Universe; Your Feet are my eternal refuge!

Kaṇturakkū mahādēvī bhakti nalkū kārtyāyanī
ennu mennum nin pādaṅgaḷ enikkāśrayam
Kaṇ turakkū mahākāḷī bhakti nalkū bhadrakāḷī
ennu mennum nin pādaṅgaḷ enikkāśrayam

Open Your eyes, O great Goddess; grant me devotion, O Kartyayani, Your Feet are my eternal refuge. Open Your eyes, O Mahakali; grant me devotion, Bhadrakali, Your Feet are my eternal refuge.

MAUNATTIL IRUNTU

Maunattil iruntu pārttāl
teriyum tāyē un mukham

Manattai nilai nirutti aympulanai aṭakki
Dhyāna mēṭaiyil dinamum nī amarntu

O Mother, when one meditates in silence, making the mind one-pointed, with all the five senses well controlled, then he can behold Your Divine face.

Iṅkē iruntu nān un tirupukkazh pāṭa
eṅkō iruntu nī ennai paṇittāyē
tāyē amṛtānandamayī tāyē
tatva bōdhamē vittaka vēdamē
śaktiyin rūpamē tāyin mukhamē (2x)

O Amritanandamayi! Sitting here I am singing Your glories; from some-where You bestow Your blessings. You are the essence of all philosophies, the repository of the Vedas; Your face is that of the Goddess Parasakti.

Ettannai ārukaḷ eṅkeṅku ōṭiyum
attanai nadikaḷum kaṭalinil sangamam
buddharum karttarum kṛṣṇanum allāvum
bhaktiyil pārkkayil ōrinam ōrkalam

All the rivers, irrespective of where they flow, finally merge into the ocean. Buddha, Christ, Krishna & Allah, when seen through the mind full of devotion, are in reality One.

Ittanai māndaruḷ ettanai pirivukaḷ
palamata pirivukaḷ ulakil sarivukaḷ
sarivukal varukaiyil uravinil pirivukaḷ
ulakinil anaivarum oru tāy kuzhantakaḷ (2x)

Oh! How many classifications of castes exist among the people! These divisions are the short comings of the world. When such divisions exist, the harmonious relationship among people is lost. Remember, all are the children of One Universal Mother.

Atiloru kuzhantai nān ariyā siruvan nān
puriyā bhaktiyil paṭiyēri varupavan
irulvazhi nīṅkiṭa arul vazhi ōṅkiṭa
urupaṭiyākiṭa marupaṭi marupaṭi

I am also an innocent child among Your children, trying hard to tread the difficult path of devotion. O Mother! I seek Your blessings to dispel darkness ahead of me, to advance on the spiritual path, and to gain purity of mind.

Tiruppaṭi ērinēn tirumukham teṭinēn
amṛtānandamayī tāyē
un aruladinam tanai tēṭiyē vandēn tāyē
un arulaṭanai tēṭiyē vandēn tāyē

O Mother Amritanandamayi, I have come to Your abode, to behold Your divine face and seek Your blessings.

MAYILONTRU ĀṬUTU

mayilontru āṭutu
manam unnai tēṭutu
kuyil pōla pēśiṭum
kumaran kural kēḷkkutu

Oh Muruga! I see your vehicle, the peacock, dancing in my mind, remembering you, searching for you. It even hears in faint your lovely voice which is so sweet as a cuckoo-bird.

vēlonṭru tōnṭrutu
vinai tīrppēn entrutu
pāl pōntru manamellām
paḷiṅk pōle oḷirutu

Your weapons appearing before us say, "I will protect all of you." Seeing this, all the innocent hearts rejoice in happiness

tēronru aśaiyutu
tirukāṭcci teriyutu
pār entu śollutu
bhaktar manam urukutu

Seeing the blessed sight of your chariot coming forth gently, the hearts of the devotees are highly elevated.

śēval ontu āṭutu
śentil mukham kāṭṭutu
sēvippōrkaḷ śeyalellām
jayam enrē muzhaṅkutu

While the resounding sound of the temple bell fills the air, the devotees are intoxicated with devotion, which appears to prove that selfless service is always successful.

kaṭal aṅku olikkutu
kavitayumē pirakkutu
kantan mukham kaṇṭa uṭan
kaṇkaḷ mazhai pozhiyutu

Even when the waves of the ocean uproar it reminds the devotees of hearing the praise of the Lord. At last seeing his divine form, the eyes shed blissful tears.

vēl murukā vēl murukā vēl murukā vēl vēl (2x)

MŌHANA MURAḶI MŌHITAMEN

Mōhana muraḷi mōhitamen manam
mōhana vṛndāvana kṛṣṇa
Nin amṛtādhara cumbanam ēlkkān
ñān oru murali kayākām kṛṣṇa
ñān oru murali kayākām

My mind is enchanted by the magical flute of Krishna, the enchanter of Vrindavan. To receive Thy nectarine kiss, I will become a flute, O Krishna, I will become a flute.

Prēmila rāgam utirtten jīvane
rādhika yākkū murārē
Cintakaḷ gōpikaḷāy nin cuttinum
rāsa līlaykku varaṭṭe!
kṛṣṇā rāsa līlaykku varaṭṭe!

O Murare, make me a Radhika (another name of Radha) by playing the melody of Love. May our thoughts become gopikas and may we come for the rasalila, O Krishna, come for the rasalila.

Saundarya dhāmamē nin madhu cintayil
manavum nāvum niścalamāy
Pinne eṅgane ninne kīrtticciṭum
prēma sudhārasa mūrttē kṛṣṇā
prēma sudhārasa mūrttē

O embodiment of Beauty, dwelling in your sweet thoughts, my mind has become still and I am rendered speechless. How then can I sing Thy glory? Embodiment of nectarine Love, O Krishna!

MṚDULA NĪLA KAḶĒBARĀ

Mṛdula nīla kaḷēbarā - ghana
kuṭilakuntala kōmaḷā
kuvalayōpama lōcana - chala
makara kuṇḍala maṇditā
Mṛdula nīla kalēbarā

O Lord with a soft blue-hued body, O beautiful One with thick curly hair, O lotus-eyed One, adorned with the swaying fish-shaped earrings!

Aruṇa bimba phalā dharā - madhu
madhura mṛdu hasitānanā
Adhara dhṛta muralī yutā - nava
tuḷasi hāra suśōbhitā
Harē rāma rāma harē harē
harē kṛṣṇa kṛṣṇa harē harē

O Lord, with lips of the color of the rising sun, whose face is lit with a honey sweet smile, who has a flute on his lips, who is resplendent with a garland of fresh tulasi leaves.

Mṛdula nīla kalēbarā (call only/unison)
Malaya candana carcitā - śata
madana kōṭi manōharā
Laḷita lāsya vidhāyakā - madhu
bharita rāsa rasēśvarā (Harē rāma rāma)

O Lord, the One who is adorned with sandal paste from the Malaya mountains, who is as beauteous as millions of Kamadevas (God of Love), who engages in the sportive dance, You are the nectarine bliss of the rasalila.

Mṛdula nīla kalēbarā
Paśupa bāla parāt parā - sura
muni supūjita sundarā
Yadu kulācala dīpakā - bhava
bhaya vibhañjana nandanā (Harē rāma rāma)

O cowherd boy, the Ultimate One, O beautiful One worshipped by sages and Gods, You are the Light of the Yadava clan, O Nandana, You are the destroyer of the fear of samsara.

Mṛdula nīla kalēbarā
Vraja vadhūjana jīvanā - mama
hṛdaya maṇḍa pamaṇḍanā
Jayatu yādava nāyakā - śubha
vibhava saukhya vidhāyakā (Harē rāma rāma)

You are the very life of the women of Vraja; You are the one who adorns the chamber of my heart. Victory to You, the Lord of the Yadavas, the bestower of prosperity and happiness.

MṚTYUÑJAYĀYA NAMAḤ ŌM

Mṛtyuñjayāya namaḥ ōm
Tryambakāya namaḥ ōm
Lingēśvarāya namaḥ ōm
Sarvēśvarāya namaḥ ōm
Ōm namaḥ śivāya namaḥ ōm (4x)

Salutations to the conqueror of Death! Salutations to the Father of the three worlds! Salutations to the Lingeshvara (who is worshipped in the form of Shiva lingam), Salutations to the Lord of all beings! Salutations to the Auspicious One!

MUJHĒ DARŚAN DŌ BHAGAVĀN

Mujhē darśan dō bhagavān
Śrī kṛṣṇa candra bhagavān

O Lord, please bless me with Your vision! O Sri Krishna!

Tū jānat sab antaryāmi
Dījō mērē prabhū amṛtavāṇi

O Lord, being the indweller of all beings, You know everything, Please let me hear Your Divine words.

Tū hī mērē ātmārām kṛṣṇā
Dūr karō mērē man kē kām kṛṣṇā

O Krishna, You are my innermost Self, please cast away all desires from my mind.

NAMŌ BHŪTANĀTHĀ NAMŌ

Namō bhūtanāthā namō dēva dēva
namō bhaktapālā namō viśvanātha

Salutations to You, O Lord of Bhutas (Lord of Creation), Lord of the Gods, salutations to the protector of devotees, the Lord of the Universe.

Sada suprakāśā namō pāpanāśa
kāśi visvanāthā dayāsiṇdhu dātā
Namō pārvatī vallabhā nīlakaṇṭhā

Salutations to the ever-effulgent One, the destroyer of sin, the Lord of the Universe, the Lord of Kasi, the Ocean of mercy, the Lord of Parvati, the blue-necked One, who is the essence of the Scriptures and of the world, the ever dispassionate One.

Bhavā vēdasāra sadā nirvikāra
namō lōkapālā namō nāgalōla
Namō pārvatī vallabhā nīlakaṇṭhā

Salutations to the One who protects the world, to the Lord, who is fond of snakes, to the blue-necked One, the Lord of Parvati, the ever dispassionate.

NAMŌ NAMASTĒ MĀTAḤ SARASVATĪ

Namō namastē mātaḥ sarasvatī
amṛtamayī ānandamayī
Namō namastē nāda śarīriṇi
hamsa vihāriṇi namōstutē

Prostrations to You again and again, O Mother Saraswati! O Amritamayi (embodiment of immortality), O Anandamayi (embodiment of bliss), prostrations to You! O the embodiment of Nada (Divine Sound), salutations to You, who rides on a swan (Goddess Saraswati).

Śvētāmbara dhara kēsa ghanāmṛta
patmālaya rasa manōhari
Prāṇava mayī sacinmaya rūpiṇi
jyōtirmayī tē namō namaḥ

O white clad One with a flowery cascade of hair, the beautiful One who delights in residing on the lotus flower, who is the form of Pranava, and the Sat and Chit (existence and consciousness).

Jnānamayī saṭ granthamayi śubha
sapta svaramayī namō namaḥ
Vīṇāpāṇi suhāsa māyimē
dēhi śivam tē namō namaḥ

O effulgent One, salutations to You, who is full of wisdom, who dwells in holy books, who is the form of the auspicious seven notes of music, One who holds the veena, who sports a sweet smile, the indweller of all.

ÑĀN ŚOLLUM MANTIRAM

Ñān śollum mantiram ōm śaktiyē
Śaṅkaran nāyakiyē śaṅkari saundariyē
śaraṇam śaraṇam śaraṇam

I am chanting the mantra 'Om Sakti'. O Sankari, the consort of Lord Shiva, the beautiful One, You are my refuge.

Arul mazhai pozhikinṭa karumāri tāyē
tāyē ādi parāśakti nīyē
arivum tiruvum tantu poruḷum pukazhum tantu
avaniyil vāzhntiṭa arulvāy tāyē

O Karumari (Goddess with a dark complexion), who showers the rain of grace, You are none other than Goddess Adi Parasakti. Bless me for my total well-being and let me live in the world happily.

Kaṇkaḷil śāntamum kaiyinil śūlamum
koṇṭavaḷ kōla vizhi annaiyē tāyē
tāyē tāyē tāyē tāyē
ādiparāśakti tāyē tāyē
kantanil tāyum nī
karuṇaiyil vaṭivum nī
mayilailiyil amrarntanal
daivam nīyē

The peaceful eyes, a spear in the hand, beautiful eyes; such is the form of my Mother who is Goddess Adi Parasakti. O Mother of Skanda (Lord Muruga)! You are compassion incarnate, the beloved deity of the temple in Mylapore.

NANDA NANDANĀ

Nanda nandanā nanda nandanā
nanda nandanā sundara vadanā
Nanda nandanā nanda nandanā
nanda nandanā vandita caraṇā

O Son of Nanda, with a beautiful body, we bow at Your Lotus Feet!

Sundara vadanam vandē naṭavara
nanda kumāram vandē
Paṅkaja nayanam vandē madhu maya
mangaḷa dhāmam vandē

Obeisance to the One who has a beautiful body. Obeisance to the elegant dancer. Obeisance to the darling Son of Nanda. Obeisance to the lotus-eyed.Obeisance to His holy sweet abode.

Mañjuḷa caritam vandē bhava bhaya
bhañjana nipuṇam vandē
Kuñja vihāram vandē janamana
rañjana śīlam vandē

Obeisance to the sweet story of His divine lilas. Obeisance to Him, who is dexterous in destroying the fear of samsara. Obeisance to Him, who roams in the groves. Obeisance to His habit of pleasing the hearts of people.

Gōkula pālam vandē giridhara
gōpa kumāram vandē
Vēṇu vilōlam vandē vrajajana
jīvana sāram vandē

Obeisance to Him who looks after the village of Gokul. Obeisance to Gopakumara, who lifted the mountain Govardhana. Obeisance to Him, who plays the Flute. Obeisance to Him who is the very life of the people.

Kāḷiya damanam vandē kalimala
mōchana caraṇam vandē
Kōmaḷa rūpam vandē kavikula
mānasa cōram vandē

Obeisance to Him who hushed the pride of Kaliya. Obeisance to His Feet that dispel the impurity of the Kali Yuga. Obeisance to His enchanting form. Obeisance to Him who steals the hearts of poets.

Nārada vinutam vandē nirupama
nīla śarīram vandē
Vēda vihāram vandē yadukula
rāja kumāram vandē

Obeisance to Him who is worshipped by Narada. Obeisance to His gorgeous blue body. Obeisance to Him who resides in the Vedas. Obeisance to Him who is the Prince of the Yadu clan.

NANDA NANDANĀ HARĒ

Nanda nandanā harē
sundarā nanāmbujā)
indirā manōharā
vanditāmghri paṅkajā

Kuñcitāgra kundaḷā
lōla pimcikā dharā
gōpi candanāṅkitā
gōpa sundarī priyā

Nīla lōla lōcanā
cāru hāsa mōhanā
vēṇu nāda lōlupā
rāsa kēḷi lālasā

Candanādi carccitā
vaijayanti bhūṣitā
pīta vāsa vēṣṭitā
mōda sāndra vigrahā

Rāsa narttanā lasā
vāsavādi pūjitā
rādhika dhipā vibhō
vāsudēva tē namō

nanda nandana	Son of Nanda
sundarananambuja	One with a beautiful lotus face
indira manohara	One who enchants the mind of Lakshmi
vanditāmghri pankajā	One whose Lotus Feet are the objects of worship
kuñcitāgra kundala	One who wears curved earrings
lola pimcikā dharā	One who wears waving peacock feathers
gopi candanankita	One who wears sandalwood paste
gopa sundaripriya	Beloved of the beautiful cowherdess of Vrindavan
nila lola locana	One with tremulous blue eyes

caru hasa mohana	Captivating with a beautiful smile
veṇu nada lolupa	One who is eager to play the flute
rasa keli lalasa	Who is fond of the dance with the gopis. (rasa dance)
candanādi carcitā	Smeared with sandalwood paste and other ointments
vaijayanti bhusita	One who is adorned with a necklace
pīta vāsa veśṭitā	One who wears a yellow garment
moda sāndra vigrahā	Embodiment of the essence of happiness
rāsa nartanālasā	Tired after the Rasa dance
vāsavādi pūjitā	Worshipped by Indra and other Gods
rādhikadhipā vibho	Lord of Radha, Lord Vishnu
vāsudeva te namo	Salutations to You, O Krishna

NINNE PIRIYUNNA

Ninne piriyunna durvidhi ōrttu ammē
ñān etra vilapicu nī aṛiññō?
ninne piriyunna durdiva saṅgaḷe
ōrttu pazhicatum nī aṛiññō?

Thinking about the ill-fated separation from You, Amma, how much have I lamented, did You know? How I cursed the anguished moments of separation from You, did You know?

Inne nikkēkum ennamma tan darśana -
mennōrttu kēṇatum nī aṛiññō?
Ninne marakuvān uṇṭāya kāraṇam
ōrttu kara ñatum nī aṛiññō?

How I wept painfully, wondering when You would bless me with Your vision, did You know? How I wept thinking about the cause of my forgetfulness of You, did You know?

Yōgyata keṭṭoru putri ennōrttu
ñān etra vilapicu nī aṛiññō?
Yōgyata illāta kāraṇam amma nī
darśanam ēkāttatōrtu kēṇu

Thinking that I am an unworthy daughter of Yours, how much have I lamented, did You know? I wept, thinking that I was denied the vision of You, as I was not befitting for it.

Prēma vihīna yāmī paital amma tan
prēmate lābhippān etra kēṇu
Ninne nirantaram cintikkān ākātta
kāraṇam ōrtu ñānetra tēṅgi

Oh, how much this child, who is bereft of love, wept for gaining Your love. Oh, how much have I wept thinking about my inability to remember Thee constantly.

Ennile kuññinu mātṛtva mūṭṭiya
vātsalayam ōrtu ñānetra tēṅgi
Nin maṭitta ṭilen tala cāycu saṇkaṭa
kaṇṇīr ozhukkiya tōrtu tēṅgi

Oh, how much have I wept remembering Your motherly affection for this child. Oh, how much have I wept, remembering the tears I shed, laying my head on Your lap.

NIZHALINTE PINNĀLE

Nizhalinte pinnālē ñān alaññu kaṣṭam
nizhaline satyamāy ñān ninaccu

Niravadya mōhinī ennammē ninte
nizhalākum māyayil tāzhttiṭalle

I pursued the shadow, alas, thinking it to be the Reality. O most enchanting Mother, please do not delude me by Your maya which is only Your shadow.

Madhura maruppacca tēṭiyōṭi ninte
kara kāṇa marubhūvil peṭṭitammē
Karuṇāmayī varū eriyumen jīvitam
kara valliyil cērttu kākkuk amme

Deluded by a mirage, I was trapped in Your vast and endless desert. O compassionate Mother, please hold me closely in Your arms and save this desperate soul.

Malarvāṭi maraṇattin keṇiyāyī kaṣṭamī
avaniyil tēntēṭi ñān taḷarnnū
Kara kaviññ ozhukum nin prēm āmṛtattinal
putujīvanēki nī kāttiṭaṇe

I am exhausted by my search for honey in this flower garden of the world. The flower garden turned out to be a death trap. Please grant me a new life to enjoy the nectar of love flowing abundantly from You.

Jīvaṇṭe jīva nām enteyammē niṇṭe
jīvāmṛtam nalki rakṣaceyyū
Prēma taramgiṇī ninn alayāyi ñān
prēma samgītam pozhicciṭaṭṭe!

Mother, who enlivens all beings, please save me by bestowing the immortality of the Self. O River of Love! Let me be one with You and bring forth songs of love.

ŌM AMṚTEŚVARIYAI NAMAḤ

Dhyāyāmo-dhavalāvaguṇṭhanavatīṁ)
tejomayīm-naiṣṭhikīṁ
snigdhāpāṅga-vilokinīm bhagavatīṁ
mandasmita-śrī-mukhīṁ
vātsalyāmṛta-varṣiṇīm sumadhuraṁ
saṅkīṛttanālāpinīṁ
ṣyāmāṅgīṁ madhu-sikta-sūktīṁ
amṛtānandāmikāmīśvarīṁ
Ōm amṛteśvariyai namaḥ (4x)

Pūṛṇa-brahma-svarūpiṇyai
saccidānanda mūrttaye
ātmā-rāmāgragaṇyāyai
yoga-līnāntarātmane
Ōm amṛteśvariyai namaḥ (4x)

Adorations to Amma, who is the complete manifestation of the Absolute, who is existence, knowledge and bliss embodied, who is supreme among those who revel in the Self, whose inner Self (pure mind) is merged in Yoga (the union of the individual Self with Brahman).

Antar-mukha-svabhāvāyai
turya-tuṅga-sthalījjuṣe
prabhā-maṇḍala-vītāyai
durāsada-mahaujase
Ōm amṛteśvariyai namaḥ (4x)

Adorations to Amma, whose very nature is inwardly drawn, who dwells in the top-most plane of consciousness known as 'turiya,' who is totally surrounded by divine light, whose greatness is unsurpassable.

Vāṇī-buddhi-vimṛgyāyai
śaśvad-avyakta-vartmane
nāma-rūpādi-śūnyāyai
śunya-kalpa-vibhūtaye
Ōm amṛteśvariyai namaḥ (4x)

Adorations to Amma, whom speech and intellect cannot apprehend, whose path is eternally non-defined, who is devoid of name and form, to whom the yogic powers are of no importance (like the whole world is unimportant when in dissolution).

ŌM BHADRA KĀḶI

Ōm bhadra kāḷi namō namā
śrī bhadra kāḷi namō namā
Ōm bhadra kāḷi śrī bhadra kāli
jaya bhadra kāḷi namō namā

ŌM JAGAD JANANĪ DĒVĪ MĀTĀ

(ŌM AMṚTĒŚVARI DEVI MATA)

Ōm jagad jananī dēvī mātā (ōm amṛteśvarī dēvī mātā)
Ōmkāra rūpiṇī dēvī mātā
Abhaya pradāyinī dēvī mātā
Dēvī mātā dēvī mātā
Anātha rakṣakī dēvī mātā (2x)

O Mother Amriteshwari, You are our Supreme Goddess! You are of the form of pranava (OM). You give us protection (from the evils of the world). Mother who protects those who are helpless.

ŌMKĀRA DIVYA PORŪLE VIII

Ōmkāra divya porūle varū
ōmana makkaḷe vēgam
Ōmanayāyi valarnām ayaṅgaḷ nīkki
ōmkāra vastu āyi tīrū

Come quickly, darling children, you who are the Essence of OM. Break away from all the shackles that you have carefully nurtured, and become one with the sacred syllable OM.

Ālasyam dūratteriyū - karma
vīryam prakāśi cidatte
ārṣa cētassil ninnāgōla sīmakal
bhēdicha śamkholi kēlppu

Discard all indolent tendencies. Let the eagerness to act be like a beacon spreading its bright effulgence beyond all boundaries.

Ponnōmal makkaḷē niṅgaḷ - ennum
ammakku pontāra kaṅgaḷ
tanniṣta bhāvam vadiññātma samyamam
manninnu māthrika yākkū

Darling children, you are Mother's bright stars forever. Give up self-indulgence and make your self-control a role model for the whole world.

Vēda vijñanam vediññu - makkaḷ
lōka vijñanattil mātram
dattāva dhānarāyi tīrnāli jīvitam
mutterā tulloru cippi

If you were to turn your back on vedantic knowledge, and immerse yourself in the pursuit of mundane knowledge, your existence will be like an oyster shell which does not contain a pearl.

Ātmīya cinta tannīrpam - vēri
nūrjjamāy tīratte yennum
satya dharmaṅgaḷ tan hṛdyānu-bhūtikal
nityam talirttu puśpikkān

Let the contemplation of the Self take deep roots within you. The ecstatic inner experiences of Truth and Dharma will blossom in due course.

Vākku mahantayāl makkaḷ - vyathā
mātsarya budhiye rāte
nirdhūta kanmara cētassōte porum
kartavya mācari cīdū

Children, do not encourage egotistic competitiveness to grow within you. Perform your duties diligently always.

Ātma prakaśam parannu - bhāva
śudhi yārnnōjassu narnnu
ātmaikya bōdhattāl makkaḷē yētilum
svātmānu bhūti valartū

Let your spiritual radiance spread all around; acquire inner purity he ojas (spiritual energy) be awakened. Let the awareness of the oneness of the Self grow in every situation, and let that be your constant companion.

Pātippatiñña sangītam - pōle
vātātta nīrcōla pōle
snēham manassin svabhāva māyi tīranam
nīrum manssukal kennum

Let love become the ingrained essence of the mind - like a song that has been sung many times and is remembered effortlessly, like a river bed that never dries up and sustains a constant flow of the stream. This will be a soothing balm for the seething mind.

Cenninam cintāte makkaḷ - karma
samgara māduka nityam
tannilum tarnnore tannōla mettippān
tannettān arpikka makkaḷ

Fight your karmic battles every day without bloodshed metaphorically). Dedicate yourself to the mission of uplifting those who are less fortunate than you.

Enniyāl tīrāt tanartham - kandu
kanmiri cīdunnu martyan
ārtiyōdetti piṭikkunna tokkeyum
cīrtha dukkum kāla sarppam

Man is blind to the innumerable undesirable things that appear attractive at first sight. Know that the things that you reach out to grab are like hidden coiled snakes.

Indriya mātrā bhimanam - nindyam
hanta jīrnicu pōm dēham
ēkagra mākum manassinte śaktiye
vellānetir śaktiyilla

To be proud of the body, and the power of the senses - how pathetic that is! Alas, the body will decompose into its constituents one day. Know that there is no power that can suppress the power of a one-pointed mind.

Ārakkatal saumya śāntam - sadā
tīrakkatal kṣōbha pūrnam

dhyānalīn ātmāvu śāntam, vikāranga -
lālum manassu vikṣubdham

The deep ocean far from the shore is calm and peaceful. But its waves near the shore are restless. The mind immersed in meditation is at peace; that trapped in its emotions is turbulent.

Sampal samrudhika lellām - innō
nāleyo kaicōrnu pokām
īśvara prēmam labhicāl naśikkilla -
tāsvāśa mullil nirakkum

All the amassed material wealth will slip through your hands sooner or later. If you attain love of God, it will not (slip through your hands); it will fill you with contentedness.

Nādinte kāval bhadanmār - makkaḷ
nādinte svatva mulkollū
raśtra dehattinte ārōgya pūrnatakk-
ātmārtha sēvanam ceyyū

Children, you are the protectors of the nation. Imbibe the ethos of the nation. Serve it selflessly, so that its institutions remain healthy.

Onnico rotta manassāyi - dēśā
rakśakku munnitti rangū
inn ōlamārjica samskāra dhāraye
nirvighnam munno torukkū

Come together and protect the cultural legacy that you have inherited. Let that cultural stream continue to flow uninterrupted.

Nammē parikkunn avarkum - uḷḷāl
nanma nērnīduvin makkaḷ
nanmakkaḷ kānān kariyunna kannukal
mannil apūrva mānennum

Children, pray for the welfare of even those who heap abuse and blame on you. Know that the eyes that can see the goodness in others have always been rare on this earth.

Dharma samsthāpana karmam - ceyyān
vannavar conna tōrkumbōl
svantamen ōrtatil bandham valartunna
chintakal ellām anartham

When you remember the words of those who were born for the only purpose of preserving Dharma, you will see the futility of tendencies that reinforcc the sense of "me and mine".

Ajñāna ghōrāntha kāram - hṛttil
mūcudum mūtti-tarakke
dēham dehikkunna tānenna riñjittum
dēhōha bhāvam sajīvam

When the darkness of ignorance predominates in the heart, the idea "I am the body" flourishes strong and healthy, in spite of the knowledge that the body will be burnt some day.

Nammal niyantri cidēntum - śakti
namme niyantri cidunnu
dhīra karmaṅgaḷ kinangēndum śaktikal
nīca karmaṅgaḷ kinangi

The shaktis (energies) that ought to have been controlled by us, reign supreme over us. Those shaktis which were meant to be devoted to positive actions, are, alas, wasted in inferior pursuits.

Niścala citrangal pōle - makkaḷ
niśkriya rākā tirikkū
ellāru mellārkku mennōrrta lambhāva
mellām kuda ñeriññīṭū

Children, do not be actionless like still-life pictures. Remember the axiom "One for all, all for One", and discard indolent tendencies.

Dīnaril ullaliv ullōr - svantam
dīnata yellām marakkum
kāruṇya nīhāra śīkara dhārayayi
jīvita manyārtha mākkum

Those who have compassion for the poor and the hapless, forget their personal problems. They dedicate their life to the betterment of others, a succession of moments filled with concern for others.

Cummāto rēda thorikkal - vannu
ninnu pōnnōralla nammal
janmangal etrayaō pinnitta namatin
uḷḷariññ uḷḷunarēṇṭōr

Our life was not meant to be spent merely eking out a humdrum existence. Having had innumerable life-times behind us, it is essential to wake up now and know the purpose and deep significance of this incarnation.

Tannuḷḷil tangunna śakti - tanne
tānākki nirtunna śakti
tanēyunaril lunarti yuyar tanam
tanne svayam tānriyān

The shakti that resides within you, the shakti that maintains you the way you are, that shakti will not wake Herself up (in a spiritual sense). She needs to be awakened if you want to find out who you are.

Māyā kadhīśan mahēśan - mahā
māyā kadhīnan manuśyan
mōha pāśam kontu māyā bandhi kunnu
śōka samsārattil namme

The Lord reigns supreme over maya, and man is but a slave to Her. Maya binds us to samsara (mundane existence) with the ties of infatuation.

Ārṣa sidhantanga lellam - martya
jīvitā ślēshika lallo
jīvana dharmavum mōcana marmavum
mēlippatam sarga kāvyam

The spiritual philosophies, when understood, are so beneficial in your life. When the understanding of Dharma, and the secret of liberation meet, they produce a joyous symphony.

Vyakti vairaṅgaḷ vediññāl - hṛttil
śudha cai tanyam vilaṅgum
muttitarakkā tasūyayum spardhayum
sacil prakaśam telikkū

When personal animosities are given up, consciousness will shine in the heart in its pristine purity. When jealousy and enmity do not put down roots in the heart, the light of 'satchit' (Existence-Consciousness Absolute) will burn bright.

Māmuni sattaman māril - ninnum
āvahic adhyātma dīpam
āyirattāntukal kaipakar nātmāvi -
lālijvalikkayā ninnum

The light of the Self is like a torch that has been passed down to us from the times of the great ancient seers. It has changed hands many times over a period of thousands of years and still burns brightly in our souls.

Ēriyāl nūttantu kālam - dēhi
dēha nīdttil vasikkām
nīdam vediññakkili parakkaum mumbe
tēdiyal arkkum piṭikkām

The indweller will at the most live up to a hundred years in the nest of the body. Anyone can search for That before that bird flies away from the nest, and attain That.

Unduran gānalla janmam - lakṣyam
santānā saubhāgya mallā
bhōga sampattum praśastiyu mōrkkukil
yōga sampattānu mukhyam

This life is not meant to be frittered away in sleeping and eating, nor is the procreation of progeny the ultimate goal of this life. Remember that (acquiring) the wealth of bhoga(sensual enjoyments), and fame are secondary only to the wealth of yoga.

Ñāval param tinnu tinnu - nāvu
nīlicapōl martya cittam
śīlichatām bhōga lālasa cintayāl
klāvica tan niram kettu

The mind is colored by external influences, like a tongue that turns blue after eating a good number of 'nyaval' fruits. The obsession with pursuing pleasurable things becomes a habit and permanently stains the mind.

Vaidika cintā tarangam - viṣva
meṅgum paranno rukatte
martyan mahēśanāyi mārum vimōcana
śakti mantram jayikkatte

Let the flow of spiritual thoughts fill up the whole world. Let the mantra imbued with the power to liberate, which can transport man(from his limitations) to Supreme Lordship, be victorious.

Kānān kotikunna tatvam - nēril
kantālum kānāttatentē ?
tanne svayam kānum kanninte kārcayil
anyanum tānu monnākum

Why do you fail to see the Truth that stares you right in the face - in spite of your ardent desire to see it? In the eyes of one who can truly see himself, the "other" is not an entity separate from oneself.

Dūrattu tēdunna daivam - tante
cārattitā vasikkunnu
martya rūpattil dayārha bhāvattil nin
ārcanam kāmkṣicu nilpū

The God that you are seeking, all the while imagining that He is far away, dwells so close to you. He stands right beside you in a human form, full of compassion, waiting for your recognition.

Tāngum tanalum illāte - koṭum
yātana tinnum janatte
pādē marakkum narādhaman mārarum
pāpikal ennōrka makkaḷ

Those who are totally unconcerned about the existence of others living in abject misery without any support or hope, are indeed sinners. Remember this, children.

Kānana cōlakal pōle - bhāva
sāndra gānāmṛtam pōle
jīvita manyark unarvin anusyūta
kāhala mākatte yeṅgum

Let your life be like a clarion call for awakening others, beautiful like a meadow in the wilderness, like the nectarean flow of music filled with poignant feelings.

Samsāra vṛkṣa talappil - pūttu
kākkunna tēn kaniyunnum
martya samūham sukha duḥkha sammiśra -
metrayō janmaṅgaḷ ennum

Humanity which loves to pluck and sample the sweet fruits growing on the tree of samsara (mundane existence), will tally up many life-times of it, all of it an uneven mixture of happiness and sorrow.

Nāvinte svādōrtu pāyum - manam
nērinte svādarivīla
ātma rasattinte svādariññāl pinne
āru rasangalum kaikkum

The mind that rushes to satisfy the tasty demands of the tongue, will never savor the Truth. When the ambrosia of the Self is tasted once, the six classical tastes will all seem bitter.

Yāgāgni kettu pōyi pakshē - hōma
dhūmam vamikkunnu cundil
sōmarasam pōymaraññu madyā-sakti
sōma lahriyāyi māri

The sacrificial fire is no longer kept up in households; but the smoke of the oblations emits now from your mortal lips! The juice of soma (which used to be offered to the deities) is no longer to be found, but the inebriation of wine has taken the place of the intoxication of soma!

Uḷḷinn ulayil jvalikkum - daiva
sankalpa śakti tan tīyil
paṅkaṅgal ellāmakannarka shōbhavāy -
cullam paramvyōma mākum

In the fire of divine sankalpa shakti (divine power of will) that burns in the inner furnace, all differences will be consumed, and the all-embracing spiritual radiance will be like an boundless supreme expanse.

Vaidika mantra dhvaniyil - muṅgi
kātum karalum kulirttu
kāla dēśaṅgaḷ kadannettum ātmasan
dēśattil muṅgatte viśvam

Let the ears and heart exalt in the sounds of Vedic chanting; let the whole world be flooded with that joyous message, the differences in cultures and times notwithstanding.

Śīlakkēdērum śiśukkal - svantam
mātāvin cēlattalappil
kaividāte porum ñan nukērunna pōl
tēduvin daivatte makkaḷ

Children, seek God like babies who hang on to their mothers' aprons, never letting go, and constantly plead for attention.

ŌMKĀRA DIVYA PORŪLE X

Ōmkāra divya poruḷē - varū ōmana makkaḷē vēgam
Ōmanayāy vaḷarnnā mayaṅgaḷ nīkki
ōmkāra vastuvāyu tīrū ōmkāra vastuvāy tīrū

Come quickly darling children; you are the essence of Om. Removing all sorrows, grow to be adorable and become one with the sacred syllable Om.

Vēdō jvalānta sandēśam - lōka
vēdiyil kīrttikka makkaḷ
kōṭi yabdaṅgaḷ kazhiññālu millati-
nnētum svarasthāna bhēdam (2x)

Children, sing the shining spiritual message of the scriptures! There will not be a wrong note in it even after millions of years.

Āyōdhanaṅgaḷ vēṭiyū - makkaḷ
ātma maitrikkāy śramikkū
āyōjanāhvāna mantra toṭādarāl
bhāviyi vārtte ṭuttīṭū (2x)

Children, give up fighting and strive for friendship amongst you. Mold the future, chanting the mantra of unity.

Āśayāyō dhanam vēṇam - martya
jīvitōt karṣattin ennum
āyudh āyōdhan ōtsāham manassinte
āsura vṛtti yāṇōrkkū (2x)

There should be the fight of ideas for the enrichment of life. Remember that fighting with weapons only shows the demonic side of the mind.

Vāḷmuna tumbil koruttī - lōkam
tankāl cuvaṭṭil taḷaykkān
āḷunna hantaykku pērilla pārinte
śāpamāṇām anōvṛtti (2x)

The ego that surges ahead to bring the whole world to its feet at the point of a sword has no other name - it is the curse of the world.

Uśappūvilar paṇam vēṇam - sadā
sadgurōr ājñānukūlam
sadguru prēmauṣadha tālanānmāvi -
lātmā bhimānam śamikkum (2x)

There should be complete surrender in the heart to the wish of the satguru. The medicine of love for the satguru will cure the pride that is in the unrealized self.

Vīṇvā kuraykkolla makkaḷ - kāmbum
nāmbum ārnnīṭaṭṭe vākkil
viśvā sadarppaṇa mākaṇam vāṅmayam
viśvaika śaktikka dhīnam (2x)

Children, do not speak empty words. Let there be substance in your words. Speech should be the mirror of faith; it should pay homage to the Supreme Power.

Ōmanicc amma vaḷarttām - ōrō
kālccōṭum amma teḷikkām
ōtunnavākkinte bhāvārttham uḷkkoṇṭu-
pōyāl manaḥ kaṇturakkām (2x)

Mother will bring you up as Her darlings. She will clear your path in each step. If you take in the meaning of Her words and go forward, She will open your mind's eye.

Duḥkhaṅgaḷeṇṇi niratti - daiva
śraddha kṣaṇikkēṇṭa makkaḷ
ujjvala prēma svarūpanāṇ īśvaran
hṛttil manaḥ kaṇturakkām (2x)

Children, there is no need to attract God's attention by enumerating your sorrows. He is the embodiment of shining love, the supreme essence that fills your heart.

Antaramgatt inte tēṅgaḷ - ennum
anyakār yārttha mākumbōḷ
anya kāruṇyamām puṇya tīrtthttinte
kaṇṇunīr uḷḷam viḷakkum (2x)

When your heart sobs only for the sake of others, the sacred tears of that compassion will cleanse and brighten you within.

Anpezhāneñcham dharippōr - śava
mañcam cumakkunnu pāzhē
dīnērāṭ uḷḷaliv uḷḷavarāy makkaḷ
vāzhta peṭaṭṭeyī maṇṇil (2x)

Those who carry a heart without love are carrying the load of a corpse. May you children be celebrated as having hearts that melt for those who suffer.

"Bhūtam" vaḷakkūrāy māri - "vartta-
mānam" namukkinna dhīnam
"bhāvi" kayyettā vidūratt irikkunnu
nēṭaṇam nēṭēṇṭatipōḷ (2x)

The past is dead and buried; the future is beyond the hand's reach. The present is in our control; whatever is to be gained, we should gain right now.

Āśā patamgamām uḷḷam - bhōga
mādhvīrasattil mayaṅgi
kāzhcayum prajṇayum pōy maraññōrāte
kūmbumā pūvilōṇantyam (2x)

The mind that is the butterfly of desire is lured by the honey of enjoyments, losing its sight and its sense, comes to its end as the flower of the senses closes its petals around it.

Lakṣyam mikavutta tiṅkil - mārga
vighnaṅgaḷ ētum nissāram
mṛtyuvin mēlkkōy mattaṭṭi takarttuko-
ṇṭātma lābham kaivarikkū

If the goal is high, the obstacles on the way are nothing. Children, break the dominion of death and gain the knowledge of the Self.

Tapta smaraṇa kūṭāte - bhōga
tṛpti pradamalla lōkam
pūmettayum kanal cūḷayum kaimāru-
mī mahāsam sāravīthi

The world does not give satisfaction of the senses without at the same time also giving burning memories. The great path of life alternates between beds of roses and burning furnaces.

Jīvitam kaykkum ennālum - karma
śuddhiyāl tūvamṛt uṇṇām
vēdanayil ninnu kāykkum vimōchana
mūlya bōdham svādiyattum

Even though life is bitter, one gets to enjoy nectar through the purity of one's actions, and the sense of liberation one gains through pain, adds taste.

Krōdham varumbōḷ kṣamikkān - vēṇṭum
vīryam manassinnu vēṇum
vīryam karuttezhum gāṇḍīvamā ṇatu
dharma jayikkān kulaykkām

The mind should have the strength to forgive when anger rises up. That strength is a mighty bow that can win the battle for dharma.

Kāpaṭyam uḷḷil potiññum - viśva
mānavan tānennu nāṭyam
mānava maitriyum viśva mataikyavum
nāvil cetumbicca mantam!

Some pretend to belong to the whole world, at the same time hiding deceit inside. Universal friendship and unity of all faiths are slogans that have rotted on their tongue.

Mānavaikya tinte mēnma - atya-
rārum paṭhippicci ṭēṇṭā
janmanā nāmatil tan mayarāṇ āru-
manyarall ātma bhāvattil

No one needs to teach us the greatness of the unity of mankind. We are attuned to that at birth; in the state of the Self, no one is alien.

Lōka morārādya puṣpam - dēśa-
mōtōnnum ōrō daḷaṅgaḷ
bhinnamall ammaykkatōrō
bhamgiyārnnō manikkēṇum

The world is a flower to be worshipped. Each country is a petal in it. For Mother no petal is different from any other. Each is to be loved.

Tulyamām svātantryam ārkkum - ārṣa-
sandaśa sāramat ōrkkū
uccattilud ghōṣaṇam cheyka nām divya
mānavai kyattinte mantram

Remember that, "equal freedom for all", is the message of the ancient sages. Let us proclaim aloud the mantra of unity of all mankind.

Āzhattil ādaravōṭe - namme
nāmari yumbozhē nammaḷ
ārṣapratibha tan satyā nubhūtiyil
martya svātantryam svadikkū

Only when we know ourselves in depth we will get the experience of truth that the ancient sages visualized, and enjoy human freedom.

Uḷḷam prabhā pūrṇṇam ākum - uṇma
namme karam tannuyarttum
uḷḷeriyum jñāna dāhāgni tīvramāy
uṇmatann ulviḷi kēḷkkum

Our hearts will shine; truth will give us a hand and raise us up. The desire for knowledge will burn stronger and we will hear the call of truth inside.

Uḷveḷiccam vīśi makkaḷ - varṇṇa
bhēda vidvēṣam veṭiññu
pārinte pūm ukhattāḷi jvalikkunna
ponviḷakkāy prēśābhikkū

Children, forgetting the differences of caste or color, spread the light that is in you and be a golden lamp that shines brightly on the porch of the world.

Onnikka makkaḷ manassāl - lōka
nanmaykku nēdikka namme
caitanya dīpta māmun mukta cētassil
vārnn ozhukaṭṭe svarganga

Unite, children, and dedicate yourselves for the welfare of the world. Let the heavenly stream of Ganga flow in your radiant, liberated heart!

Anyartan kaṇṇīru kāṇkē - manam
kallāyuray kunna makkaḷ
madyōtsavattāl gṛhacci dravum nāṭi-
nuḷttēṅgalum vilaykkunnu!

Those children whose heart hardens like stone when they see the tears of others, are causing family breakdown and distress in the country by their indulgence in drinking.

Ḍambhum kuśumbum muḷacchu - hṛttil
"daṇḍakāraṇyam" tazhaykke
ūḷḷile paital karaññu viḷikkunnu
kāṭaruttā śvāsamēkū

When pride and jealousy sprout inside, the heart becomes a wild forest. The child in your heart is crying for help; cut down the forest and rescue the child.

Aiśvaryam kaivarum nēram - garvvu
kāṭṭāte dharmam pularttū
dharmam pularttuvān kaivannora iśvaryam
daiva kāruṇya mennōrkkū

When prosperity comes, do not be proud of it; nurture dharma righteousness) with it. Remember that the prosperity that is given for the spread of dharma is a grace from God.

Puṇya karmmattāl manuṣyan - kivya
lōka bhōgaṅgaḷum nēṭrum
eṇṇa tīrnnālkkeṭum dīpam kaṇakku tan
puṇya mattiṅguṭal tēṭum

By doing meritorious acts, man gains enjoyments in heavenly worlds. When the merit is exhausted, he returns to take a human body, as the lamp that goes out when there is no more oil.

Tāzhmayil jīvikka makkaḷ - hṛttil
ārātirikkaṭṭe vīryam
martya janmattinte vāg dattalakṣyattil
śraddha tannastram kulaykkū

Children, lead humble lives. Let not courage fade from the hearts. Point the arrow of sraddha (faith) at the promised goal of human life.

Ōm ennorēkā kṣaratte - sarvva
vēda vumādari kunnu

ātma pratīkamī nāda bījam koṇṭu
ātma hṛdantam teḷikkū

All the Vedas celebrate the single syllable Om. Brighten your heart with this sacred kernel of sound which is the symbol of the Self.

Arccan āsūnamāy namme ' svayam
arppaṇam ceyyuvin makkaḷ
lōka kāryārtthmāy nēdiccu jīvitam
cāritārtthyam pūkiṭaṭṭe (2x)

Children, offer yourselves as the flowers of worship. May you gain fulfillment by leading your life in service of the world.

Jñāna dānattin caritram ' divya
snēha dānattin caritram
āyirattāṇṭukaḷ mudraṇam ceytorī
nāṭin mukam nitya ramyam (2x)

The face of this country is ever beautiful from its history of thousands of years of the gift of love.

Snēhanūl nīḷattil nūlkkām ' atil
dēśa sauhārddam korukkām
varṇṇā bhamārnnorā hāram uḷkkāmbile
ōmkāram ūrttikku cārttām (2x)

Let us spin a long thread of love and make a garland from the flowers of friendship for all lands; let us offer that brightly colored garland to the deity of Om in our hearts.

Aikyattinākātta karmam ātma
saughyattin ennum taṭastham
lakṣyam pizhaccu nērkkettum śaram kaṇa-
kāpattaṇaykkuma dharmam (2x)

Actions that do not bring unity are always a hindrance to inner happiness. Unrighteous actions will always bring peril, like an arrow that has missed its mark and comes back at you.

Toṭṭutoṭṭill ennamaṭṭil - mṛtyu
toṭṭupinnālē carippū
appappōḷ namme viḷiccuṇ arttum tante
nitya sānniddhya teyōrkkū (2x)

Remember that death is always walking behind, at touching distance. From time to time it will wake us up and remind us of its presence.

ityam nirantaram hṛttil - bhakti
śraddhā vivēkam viḷakki
tatva masīlakṣya sārasava svamām
muttāyi śōbhikka makkaḷ (2x)

Children, cultivate devotion, faith and wisdom within, and shine like pearls becoming the essence of the statement, Thou art That.

Dhyāna prakāśattil ūṭe - dvandva
vairuddhya bhāvaṅgaḷ māyum
dhyān ōrjjarēṇukkaḷ dharmōd dhṛtaṅgaḷām
karma tinuḷkkaru tēkum

In the light of meditation, the sense of duality and the sense of opposites will vanish. The energy gained from meditation wil give the inner strength for actions that enhance dharma.

**Vīṇayil nādam kaṇakkē - prāṇa
tantriyil ōmkāram ōlān
vēṇam nirantar ābhyāsam svaramṛta-
pānam tuṭarnnāra mikkū**

For the music of Om to emerge constantly from the strings of the heart, just as the notes from the string of a veena, constant practice is needed. Revel in the enjoyment of the nectar of that sound.

**Toṭṭāl trasikkunna śkti - martya
hṛttil niguḍham vasippū
mītē manōvṛtti mūṭi pataykkayā-
lōrātiri kayāṇārum**

In the heart of man resides the secret power that springs to life at a touch. We remain unconscious of this because of the covering imposed by the working of the mind.

**Dhyānattil vērukaḷāzhtti - karma
śākhakaḷ lōka tulartti
jīvitam ākum mahā vṛkṣam ēvarkku-
mēkaṭṭe śītaḷa ccāya**

Sinking its roots in meditation and spreading out good actions as its branches, let the great tree of life give cool shade to everyone!

**Sīmayattuṇ maye pulkū - uḷḷam
saumya bhāvōjvala mākkū
sauvarṇṇa phullā ravindam kaṇakkutan
uḷḷam malarkke viṭarttū**

Children, embrace truth with no conditions; make your heart shine with that gentle spirit and let it open up like a full golden lotus blossom.

Divya mātāvin karattil - iḷam
paital āytīrān kotikkū
jīvitād dhyāyṅgaḷ ōrōnnu manyarkku
mātṛ kādar paṇam ākkū

Yearn to be a little baby in the hands of the Divine Mother! Make every chapter of your life an ideal mirror for others!

ŌMKĀRA DIVYA PORŪLE XI

Ōmkāra divya poruḷē - varū
ōmana makkaḷe vēgam
Ōmanayay vaḷarnnā mayaṅgaḷ nīkki
ōmkāra vastuvāy tīrū

Come quickly darling children, you who are the divine essence of Om. Remove all sorrows, grow to be adorable and merge with the sacred syllable Om.

Ātma vipañcikamīṭṭi - snēha
gānaṅgaḷ ālapiccīṭū
nīrum manassukaḷ kāśvasa tīrtthamāy
snēhardra gānam pozhikkū!

Sing songs of love in the veena of the Self. Be the holy water, consoling the burning hearts with your melting song of love.

Lōla vikāraṅgaḷētum - krōdha
vēnalil vāṭinnaḷarum
vēru ventūrnnupōm jīvita vallikaḷ
snēham taḷiccal taḷirkkum

The tender feelings will dry up in the summer heat of anger. Just like the roots of the creepers will be destroyed by the summer sun, life will be destroyed by anger. Both will be rejuvenated if you sprinkle them with love.

Vēdam viḷaññorī maṇṇil - bheda
bhāvam viḷayunnat entē?
snēhattin pūntēn ozhukkil innīmaṇṇu
kōrittari kāttat entē?

In the land the Vedas sprang forth, why is the feeling of duality growing? Why don't our hairs stand on end when the honey of love is flowering in this land?

Kāyphalam nalkātezhikkum - verum
pāzhcceṭi yākāyka makkaḷ
kāykkilum kayppum kavarppum vitaykkunna
jīvitam nāṭinnan arttham!

Children, don't become like trees which do not yield fruit. Even if it bears fruit, the bitter and sour life produced ruins the country.

Oṭṭupēr namme stutikkām - pinne
oṭṭupēr namme duṣikkām
nammil namukkātma viśāsam uṇṭeṅkil
raṇṭum namukkonnu pōle!

A lot of people may sing our praises and a lot of people may condemn us. If we have confidence in our own selves, both of these are equal to us.

Sattatan lāvṇyalāsyām - hṛttil
nityavum kaṇṭā svadikkū
cuṭṭunōvin cuṭukaṇṇīrināy vṛthā
svapnaṅgaḷ neyyāyka makkaḷ

Try to enjoy the divine consciousness dancing in your hearts daily. Children, don't build castles in the air for the result will be only burning tears shed out of pain.

Samgharṣa vahniyil nīri - kāñña
kaṇṇīr ozhukkēṇṭa makkaḷ
vātsalyam ūṭṭittal ōṭuvā nammayu -
ṇṭātma dhairya tōṭeṇīkkū

Struggling in the fire of tension, don't shed tears my children. Lift yourself up with courage as Mother is there to feed you with love.

Mālinya millātta kaṇṇil - viśva
mākeyum caitanya dhanyam
nāma rūpaṅgaḷ pratītiyāṇ ōkkeyum
māññupōm vṛttikṣayattāl

In a pure eye, the whole world appears rich with consciousness. When the thoughts die away, the mirage of names and forms will vanish.

Kāla perumpāmbu namme - melle
vāykkuḷḷil ākkunnu gūḍham
āyussar unnatum ōrā tahōrātram
āhanta! teṭunnu bhōgam

Death, like a python, slowly and secretly swallows us. Ignorant of approaching death, we look for sensual pleasures day and night.

Ōṭittaḷarnna manassu - svantam
jīrṇṇava pussum cumannu
jīvitam ākumazhu kucālil nīnti
pōkunnu mṛtyuvin pinpē!

The dissipated mind, as if weakened in a running race and carrying its deteriorating body, swims in this life, like the sewage in the drain, followed by death.

Ōrttālīsam sāramōṭi - ennum
antakan tīrttapūvāṭi
ātmāvil ātmāvuṇar navark ātmāvil
kāṇāmit ānanda vāṭi

If we discriminate, the splendor of the world is always a garden made by the god of death. Those who are awakened in the Self will see this world as a garden of bliss.

Uḷḷinte kāṭṭil timarppū - krūra
jantukkaḷ nityam yathēṣṭam
ōrō manassinte puttilum vidvēṣa
sarppam viṣamcītti nilpū!

In the jungle of the mind, a lot of wild animals carouse daily. In the anthill of the mind lies the snake of hatred which spits poison all around.

Nūlizhay ōrō nazhiccu - cennāl
kāṇān kazhiyilla vastram
saṅkal vēraruttāzha tilettiyāl
kāṇillatēpōl manassum

If the threads are removed, the cloth cannot be seen. Likewise, if we destroy the roots of thought, the mind also will be unseen.

Kūṭṭile paiṅkiḷiyākā-tātma
sattatan mōcanam tēṭū
pāṭattu punnelkkanir kōtti mānattu
pārum panamtatta pōle!

Do not try to be like a bird in a cage. Look for the freedom of truth of the Self, like parrots enjoying grains in the open field, who are free to fly in the sky.

Kāzhcakaḷ kaṇṭu kaṇṭiṅg - makkaḷ
kaṇṇā yatōṅgā marannu
lakṣyam purattall aṭuttāṇ akattāṇ-
naśvar ātmānanda vastu

Children, seeing the scenery here and there, you have forgotten your inner eye. The goal is not outside, it lies inside as the blissful Self.

Kūṭevann īṭill oraḷum - antya
kālattu bandhukkaḷ pōlum
bhāṇḍam murukk ēṇṭanāḷ varum pōnkina-
vellām atōṭasta mikkum

Nobody will come with you at the time of death, not even your relatives. You will have to tie up your bundle one day and all golden dreams will vanish.

Oṭṭum nin aykkātirikke cuṭṭu
nōvētti duḥkham tiḷaykkum
addhyātma labdhiyala llāteyār illa
nīrum manaḥ klēśamārkkum

Sorrow will boil up causing burning pain without our knowledge. Without Self-knowledge, the burning mental agonies will not cool.

Mārggaṅgaḷ ellām aṭaññu - raudram
āḷippaṭarnnu kattumbōḷ
rakṣa yārōnnārtta kakkāmbu vēvunna
lakṣangaḷ āṇinnu cuttum!

When all the ways are closed and the fire of violence spreads, thousands of people in mental agony will look for help.

Jātiyē pūjiccuraññu - svantam
vīṭinnu tī koḷuttunnu
lābhavītatt inte kaikaṇa kilkatti
yāḷunnatārṣa samskāram

Adoring the caste system, people set fire to their own houses. The culture of Bharat (India) is burning in greed and self-interest.

Ādarśavādam muzhakkumtellum
ācarikkillattinleśam
jīvitam ācāraniṣṭhamalleltulōm
ādarśavādam nirartmam

People talk about idealism but do not practice even a bit of it. If life is not established in practicing those ideals, talking about idealism is useless.

Samvāda satraṅgaḷ vēṇṭa - cīrum
vagvada sīlkkāram veṇṭa
bhāvāt makaṅgaḷ āmādarśa śuddhiyil
ātmavīryam trasikkaṭṭe!

There is no need of gathering to argue and shout. Let the valor of the Self become prominent in the expression of sincere and pure ideals.

Ātma saurabhyam tuḷumbum - vākki-
larkkum viṣvāsam janikkum
tannil tanikkilla viśvāsam eṅkilō
pinnāratil kāmbukāṇum!

Everyone will believe in a fragrant word uttered by the Knower of the Self. If one has no faith in oneself, who will value them?

Mādhurya mūrum vacanam - jīva
kāruṇya mūrum nayanam
ādarśa dīpam jvalikkunn ōruḷḷavum
mānava maitrikku mānam!

The words dripping honey or sweetness, eyes shedding compassion towards beings, a heart in which idealism is burning, these are a ladder for uniting the human beings in friendship.

Ētō bhayattinte puttil - martya
lōkam vitaccu nilkkunnu
anyante jīvitam taccuṭaykkān kaika-
ḷanyōnayam vāḷōngiṭunnu!

The human world is shivering with some sort of fear. Their hands bear swords to destroy others' lives.

Kātōrttu keḷkkuvin makkaḷ - lōkam
tīgōḷ amāyuruḷ unnu
ātmaikya millāte nētram cuvappiccu
nērkkunēr garjjicciṭ unnu!

Hear carefully my children, the world is spinning like a burning globe. The eyes are reddened in anger and people roar, devoid of unity in the Self.

Tanne tyajikkātta tyāgam - tyaga
mallatum poḷḷunna bhogam
"ellām tyajiccavan ña" nenn ahantayum
makkaḷe bandha namārggam

If you are not giving up your ego, it can't be called renunciation, it is like being burnt up in sensual gratification. Even thinking egoistically that "I am a renunciate" is the blinding path.

Dānattil ñānenna bhāvam - ninnal
ceyyunna karmam duṣikkum
sthānattinum svargga lābhattinum nammaḷ
ceyyunnatum svārttha karmam!

If you develop the "I am giving" feeling in charity, that work will become impure. If we work for power and for attaining heavenly pleasures, that is also a selfish work.

Svanta māyōnnu milleṅkil - makkaḷ
anyarkku pinnentu nalkum?
anya duḥkhattil manam tapi kāttavar-
kanyamām ātma sambattum!

If you have nothing of your own, what will you give to others? If your heart is not burning for others' suffering, you won't get the treasure of the Self.

Ceyyunna tellāma śuddham - nammaḷ
kōyyunna tellām anarttham
ceyyām manassinte kaṇṇāṭiyil nōkki
koyyām kalarppatta puṇyam

All acts we do are impure and what we yield is also useless. If you work seeing the mirror of the mind, you can yield pure merit.

Nāriye pūjicca puṇyam - inn
nārakī yāgniyil vīzhtti
māna kṣayttinte kāṭṭutī kattunnu
nāṭeṅgum innatin tēṅgal!

Merit acquired by worshipping women has been thrown into the fire of hell. The wildfire of their fall of virtue is burning and their crying can be heard all over the country.

Satyatte sambattināyi - vātu
veykkan maṭikkātta lōkam
satya niṣṭhakkāy samarppicca jīvita
śuddhi inn ārōrttiṭunnu!

Today's world will not hesitate to give us truth for money. Who is thinking today of a pure life surrendered for Truth?

Nālāṇṭu nannāy śramiccāl - ārkkum
nēṭam nijānanda lakṣyam
nalkāmurapp amma cūṇṭunna nērvara
nīṅgāte nīṅgiyāl mātyam!

If one tries very hard for four years, one can attain the goal of bliss established in the Self. Amma will certainly give you this, if you will move along the path, without breaking the straight line drawn by Amma.

Veda sūktaṅgaḷ pukazhtti - "gītā
māta"yum kīrtticcu pāṭi
ātma sūryōdaya pōnnuṣaḥ sandhyaye
pērttum atēttēttu pāṭu!

Sing and praise Vedic hymns and "Mother Gita" repeatedly, of which the sun of the Self will dawn.

Bāhyanetyam pintiriccu - śraddha
antarātmā viluraccu
annukaṇṭ atbhutum inn umataṅgane
maṅgātta māyātta satyam!

Firmly turn your external eye into the internal Self. The wonder which was seen before is the same shining eternal truth even now.

Uḷḷile daiva sanniddhyam - namaḷ
uḷḷapōl kaṇāttat entē?
Uḷḷil manassilla tanyavastu kaḷe
nuḷḷi kōriccu nilkkunnu!

Why don't we see the presence of the inner Self the way it exactly is? Our minds are not turning inside, instead, it goes after tasting external objects.

Pūvam pasādavum vāṅgi - dēva
prītikkay kaṇikka nalkam
uḷḷile śrīkovil taḷḷittur annuḷḷu
kaṇuvān dhairyam illārkkum!

You can receive flowers and other things offered to God and give money instead, but nobody is brave enough to open the Sanctum Sanctorum inside themselves.

Svantam hṛdantam marann - svarga
vātilil muṭṭeṇṭoraḷum
illāta vātil turakkān orumbeṭā
iḷḷam turakkān pathiykkū

Do not knock at the door of heaven forgetting your own heart or Self. Instead of trying to open the door, which does not exist, learn to open your own heart.

Dūrattūnn ārānum vannāl - namu
kārennatōrān tiṭukkam
"ārutā"nennalla - ārā ṇatennaṇ
ārayuvān namu kiṣaṭam!

If somebody comes from far away, we are eager to know who it is. We like to enquire, "who is it?", instead of enquiring, "who am I?"

Kāla koṭuṅkātt aṭikkum - dēham
ētu nērattum patikkum
ātma lakṣyattil manassu veccīlōka
līlayil sākṣyam vahikkū!

The body will fall when the cyclone of time blows. Try to fix your mind on the goal of the Self and be a witness in the play of this world.

Nāl āśramaṅgaḷ vidhiccu - saumya
jīvitam nammaḷ nayiccu
mṛtyu mārgga tinnetirē cariccu nām
mukti pīyūṣam svadiccu

Four ashramas (stages of life) were ordered and we lived a peaceful life. We tasted the ambrosia of liberation, walking against the path of death.

Cōdicca varkkēkiyētum - nammaḷ
pētal ābhaṅgaḷ ōrkkāte
pratyu pakāram kōti callayēv arkkum
'svasti'yī nāṭinte dharmam

Without seeing the loss and profit, we gave everything to those who asked for it. This country never longed for compensation, as its duty was only wishing for peace to all.

Ellām marannu pōyinn - lakṣyam
indriy ārtmaṅgaḷil taṅgi
kāṇunnat okkeyum durnim ittaṅgaḷāy
kālakkēṭ ennatin bhāṣyam!

We have forgotten everything and are living for sensual gratification. Whatever we see, has become a bad omen and can be called the misfortune of time.

Jīvitam naivēdyam ākkū - manō
nākkilayil nivēdikkū
ātma svarūpikaḷ makkaḷē niṅgaḷā
tīkkanal ūtitteḷikkū!

Let your life be an offering to God placed on the leaf of your mind. Children, you who are the embodiment of the Self, try to kindle that spark of fire.

ONNU TIRIÑÑIṄGU NŌKKAṆĒ

Onnu tiriññiṅgu nōkkaṇē kṛṣṇā (2x)
ente ponnin ponnāra nīlakār varṇṇā
kṛṣṇā kṛṣṇā kṛṣṇā

Kindly turn around and cast a glance at me, O my dear darling Krishna, who has the complexion of the dark rain clouds.

Mañña pītāmbara paṭṭuṭuttu
maṇṇil puraṇṭoru dēhavumāy
Añjana kaṇṇukal cimmi cimmi
piñcu karaṅgaḷil veṇṇayumāy
onnu mariyāte puñcirikum
kṛṣṇā kṛṣṇā kṛṣṇā

Clad in fine yellow silken robes and the body smeared with dust, the dark eyes blinking occasionally, holding butter in those tender hands, smiling in all innocence, O Krishna! Krishna! Krishna!

Pica vecu nī melle naṭannu
tetti pūmāla kalāke ulaññu
Accyutā nīyaṅgu muttatt iraṅgi
maṇṇu vārittinna paitalallē
amma kaṇṭaṅgati śayiccu
kṛṣṇā kṛṣṇā kṛṣṇā

Toddling slowly with swaying steps, the flower garlands fluttering, Achyuta, are You not the child who stepped into the courtyard and ate mud? The mother (Yashoda) saw You and was wonderstruck (having seen the whole cosmos in the mouth of Krishna). O Krishna! Krishna! Krishna!

ORU KOCCU KUÑÑINTE

Oru koccu kuññinte tanuveni kunṭeṅkil
entoru bhāgya māyēne (2x)
Ōṭiyaṇaññu ñān āmaṭittaṭṭil
vīṇu rasiccu pōnnēne (2x)

Oh, how lucky I would have been if I had the body of a little child! I would then run up, fall into that lap, revel and romp!

Ā veḷḷa cēlatan tumpu piṭicu ñān
picca naṭannu pōyēne (2x)
Mattoru kuññine talōli cennāl ñān
śāṭhyam piṭicu kēṇēne (2x)

Taking hold of one end of that white garment, I would take some steps! And if another child was petted, I would cry in insistent protest!

Cāruta yārnorā mukha patmam vīkṣiccī
lōkam marannu ninnēne (2x)
Ōnnenne nōkki nī hasiccennu vannāl

tuḷḷikkaḷi cirunnēne (2x)

I would stand watching that beautiful lotus face, forgetting this world! And if I got a glance and a smile, I would dance with joy!

Kuññikka raṅgaḷ koṇṭā linganam ceytu
kinnāraṅgaḷ paraññēne (2x)
Viṭṭiṭṭu pōkan udyami cennāl
vaṭṭam piṭiccu ninnēne (2x)

I would embrace Her with my little hands, and make sweet baby talk. And if I were about to be left behind, I would throw a tantrum!

Enne kaḷippiccu nī maraññennāl
poṭṭi karaññu pōyēne (2x)
Kaṇṇuruṭṭi nī pēṭippi cennāl
vitumpi karaññu ninnēne (2x)

If You were to fool me and disappear, I would break into tears. If You rolled Your eyes and scared me, I would stand there sobbing.

Kōpam naṭiccu nī talliyāl pādattil
muruke puṇarnnu kēṇēne (2x)

And if You feigned anger and pushed me, I would hug Your feet tightly and weep!

ORU KOCCU PULNĀMBIN

Oru koccu pulnāmbin tunpattiṅgi-ttunna
oru maññu tuḷḷiykku tulyan ñān
oru maññu tuḷḷiykku tulyan ñān

Kṣaṇanēram nila ninnu takarumī himakaṇam
ulakattin katha yentariññu - neṭiya
kālattin gati yentaṛiññu?

I am a dew drop at the far edge of a tiny leaf of grass, alive a while, aching, tremulous, delicately poised, dripping, emptying, and will be no more. Poor me, can I scan the meaning of the mystery of the mazy world, time's ceaseless motion, its drift, thrust and goal? Cramped in the world, bound in time, can I see the Truth transcending world and time?

Oḷḷiyum nizhalum menayunna rūpaṅgaḷ
sthiramennu ñān ōrttiṭunnu - satya
dhanamennu ñān ōrttiṭunnu
Oḷi māññāl nizhal māyum
nizhal māññāl marayum nāl
kamanīya rūpaṅgaḷ ellām - kaṇṇum
karaḷum kavarunnat ellām

Crazy and deluded, I take for real what light and shade shape and throw up fleeting chimeras; I take for stable what their endless play conjures up: frothy nothing. Light casts shadows, shade ceases when light is no more. Ah! The myriad forms, all comely, spring into sight in light but where are they when the light illumines them not?

Viriyunna pūviṇṭe azhakil ñān aṛiyāte
mizhi naṭṭu mati mayaṅgunnu ente
nila maṛannanu mōdiykkunnu
Aṭarunna pūvupōla ṭarum ñān lāḷicca
cirakāla svapnavum ñānum puttan
abhilāṣa pūmoṭṭu pōlum

I gaze and gaze at the blooming flower, scented and flushed. I am enchanted, enthralled by the blossom swaying and smiling, and give it rapturous praise in my thoughtless ignorance. But what a fool I make myself not to know that frail beauty will droop and drop ere sun-down, not to know that my bursting dreams will wither and die alike.

Kālattin nīḷatte ñān onn aḷakkumbōḷ
ñānenna 'māna'vum māyum māññāl
māyum 'ñān' - 'nī'yennatellām
Kaṭalinte āzham ñān ariyumbōḷ 'ñā'nākum
'kana'vumaṅgaṭil līnamākum pinne
karakēṟān ñān illennāvum

When the 'immeasurable' time I seek to 'measure', the 'I' fades away, 'You' and 'all' are all erased. If the 'I' is not, who is to know whom? A void absolute. When the 'unfathomable' ocean I seek to fathom, I dissolve into the vast deep roaring brine together with my rod. Ah ! Then, there is no 'me' to swim ashore to tell its depth.

ORU MAṆAL TARIPŌLUM

Oru maṇal taripōlum avirāmama viṭuttē
tikavut toravatāra katha parayum
amṛtāmayī tava hṛdaya kṛpārṇṇava
madhura rasāmṛta katha parayum

O Amritamayi (Sweet, Immortal One)! Even a dust particle will forever sing the stories of the incomparable play of Your divine incarnation; it will tell the sweet, honey like, immortal story of the Compassion of Your heart, vast as the ocean.

Amṛtānandam sahaja svabhāvam
amara padam nin tirupada kamalam
Amṛtamayī tava pada malarūnnum
malayāḷ-attinum amara padam

Immortal Bliss is Your natural state. Your holy Lotus Feet are verily the abode of the gods. Oh Amritamayi! The land of Kerala, blessed by the touch of Your Lotus Feet, has also attained immortal glory.

Dāhicca maṇṇinte dāham śamipikkum
snēhāmṛta tintē dhārā pravāhamē
Mānava lōkam samārā dhanam ceyyum
pārinna dhīśa caitanyame vandanam

You are an incessant stream of Immortal Love that will quench the thirst of the land. Prostrations to You, who are the Holy Spirit that rules the Universe, and is adored by the world of humanity.

ORU NIMIṢAM EṄKILUM

Oru nimiṣam eṅkilum svarayam uṇṭō
ninakkoru nimiṣam eṅkilum svairyam uṇṭō
Iha lōka sukham tēṭi alayuvaiyram uṇṭō

O man, do you feel peace of mind for even a second while seeking happiness in this world?

Paramārtha tatvaṅgaḷ ariyāte māya tan
nizhalinte pinpē brahmiccu cāṭi (2x)
Eriyunna tī kaṇṭa śalabham kaṇakke
oru phalavum illāto ṭuṅgān tuṭaṅgunnu
Ninakkoru nimiṣam eṅkilum svaiyram uṇṭō

Without grasping the Truth, you ran after the shadow of maya (illusion). You will face the same fate as that of a moth deluded by the sight of a glowing fire.

Kṛmiyāyi puzhuvāyi izhayunna jantukkaḷ
palatāyi paṛavakaḷ mṛgavumāyi
Kramamāy uyarnnu yarnnātmā nubhūti tan
narajanma mārjjiccat entinnu nī
Ninakkoru nimiṣam eṅkilum svaiyram uṇṭō

Having evolved gradually through various incarnations like worms, crawling creatures of different kinds, birds and animals, you become a human being. What is the purpose of human life other than Self-Realization?

Atinalla manujante vilayēriṭum janmam
atinuṇṭō ravakāśa matinu vēṇṭi
Abhimāna dhana-dāra mōham veṭiññu nī
harihara parabrahma bhajana ceytallāykil
Ninakkoru nimiṣam eṅkilum svaiyram uṇṭō

Cast away pride and greed. Leave the life of illusion and spend your human birth singing the glory of the supreme Brahman. God-Realization is your birthright; don't waste away this precious life.

ORU PIṬI DḤUKHATTIN

Oru piṭi duḥkhattin kai kumbilum
netuvīrpil oṭuṅgunna kathayumāy
antikē nilkumi nin makanē
onnu kadākṣikkān bhāvam illē?

O Mother, won't You look at me with Your merciful eyes? I have been waiting near You with folded hands and heart-breaking tales full of sorrow.

Nindyayāi kaṇṭu koṇṭāy irikkām
ninne ariyātta kāranavum
Onnum ariyāte entu ceyyum ammē
onnum arivāno kelpumilla

Maybe because of my ungratefulness and my impure perception of You, I am unable to comprehend Your divinity. I have no ability to know You. O Mother, what can I do to know You?

Ammē ennulloru nītivili
nin kātil vannaṅga ḷacidillē
Āśvāsa mēkuvān ettukille ammē
sāndvana vākkukal nalkukille

I have been calling You, "Amme, Amme", a long time. Haven't these supplications reached Your ears? Won't You come to me and say a few kind words to give me comfort and solace?

ORU PIṬI SNĒHAM TIRAÑÑŪ

Oru piṭi snēham tiraññū ñān
nizhalinte pinpē naṭannū
kayy ettuvānāy oruṅgi— vīṇṭūm
piṭiviṭṭu ñān iṅgalaññū
ammē ammē

Searching for a speck of Love, I wandered after the shadows. O Mother, I tried again to reach out for it. But it eluded my grasp and I am still wandering.

Iḷakum kadanatti rayil
taḷarnnu hṛdayam jananī?
Takarum jīvan iniyum
tirayuva teviṭen jananī?
varumō nī varumō

In the lashing waves of sorrow, O Mother, my heart has become weary. My life is crumbling, where else will I search for You? O Mother, won't You come, won't You?

Azhalārnn ozhukum mizhinīr
nukarnn uraṅgātini ñān
Jananī! tiru pada malaril
uṇarān tava kṛpa yaruḷū

O Mother, bestow Your Grace that I may awaken at Your Lotus Feet, and not sleep any more, sipping the streaming tears of sorrow.

PĀHIMURARĒ PĀVANA CARITĀ

Pāhimurarē pāvana caritā
trāhi mahēśā gōpīśā
Pāhi kṛpālō vandita caraṇā
parama pavitrā gōpālā

O slayer of the demon Mura, whose life deeds are sacred, protect me! O Supreme Lord, Lord of the gopis! Give refuge, O compassionate One, of adored feet. Hail to the Divine Cowherd, most holy One!

Hṛdi hṛdi mṛdupada naṭana kutūhala
līlā mānava rāsavihārī
Janaga ṇamana vṛndāvana mōhana
prēma ayānvita muraḷī bālā

You are adept at dancing in the heart, with soft steps. Thy human form is a divine sport, You revel in the rasa dance, enchanting the Vrindavan of the devotee's minds.

Akhila carācara karma vidhāyaka
cakrā yudha dhara dharma vidhātā
Janimṛti jīvana kāḷiya mardana
samsṛti viṣa samhāri murāri

O Love Personified, flute player! You are the dispenser of the fruits of the deeds of all beings. O wielder of the divine discus, eternal champion of dharma, the basis of life and death, conqueror of the snake Kaliya, destroyer of the demon Mura, who cures the poison of worldliness.

Viraha vitāḍita hṛdaya jvālā
pīḍita rādhā jīvasu dhāmśō
Brahmānanda rasātma vikāsā
gō jīvātmā rādhā dhārā

To Radha's heart scorched by the flames of separation from Thee, You are the life giving rays of the ambrosial moon. You, the divine cowherd, the Lord of Radha and the soul, lead them to the infinite bliss of the Absolute.

PĀLANA PARĀYAṆI AMṚTĒŚVARI

Pālana parāyaṇi amṛtēśvari
pāvana pūjitē jagadīśvari

O Amriteshwari, who is always engaged in the welfare of Her children, who is the mistress of the universe, worshipped by pure souls.

Śrita janamanō rañjini śrī mannagara nāyikē
pañca tanmātra sāyakē namāmi śrī laḷitāmbikē

She who gives joy to those who seek refuge, who is the mistress of the most prosperous city, who holds the five elements as arrows, to that playful Mother, I bow down.

Patita lōkōddhā rakē kalikan maṣa nāśinī
ābāla gōpaviditē namāmi śrī laḷitāmbikē

She who raises those who are fallen, who destroys the evils of this dark age, and who is known by children and cowherds, to that playful Mother, I bow down.

PAṄKILAMĀM EN MANASSU

Paṅkilamām en manassu koṇṭaṅgaye
saṅkiyāt eṅgane ñān viḷikkum(2x)

How can I call out to You unhesitantly, O Lord, with my mind which is stained with sin?

Tīyil paticcoru pulkkoṭi tumbinu
meyyazha kāśippān entu ñāyam? (2x)

How can a blade of grass fallen into the fire claim for itself beauty of form?

Pāvana nāyiṭum aṅgunnu pāvakan
pāpiyāy uḷḷōn ñān pulkkoṭiyum (2x)

You, the holy One, are the Fire and I, the sinner, am the blade of grass.

Pātaki pōlum nin pāvana nāmattāl
pūta svabhāvanā yennu kēḷppū (2x)

I have heard that even the worst sinner will be transformed into a saintly character by chanting Your hallowed Name.

Ākayāl tāvaka nāmaṅgaḷ kēḷkumbōḷ
āke piṭayunnit en hṛdantam (2x)

Therefore when I hear Your Names, my heart trembles.

Māmaka cittattil ninne vāzhippānāy
ñān ahōrātram paṇi peṭṭallō (2x)

Day and night have I toiled to install You in my heart.

Onn iviṭattil kaṭannu vannīṭuvān
ennil kaniyuka yillē nāthā (2x)

O Lord, will You not be compassionate enough to visit me here once?

En muṭikkuttil piṭiccizhacch eṅkilum
nin aṭittāril aṇaykkuk enne (2x)

At least catching me by the hair, won't You pull me near Your lotus Feet?

PANNAGA BHŪṢAṆA PARAMA

Pannaga bhūṣaṇa parama dayālō
pārvati jānē mām pāhi
vandita suramuni sundara rūpa
indu jaḍādhara sāmbaśivā

Adorned with serpents, supremely compassionate, O Lord of Parvati, support me. Thou of beautiful form, revered by devas and sages, O Samba Shiva, whose matted locks are adorned with the moon.

Sarva śivaṅkara saṅkaṭa nāśana
garva vivarjjita sarvahara

tunga himālaya śṛnga nivāsa
gangā dhara hara jaganmaya

Bestower of auspiciousness to all, destroyer of sorrow, destroyer of all who do not forsake pride, abiding in the peaks of the high Himalaya, O Hara, who carries the Ganga and pervades the universe.

Matilaya kāraṇa natajana pālaya
kuvalaya lōcana sanātana
Praṇava sarōruha nilayā pālaya
prapañca bharaṇā māmaniśam

The cause of dissolution of mind, the protector of the devotees, The Eternal One with eyes like the kuvalaya flower, who resides in the lake of Om, Always protect me, O Sovereign of the Universe

Samba śiva hara samba śiva

PARAMA PĀVANA VADANĒ

Parama pāvana vadanē varadē
śaradambikē [amṛtavarśini] vandanam

O Mother, the One with the most sacred countenance, salutations to You, O Amritavarshini (the bestower of nectarine bliss).

Citta śuddhi tan cāru citramām
ambikē jagadambikē
Satya sundara caritē mahitē
śaradambike [amṛtavarśini] vandanam

O Mother of the Universe, You are the very personification of purity. Glorious is Your life, true and beautiful. Salutations unto You.

Śānti tan mṛdu kānti cintiṭum
ambikē jagadambikē
Ēka mātā sakala jagadā
śaradambike [amṛtavarśini] vandanam

O Mother of the Universe! Who radiates the soft light of peace. The only one Mother of the entire Universe, Salutations unto You.

Mādhurī nidhē dāna vāridhē
ambikē jagadambikē
Nirmalā kṛtē dīna vatsalē
śaradambikē [amṛtavarśini] vandanam

O Mother of the Universe! You are the treasure house of sweetness and the ocean of generosity. The One with immaculate form, who is affectionate to the poor. Salutations unto You.

Loka sēvana nipuṇa-yāyiṭum
ambikē jagadambikē
Snēha sāramē bhavya tāramē
śaradambikē [amṛtavarśini] vandanam
Vandanam! vandanam! vandanam!

O Mother of the Universe, supremely skilled in serving the world. You are the essence of Love, the star of auspiciousness. Salutations!

PARIŚUDDHA SNĒHATTE

Pariśuddha snēhatte tiraññu tiraññu ñān
rāppaka lillāta laññiṭāvē
Paramārttham entenn aṛiññu ñān entammē
nin snēham mātramāṇiṅg abhayam

Searching for pure love, I wandered oblivious to the passing of night and day. I understand the supreme Truth that, Mother, Your Love alone is my sole refuge.

Nīṛunna cintayāl en manam taḷaravē
pratīkṣakaḷ nin snēham mātramallō
Viṅgunna hṛdayattil kotikkunnu ammē
nin snēha vātsalyam ēttiṭānāy

When my mind is weary of burning thoughts, Your Love is my only hope. My anguished heart, O Mother, deeply yearns to receive Your Love and attention.

Nin snēha māṇenikkēkā valambam
mattentum nirāśayil āzhttum enne
Nin cintayilāṇṭen jīvan veṭiyuvān
ammē ī makal koticciṭunnu
ammē ī makal koticciṭunnu

Your Love is my only support; everything else will plunge me into despair. O Mother, this child yearns to give up this life, immersed in the thoughts of You.

PĀṬĪṬUM AMMĒ ĀṬĪṬUM

Pāṭīṭum ammē āṭīṭum nin
nāmam pāṭi ñān āṭīṭum
Kāḷi kāḷi mahakāḷi
kāḷi kāḷi bhairavī

Oh Mother, I will sing Your Name and dance. I will sing and I will dance. Oh Kali, Kali, Mahakali, Kali, Kali, Bhairavi (Consort of Shiva).

Kēṇu kēṇī kuññuvīṇu
karuṇa tūkū kāḷikē
Kaṇṇunīrāl kāl kazhukām
rakta puṣpaṅgaḷ ñān tarām
Karuṇa tūkū kāḷike
Āmṛtamayī kāḷikē Āmṛtamayī kāḷikē
Ānandamayī kāḷikē

Crying ceaselessly, this child has collapsed. Oh Mother Kali, show some compassion! I will wash Your Feet with my tears. I will offer Thee red flowers (flowers of sacrifice). Show some compassion, Mother Kali! O immortal and blissful Kali!

Viṅgiṭūm hṛt spandanāttāl
puṇya nāmam mīṭṭiṭām
Eṅgupōy ni eṅgupōyī
en kināvām ambikē
En kināvām ambikē Eṅgupōy ambikē
Amṛtamayī kāḷike Ānandamayī ambikē

I will chant Your holy Name, with the painful throbs of my heart. I will chant Your holy Namc. Where have You gone? Where have You gone, oh Mother of my dreams? Oh Sweet, Eternal Kali! O blissful Kali!

PĀṬUPEṬṬĒRE ÑĀN

Pāṭupeṭṭēre ñān pāmaran ākumen
mānasa kōvilil ninne vāzhttān
pāram taḷarnnu ñān vēdanayāl ammē
kātara cittanāy kēṇu vīṇṭum
tēṅgalāl uḷḷam piṭaññu vīṇṭum

I, the ignoramus, have struggled long and hard to worship You in the temple of my heart. Thoroughly exhausted, O Mother, I weep in pain with an anguished heart.

Ayyō yenikkinī vayya vayyoṭṭumē
alpavum jīvitam veccupōttān
Entini ceyvū ñān ninne labhikkuvān
ōtuka kelpilla ninnuvāzhān

Ah! Enough have I suffered, no more can I bear to prolong this life. What am I to do to gain You? Do tell me Mother; my strength is ebbing.

Pārile bhāraṅgaḷ kaṇṭu maṭuttu ñān
pārvatī! pāpiyī kuññinōṭu
Nīyum veruttuvō eṅkilī putranu
vēreṅgum illini rakṣayambē

O Mother, I am tired of the worldly sorrows. O Parvati, if you, too, begin to hate me, there is no other refuge for me.

PĀŚĀṄKUŚA DHARA

Pāśāṅkuśa dhara pāpa vināśana
pāhi dayāmaya gaṇanāthā
Śrīkara jaya praṇavām bujanilaya
śrī śiva tanaya surasēvya

Oh, Lord Ganesha, holding the noose and goad, destroyer of sin, chief of the attendants of Shiva, merciful One, protect me! Victory to the One dwelling in the Lotus of Omkara, the doer of auspiciousness, the son of Lord Shiva, who is worshipped by devas.

Pītāmbara dhara bhītivi bhañjana
cāruka ḷēbara vidhivandya
Hē rambā sukha śānti vidhāyaka
nīraja lōcana śiva sadana

Clad in yellow robes, remover of fear, beautiful bodied, bowed to even by destiny, who is the giver of peace and happiness, lotus eyed, You are the abode of auspiciousness.

Trāhi parātpara bhūri kṛpākara
mātam gānata hṛdayēśa
Rakṣa ganēśvara vighna vināśaka
sadgati dāyaka gaṇanātha

O Supreme One, verily full of kindness, please save me. Elephant faced, Lord of the heart, protect me Lord Ganesha ("chief of the attendants of Shiva"), remover of obstacles, giver of the good path.

PRANEŚVARA GIRIDHĀRI

Prāṇēśvarā, giridhāri, sarvēśvarā, vanamāli, O

O Lord of my life force, who lifted up a mountain, Lord of the Universe, adorned with a garland of wild flowers.

Ī rātriyil nīla nilāvuḷḷa ī rātriyil
Kaṇṇir kaṇaṅgaḷ koruttu ñān
certtoru mālayumāyitā kāttirippū
Giridhāri kāttirippū vanamāli kāttirippū

In this night filled with blue moonlight. In this night, with all my tears I made you a garland and I am eagerly awaiting to adorn you. Giridhari, I am awaiting you, Vanamali O.

Niśayuṭe niśśabda yāmaṅgaḷil
niśīthini pōlum uraṅgum vēḷayil
Ñān mātramennum kāttaṅgirippū
Nin pādasarattin cilamboli kēḷkkān
Giridhāri kāttirippū vanamāli O kāttirippū

In the silent quarter of the night, the goddess presiding over night is sleeping. Am I the only one who is intently waiting to hear the jingling of the anklets on your feet? Giridhari, I am awaiting you, Vanamali O.

PRAPAÑCATTIN OKKEYUM

Prapañcattin okkeyum ādhāram āyiṭum
prēma svarūpiṇi sarvēśvari [amṛteśvari]
praṇa mikkum makkaḷil prēmāmṛta kaṇam
pakarnnu nalkīṭuvān kaniyēṇamē!

O Universal Mother, embodiment of love, who is the support for the entire universe. Please shower us with the nectar of love. We prostrate before You.

Bhaktiyum jñānavum vairāgyavum ekuvān
bhavatāriṇi kāḷikē nī kaniññīṭumō?
Nin divya darśanam ennonnu mātramā-
ṇinnente lakṣyavum jagadambikē!

O Bhavatarini, Kalike, will You grace us with devotion, knowledge and detachment? O Jagadambike, my single goal is to have Your divine darshan today.

Nin kṛpā lēśattināy kaṇṇunīril muṅgumī
nin makanil ambikē nī kaniyēṇamē!
enteyī jīvitam ninniḷ samarppiccu
kṛta kṛtyanāy ammē ñān tīrniṭaṭṭe!

O Ambike, be kind to this daughter who has been crying and shedding tears for a tiny bit of grace from You. Let me feel contented and happy by offering my entire life to You.

RĀDHĀ MĀDHAVA GŌPĀLA

Rādhā mādhava gōpāla rāsa manōhara śīlā
Rāvum pakalum nin pada cintana mallātill oru vēlā

O Gopala, O Madhava, the beloved of Radha, whose very nature is beauteous Love, Day and night I do nothing other than contemplating on Your Lotus Feet.

Alayukayāṇī samsārē aśrayam ēkuka kamsarē
Akhilaṇḍ ēśvaran allē nī abhayam tēṭuka iniyāre

I am wandering in this cycle of birth and death.Grant me refuge, O slayer of Kamsa! O Lord of the Universe, in whom else should I seek refuge other than You?

Karalil nivēdyam orukki ñān kātt irikkunnu murārē
Karuṇā sāgara nallē nī - en kadanam tīrkkuka śaurē

Preparing the sweet offering of Love for You in my heart, I am arly waiting for You, O Murare (slayer of the demon Mura). Aren't You the ocean of compassion, O Krishna? Won't You dispel all my sorrows?

RĀDHAYE TŌZHARE

Rādhaye tōzhare cākān veṭiññiṭṭu
kaṇṇan mathuraykku pōyi pōlum
kāruṇya vāridhi yāṇupōl kāruṇyam

itraykku kāṭhinya mārnnatāṇō?
Kaṇṇā tāmara kaṇṇā (4x)

Leaving Radha and the Gopis to die, Krishna has left for Mathura. He is said to be the ocean of compassion, but is His compassion so merciless?

Ammiññappālil viṣam chērtta pūtana
kaṇṇene kālum kaṭhōra yennō?
Virahaviṣa jvāla tannil kariññiṭān
kaṇṇanī rādhaye talliyillē?
Kaṇṇā tāmara kaṇṇā (4x)

Was the demoness Putana who poisoned her breast milk more hard-hearted than Krishna? O Krishna, You have deserted Radha, leaving Her to be scorched by the poisonous flame of separation.

Kaṇṇane mātram ninacca tāṇō kuttam
vīṭum sukhaṅgalum viṭṭatāṇō?
Kaṇṇanu pūmāla kōrttatāṇō kuttam?
sarva samarppaṇam ceytatāṇō?
Kaṇṇā tāmara kaṇṇā (4x)

Was it wrong to have thought of Krishna alone or to have left the home and worldly pleasures? Or was it a crime to have made garlands for Krishna, or to have surrendered oneself entirely to Him?

Vṛndāvana priyā kaṇṇā karaññiṭān
kaṇṇunīr vattiyō rēzha rādha
Īrēzhu lōkattil ninne yallātonnum
vēṇṭāte kāttirikkunna rādha
Kaṇṇā tāmara kaṇṇā (4x)

Sri Krishna, beloved of Vrindavan, this destitute Radha has no more tears to shed. Desiring nothing else from the fourteen worlds except Her Lord, Radha waits for You alone.

RĀDHE KṚṢṆA

Rādhe kṛṣṇa rādhe kṛṣṇa
kṛṣṇa kṛṣṇa rādhe rādhe (2x)
Gōpi kṛṣṇa gopāla kṛṣṇa
govardhana dhāri gōvinda kṛṣṇa
Muraḷi kṛṣṇa mōhana kṛṣṇa
mañjuḷa hāsa mānasa cōrā
Mañjuḷa hāsa mānasa cōrā

Nirupama saure murāri malāri
pītāmbara dhāri kuñja vihāri
Nitya nirāmaya nirmala dēvā
nirguna saguna bhāva prakāśa
Nirguna saguna bhāva prakāśa

Nartana sundara nanda kumāra
navanita cōrā nīraja netrā
Nāda svarūpa vēda svarūpa
vṛndāvana candra vraja rāja nanda
Vṛndāvana candra vraja rāja nanda

govardhana dhāri	who lifted the govardhana mountain
mohana	beautiful
mañjula hasa	one who has a sweet smile
manasa cora	one who steals my heart
nirupama saure	incomparably mighty
pithambara dhāri	who wears yellow silk robes

kuñja vihāri	who plays in the kunja forest
nitya nirāmaya nirmala	eternal with no flaws
nirguna	with no attributes
saguna	with attributes
bhava prakāśa	who exhibits a creative aspect (human)
nartana sundara	dancing beautifully
nanda kumāra	nanda's son
nīraja netra	with lotus like eyes
nada svarūpa	nature of sound
veda svarupa	nature of vedas
vṛndāvana candra	the shining moon of Vrindavan
vraja raja nanda	son of the king of vraja

RĀDHĒ RĀDHĒ GŌVINDA

Rādhē rādhē gōvinda rādhē (2x)
Rādhē gōvinda
Muraḷi mukunda madhava
navanita cōrā rādhē śyām
Devaki nandalala

Beloved of Krishna, Lord of the cows. Flute player, Bestower of Liberation, Consort of Lakshmi. Stealer of butter. Son of Devaki.

Gokula nandana gōpāla
gopī manōhara gōvinda
Rādhē gōvinda

Son of the village of Gokul. Enchanter of the gopi's mind.

Natanamanohara rādhē śyām
giridharabālā gōvinda
Devaki nandalala

Who enchants with his dance, the child who held the mountain on his hand. Son of Devaki.

RĀDHE ŚYĀM

Rādhe śyām rādhe śyām (3x)
Vṛndāvana candra kṛṣṇa kanhaiya tu hi
āśraya rādhe gōvinda
Anātha nātha dīna bandhō rādhe gōvinda (2x)

O Radhe Shyam, the shining moon of Vrindavana, Krishna, You are my sole refuge and protector of cows. You are the lord of the destitute, You are the friend and relative of the downtrodden.

Mīra ke prabhu giridhara nāgara
dēdo bhakti ham kō mādhav
Nanda kumāra navanīta cōrā rādhe gōvinda (2x)

You are Meera's Lord, You held up the Govardhana mountain. Please grant me eternal devotion to You, O Madhava (Lakshmi's lord), O stealer of butter, Nanda's darling son, Radhe Govinda.

Bansi dhara hē śyāma gopāla
rādha vallabha rādhe gōvinda
Śyām śyām bōlō bōlō rādhe rādhe bōlō (2x)

You wear the sacred tulasi, You are dark and beautiful. O Gopala, Radha's consort. Sing Shyam Shyam, Radhe Radhe!

RĀDHĒ ŚYĀM RĀDHĒ ŚYĀM

Rādhē śyām rādhē śyām rādhē rādhē śyām rādhē śyām
Bōlō śyām gāvō śyām
Tērā nāma priya harinām
śyām rādhē śyām
Naṭavara śyām vrajaghana śyām rādhe śyām
Nācō śyām mama hṛdi śyām
śyāma rādhe śyām

Sing Radhe Shyam! Your name is certainly none other than dear Hari's name. In human form You are the greatest, You are the greatest of Gokula, O Radhe Shyam. Dance, dance, O Krishna, dance in my heart!

Hē gōvind gōpari pālak bālasakhā bālarāma śyām
govardhana giridhāri kāliya mardana vaibhava rādhe rādhe śyām

O Govinda, O Protector of cows, Friend of the boys of vraja and Balarama, You who held up the govardhana mountain, You who danced on Kaliya's head (the evil serpent), Radhe Shyam!

Gopī śyām yamuna śyām
Giridhara śyām rādhe śyām
Jai jai śyāma prēma śyām
Rasa vihāri śyām rādhe śyām

Gopi's Krishna, Yamuna's Krishna, govardhana mountain's Krishna, Radha's Krishna, victory, victory to You! O cloud colored Krishna, the embodiment of love who delights in the rasa dance!

RĀDHIKĒŚA YADUNĀTHA

Rādhikēśa yadunātha ramēśā
nīla dēha vasudēva tanūjā
Gōkulēśa guruvāyu urēśā
rāsakēḷī para gōpa kumārā

O Lord of Radhika, Leader of the Yadava clan, born of Vasudeva with a body enchantingly blue in color, O Lord of Gokula, Lord of Guruvayoor, who revels in the rasa dance.

Dīnanātha paripūrṇa kṛpālō
vēṇuvāda raṇadhīra dayālō
Rāgalōlā śaraṇāgata bandhō
dvārakā dhipa dayāmṛta sindhō

O Protector of the feeble and helpless, whose compassion is limitless, Lord of Dwaraka, adept in playing the flute, Friend of all those seeking refuge in You, Ocean of kindness.

Nandagōpa suta vandita pādā
candra bimba mukha cañcala nētrā
Mādhava madana mōhana rūpā
kēśavā madhura bhāva samētā

O Son of Nanda, O Keshava, O Madhava of beauteous form, always in madhura bhava (pleasant mood), with a face as charming as the crescent moon and enchanting eyes.

Mandahāsa yuta mangaḷa mūrttē
pītavāsa paripāvana kīrttē
Dēvakī suta mukunda murārē
bālakṛṣṇa bala sōdara śaurē

O Mukunda, Son of Devaki, Slayer of Mura, O Balakrishna of auspicious form and gentle smile, clad in yellow raiments, acclaimed for Your purity.

RĀMA RĀMA JAYA RĀMA

Rāma rāma jaya rāma (2x)
Kausalyā sukha vardhana rāma
Srimat daśaratha nandana rāma
Jānaki jīvana śrī raghu rāma
Maruti sevita tāraka rama

Kausalya sukha vardhana	One who increases the happiness of Kausalya (his mother)
srimat Dasaratha nandana	Son of the luminous Dasaratha
jānaki jivana sri raghu	Who is the life of Sita, of the Raghu dynasty
maruti sevita tāraka	One who is served by Hanuman and whose name takes one across the misery of life.

RĀMACANDRA MAHĀ PRABHŌ

Rāmacandra mahā prabhō
Raghuvīra dhīra jagatgurō

O great Lord Ramachandra! O Raghuvira, the valorous world Teacher!

Jānaki sukhadāna tatpara
mananīya manōhara
Trāhimām sukha sāgara
tava pāda paṅkaja māśrayē

Thou who art eager to bestow happiness upon Janaki, O adorable One, enchanter of hearts, Give me refuge, Thou who art the ocean of bliss. I seek refuge at Thy Lotus Feet.

Mātṛkā puruṣōttamā
tanubhāva nāśana śrīkara
Sāma gāna sukīrttitā
sarasī ruhāyuta lōcana

Thou art the ideal and foremost among men. Destroyer of body consciousness, Bestower of auspiciousness. O Lotus-eyed One!

Rāghava khaga vāhana
sukha dāyaka ghana śyāmala
Pāhimām praṇatārtti bañjana
dēhi mē karuṇāmṛtam

O Raghava, who rides on the bird (Garuda), O dark blue One, bestower of bliss, Save me, O destroyer of the sorrow of Thy devotees, Bless me with the nectar of compassion.

RĀMAKṚṢṆA HARĒ

Rāmakṛṣṇa harē mukunda murāre
pānduranga harē pānduranga harē

Hail to Rama and Krishna, who bestow liberation, who destroyed the demon Mura! Hail to Panduranga (of white color)!

Dēva dēva dēva brahmā dēva dēva
Dēva dēva dēva mahāviṣṇu dēva dēva
Dēva dēva dēva mahādēva dēva dēva

O Brahma Deva, Lord of Creation. O Vishnu Deva, Lord of preservation. O Shiva Deva, Lord of destruction.

Pānduranga harē jai jai pānduranga harē
Rāmakṛṣṇa harē jai jai pānduranga harē

Pānduranga harē jai jai pānduranga harē
Pānduranga harē pānduranga harē
Rāmakṛṣṇa harē pānduranga harē

RĀVĒRE NĪṆṬUPŌY

Rāvēre nīṇṭupōy rāvuraṅgī lōkam
rākkuyilin gītam ninnupōy
sūnyata yilente īran mizhiyiṇa
tēṭunnu vembalōṭ ammē ninne
tēdunnu vembalōṭ ammē
Rāvēre nīṇṭupōy

Long hours of the night have passed. The world is fast asleep. Even the nightingale has stopped her singing. Mother, in the pervading solitude, my tearfilled eyes are anxiously searching for You, eagerly looking for You.

Ākāśa tāraṅgaḷ ārdrarāy āmaya
magnanām enne yīkṣiccu nilppū
Enchitta śōka tarangaṅgaḷil kuḷi -
cēṅgal otukki prakṛti nilppū ammē
cēṅgal otukki prakṛti nilpū

The stars in the sky melt with empathy, as they watch me in my grief. I cannot live any longer without seeing You, my Mother, not even for half a moment, not even half a moment. And Nature, bathed in the waves of my sorrow, is holding back her cry. Oh Mother, Nature is holding back Her cry.

Ēllām ariyunna amme nin ōrmmayil
etranāḷ kēṇu karaññu
Āvill enikkini ninneyum kāṇāte
vāzhāna rakṣṇam ammē
Rāvēre nīnṭupōy

Oh, all knowing Mother, how many days have I spent crying in the sweet memory of You? Mother, I cannot live, not even for half a moment longer without seeing You - not even half a moment longer.

SĀDARAM BHAJICCIṬUNNU

Sādaram bhajicciṭunnu
ninne ñān dayānidhē
pōruvān amāntam ente
tāpahāri śrīpatē

With great reverence I worship You, Treasure house of compassion. Why this delay in coming to me? O Lord of Lakshmi, dispeller of sorrows!

Prēmamāri peytiraṅgi
śōka tāpam āttuvān
nīyozhiññu pārilanya
bandhuvilla mē harē

There is no other relation for me in this world except You, O my Hari, to quench the heat of sorrow showering the rains of Love.

Sūnu ñān bhavābdhi tannil
māzhkiṭ unnu mādhava
dēha bōdha rōgapīḍha
māttiṭum varam tarū

O Madhava, I, Your son immersed in the sea of samsara (worldliness), am crying. Bestow on me the boon to remove the tormenting afflictions of body consciousness.

Marttyanāy janiccen ikku
mṛtyuvuṇṭu niścayam
śuddha bhakti nalki mṛtyu
bādha pōkku māpatē

Having been born as a human being, death is certain for me. By giving me pure devotion, O Lord of Lakshmi, save me from the clutches of death.

SADGURUVĀY VANTUTITTA

Sadguruvāy vantutitta kāli tāyē
amṛtānandamayī dēvī nīyē
Eṅkalukku vaḷamellām taruvāy ammā
ennāḷum kāttiṭavē varuvāy ammā
ammā ammā ammā ammā

O Mother Kali, who has incarnated in the form of Satguru, as Amritanandamayi Devi. Please bestow all prosperity on us; come and protect us always.

Kārttikai nannāḷil vantutittāḷ
nammē - kaṇṇin imaipōle kākkavantāḷ
Kaḷḷa tanaṅkal pōkkavantāḷ - nam
karuttinil kuṭikoṇḍu vāzhavantāḷ

Amma, who took birth under the holy star of Karthika, has come to protect us like the eyelid shelters the eye. She has come to remove our negativities; She has come to abide in our thoughts.

Mēniyin niramō kārmēkkam - ammā
uḷḷamō tumpai pūv pōle
Nānilam vaṇaṅkum tāyavalām
nanmaikaḷ tantiṭum nāyakiyām

Her body is of the complexion of a rain cloud; but Her mind is pure white like the tumba flower. She is the Mother who is worshipped by all the four worlds. She is the Empress who bestows all virtues.

Eṅkeṅku pārttālum unṭran kōlam
ennālum ulakinile tazhaikkum śīlam
Poṅkivarum aruḷnadiyē untan kākṣi
bhūmiyil nī tarum nidhiyē eṅkal māṭśi

Wherever I look I see Your divine form, which is eternal. Your vision is like the flooding river of Grace; the treasure that You give us is prosperity and eternal happiness.

SAKALĀGAMA SAMSTUTĒ

Sakalāgama samstutē
mati mōhana vigrahē
muni mānasa śōbhanē
lalitē jagadāśrayē

O Mother, who is extolled by all the Vedas, who has an enchanting form, who shines in the minds of the sages, O Lalita, the support of the whole world.

Suravandya padāmbujē
sanakādi susēvitē
Mahitē mama tāpahē
lalitē jagadāśrayē

O You with lotus Feet, whose Holy Feet are worshipped by the Devas, who is worshipped by sages beginning with Shanaka, You who are great, who destroys attachment, O Lalita the support of the whole world!

Duritā maya bhañjakē
praṇavām budhi samsthitē
Sukhadē suranāyikē
lalitē jagadāśrayē

O Mother, who destroys all sufferings and afflictions, who is seated in the ocean of Omkara, who bestows happiness, and who is the leader of the Devas, O Lalita, the refuge of the whole world!

SANĀTANĪ SANGĪTA

Sanātanī sangīta rasikē
sarasvatī samastēśvarī ambe

O Eternal One, who relishes music, Saraswati, Goddess of all. Mother!

Parāparē pavitrē patita rakṣakī
Purātanī puṇyavara pradāyinī

The supreme One, the pure One, savior of the fallen.

Varadā bhaya pustaka rudākṣa dhāriṇī
vara varṇṇinī varadē vāgdēvatē
Muni mānasa vāsinī mumukṣuviyē dēvī
madanāśini mahēśī mangaḷa vradāyinī

The ancient One, bestower of boons and merits, who bestows protection and boons, who holds the books (Vedas) and rudraksha prayer beads (mala), the exceptionally beautiful One, Goddess of speech, who resides in the heart of sages, who favors the seekers of Truth.

Kamanīya rūpiṇī karuṇā mayīyammē
kamalē! kaṭākṣikkān kaitozhunnēn
Gagana gāminī! nigamārthadē! dēvī
girijē! guṇātītē! gatiyēkaṇam

The Goddess, destroyer of pride, bestower of auspiciousness, whose form is beautiful, who is the embodiment of compassion. O Mother! The lotus-like One, I pray for your compassionate glance. You who travels everywhere, who bestows the knowledge of the Vedas, the daughter of the mountain, beyond attributes, O Devi, show me the way!

SANTĀPA ŚĀNTIKKĀY

Santāpa śāntikkāy santatam tēṭunnū
ninpāda tirttham ñānammē
Ninkanivil lāykil enteyī jīvitam
ennuma nāthamāṇ ammē

I constantly seek the holy water that has washed Your lotus feet to reach the end of sorrow. Without Your grace I will be an orphan forever.

Anpiyann ammayen antaranga-ttinte
andhata māttān tuṇaykū!
Enmana paṅkaja pūvil innamma tan
puṇya trippādam teḷikkū!

Oh, Compassionate Mother, help me to wipe out the darkness inside me. Let me have the vision of Your holy feet in my inner world.

Ninprēma tīrthamām svarg-gangayil muṅgi
mālinya mokke akannen — manam

Santāpa mattātma sangītavum pāṭi
unmatta bhakti pūṇṭāṭaṭṭe ñān

By bathing in the holy Ganges water of Your love, my mind will become pure and free from sorrows and pains. Let me become crazy and intoxicated with bhakti (devotion) while singing the song of the soul.

SAPTA SVARA RŪPIṆI

Sapta svara rūpiṇi mṛtyujñaya mōhini
bhaktā bhaya dāyini raktām śuka dhāriṇi

O Mother, who embodies the seven notes of music, the enthraller of Shiva, who bestows protection to the devotees, who dons red garments.

Hṛddēśa nivāsini mattāpa vināśini
Sacchinmaya rūpiṇi naktam diva sākṣiṇi

O Mother! Who resides in the heart, who destroys my sorrows, who is the embodiment of knowledge and Truth, who is the witness to the passing of night and day.

Hṛnnarttana kēkini śrutyāgamā vādini
Pṛthvī paripālini mādhvī śiva kāmini

O Mother! Who is the peacock dancing in our hearts, who is praised by the Vedas and Agamas, who sustains the Earth..

ŚARAṆAM KĀḶI ŚARAṆAM

Śaraṇam kāḷi śaraṇam
śaraṇam satatam jagadamba śaraṇam
śaraṇam bhairavi bhadrē śaraṇam
śaraṇam satatam śiva śaṅkari śaraṇam

I seek refuge in You always, O Kali, Mother of the universe. I seek refuge in You, O Bhairavi, Bhadre, Shivasakti.

Pārvati śaraṇam pāvani śaraṇam
pāpa vināśini mē śaraṇam
Samasta viśva vidhāyākī śaraṇam
praśasta dakṣaki mē śaraṇam

O Parvati, You who are pure, destroyer of sins, You are my refuge. You who directs the entire universe, celebrated for Your skill, You are my refuge.

Bhakta janāvana dakshē śaraṇam
duḥkha vibhañjini mē śaraṇam
Hṛdaya vihāriṇi karuṇa paurṇṇami
śaraṇam caraṇam mama jananī

O my Mother, one who is skillful in protecting the devotees, one who destroys sorrow, give me refuge. Mother, You revel in my heart; You are the full moon of compassion; Your holy feet are my refuge!

ŚARĪRAM SURŪPAM

(GURUVAŚTAKAM)

Śarīram surūpam yathā vā kalatram
yaśaścāru citram dhanam meru tulyam
gurōramghri padmē manaścēnna lagnam
tataḥ kim? tataḥ kim? tataḥ kim? tataḥ kim?

Even though a person possesses a beautiful physical body, a good wife, wonderful reputation, and health equal to the Meru-mountain, if his mind is not absorbed in the Lotus Feet of the Guru, what is the use of all other possessions?

Kalatram dhanam putra pautrādi sarvam
gṛham bānḍavāḥ sarvamē taddhi jātam
Gurōramghri padmē manaścēnna lagnam
tataḥ kim? tataḥ kim? tataḥ kim? tataḥ kim?

Even though one possesses wife, wealth, sons and grandsons, good house and all the kith and kin, if one's mind is not absorbed in the Lotus Feet of the Guru, what is the use of all other possessions?

Ṣaḍamgādi vēdō mukhē śāstra vidyā
kavitvādi gadyam supadyam karōti
Gurōramghri padmē manaścēnna lagnam
tataḥ kim? tataḥ kim? tataḥ kim? tataḥ kim?

Even though a person is well-versed in all the parts of the Vedas and in the scriptural knowledge, even though he can write good verses and prose, if his mind is not absorbed in the Lotus Feet of the Guru, of what avail is the rest of the possessions?

Vidēśēṣu mānyaḥ svadēśēṣu dhanyaḥ
sadācāra vṛttēṣu matto na cānyaḥ
Gurōramghri padmē manaścēnna lagnam
tataḥ kim? tataḥ kim? tataḥ kim? tataḥ kim?

Even though one is well-respected in foreign countries, considered as blessed in one's own country, and is unequalled in good behaviour and character, if one's mind is not absorbed in the Lotus Feet of the Guru, of what avail is any of the other possessions?

Kṣamā maṇḍalē bhūpa bhūpāla vṛndaiḥ
sadā sēvitam yasyaḥ pādāra vindam
Gurōramghri padmē manaścēnna lagnam
tataḥ kim? tataḥ kim? tataḥ kim? tataḥ kim?

Even though a person's lotus feet are ever worshipped by the great king of kings on earth, if his mind is not absorbed in the Lotus Feet of the Guru, of what avail is any other possessions?

Yaśō mē gatam dikṣu dāna pratāpāt-
jagadvastu sarvam karē yat prasādāt
Gurōramghri padmē manaścēnna lagnam
tataḥ kim? tataḥ kim? tataḥ kim? tataḥ kim?

Even if I attain glory all over, even though all the things of the world are under me, if my mind is not absorbed in the Lotus Feet of the Guru, of what avail is any of the other possessions?

Na bhōgō na yōgō na vā vājirājō
na kāntāmukhē naiva vittēṣu cittam
Gurōramghri padmē manaścēnna lagnam
tataḥ kim? tataḥ kim? tataḥ kim? tataḥ kim?

Even if a person's mind is not attached towards any Yoga, or wealth like horses, not absorbed in the beautiful face of his beloved, but if his mind is not absorbed in the Lotus Feet of the Guru, of what avail are all his other renunciations?

Araṇyē na vā svasya gēhē na kāryē
na dēhē manō varttatē mē tvanarghyē
Gurōramghri padmē manaścēnna lagnam
tataḥ kim? tataḥ kim? tataḥ kim? tataḥ kim?

Even if my mind is not anxious of the peace in the forest or anxious of my own home, or agitated with any particular activity, or anxious regarding my own body; yet, if my mind is not absorbed in the Lotus Feet of my Guru, of what avail is any other possession?

Anarghyāṇi ratnāni muktāni samyak
samālimgitā kāmini yaminīṣu
Gurōramghri padmē manaścēnna lagnam
tataḥ kim? tataḥ kim? tataḥ kim? tataḥ kim?

Even if I find in my possession precious stones or pearls, and well decorated and dressed lovable bride, yet if my mind is not absorbed in the Lotus Feet of my Guru, of what avail are any other possessions?

SARVA CARĀCARA JANANĪM

(AMṚTĀṢṬAKAM)

Sarva carācara jananīm kāḷīm
ādyā śaktīm jagadā dhārām
cāyārūpa vilōlāmambām
amṛtānanda mayīm praṇamāmi)

Prostrations to Amritanandamayi, the embodiment of eternal bliss, the Mother of all living beings, animate and inanimate, the primordial power, the support of the worlds, Goddess Kali, the One who plays as the object and its shadow, as the truth and the illusion.

Nīlāmbuda sama mangaḷa varṇṇām
śētvām baradhara pāvana rūpām)
sṛṣṭi sthitilaya nilayām durgām
amṛtānanda mayīm praṇamāmi

Prostrations to Amritanandamayi, the embodiment of eternal bliss, the One with auspicious complexion of blue clouds, the holy One who dons white robes, Goddess Durga responsible for creation, preservation and destruction.

Bhakta janārtti harām śiva rūpām
duṣṭaja nārttikarī matighōrām
śūla kṛpā ṇadharām mama bhadrām
amṛtānanda mayīm praṇamāmi

Prostrations to Amritanandamayi, the embodiment of eternal bliss, who dispels the sorrows of devotees, whose form is auspicious, the terrifying One, who wields the trident and sword, the auspicious One.

Sāgara kūlē lasitām śyāmām
māyā sāgara tāraṇa tariṇīm
akṣā bharaṇa vibhūṣita gātrīm
amṛtānanda mayīm praṇamāmi

Prostrations to Amritanandamayi, the embodiment of eternal bliss. The dark complexioned One, who revels along the sea coast, who takes one across the ocean of transmigration, the One adorned with divine jewelry.

Snēhā lōka sumōhana vadanām
karuṇārdrānata nayanām ramyām
śrita janapālana vyagrām saumyām
amṛtānanda mayīm praṇamāmi

Prostrations to Amritanandamayi, the embodiment of eternal bliss, whose glance is full of love, whose face is charming, whose beautiful eyes are filled with compassion, who is eager to protect those who depend on Her.

Bhakti jñāna virāgada varadām
sādhaka citta viśuddhi dahāsām
nityā nitya vivēkō lasitām
amṛtānanda mayīm praṇamāmi

Prostrations to Amritanandamayi, the embodiment of eternal bliss, who bestows devotion, knowledge and dispassion, who purifies the hearts of the aspirants, who revels in the discrimination of the eternal and non-eternal.

Sanyāsāśrama dharma vidhātrīm
brahmajñāna sudhārasa dhātrīm
bhasmālēpana śōbhana phālām
amṛtānanda mayīm praṇamāmi

Prostrations to Amritanandamayi, who gives sannyas initiation, who bestows the nectar of the absolute knowledge, whose shiny forehead is adorned with sacred ashes.

Bandha vimōcana śilām lalitām
bandhura māyā rasikāmambām
saṭ gururūpa dharām sarvajṇām
amṛtānanda mayīm praṇamāmi

Prostrations to Amritanandamayi, who is the Goddess Lalitambika, whose habit is to free from bondage, who creates bondage and liberation by her maya, whose divine play is this creation, who has taken the form of the true realized guru, who is omniscient.

SARVA MANGAḶE

Sarva mangaḷē sadguru mātā
amṛtānandamayī mama janani
Sarva śobhanē śobhana rūpiṇi
garva vināśini namō namaḥ

O Mother who is the embodiment of auspisiousness, who shines in all brightness, Who has a resplendent form and who destroys pride, O Satguru Mata Amritanandamayi, salutations to You!

Bhava bhaya mōcini trāhi mahēśvari
nikhila nirāmaya nirañjini
Mangaḷa rūpiṇi manalaya kāriṇi
mangaḷa dāyini namō namaḥ

O Great Goddess, who liberates us from samsara, who is the bestower of all happiness, with the auspicious form, who is the cause of the dissolution of the mind, who is the bestower of auspiciousness. Please save me, O Maheswari, I bow to You!

Prēma payasvini karuṇā vāhini
māyā vibhañjini namō namaḥ
Sakala suhṛd tava padambujam mē
śaraṇam śaṅkari namō namaḥ

O Mother who feeds Her children with the milk of Love, who is the river of compassion, destroyer of illusion, salutations! O Shankari, Your Lotus Feet are the refuge of all, salutations!

Janamana hāriṇi hamsa vihāriṇi
janimṛti nāśini namō namaḥ
Brahmapadam tava parama padam mē
śaraṇam śambhavi namō namaḥ

O Mother, who captivates the minds of the people, who rides on a swan, who puts an end to the cycle of birth and death, I bow to You. O Shankari, my sole refuge is Your sacred Feet, attaining which is attaining Brahman, the Ultimate, the Highest of all.

SIṄKĀRA KĀVAṬIYIL

Siṅkāra kāvaṭiyil cintai makizhum vēlā
cikkal kaḷai nīkki entan cittamellām nirainti ṭuvāy
Unaiyanti vēru tuṇai ulakattil yārumilai
Umai yavaḷin maintanē uruti yuṭan śollukirēn

O Lord Muruga, who is pleased by the beautiful kavadi dance, Remove the obstacles (on my spiritual path) and fill my heart with Your divine love. I have no refuge in this world other than You. O son of Uma ! I am perfectly sure about this.

Bhakti yuṭan pāṭiṭum en pāṭaltanai kēkkaleyō
paritavikka vaikkāmal pakkam vantāl ākātō
Kantā enakka tarum ennai kāppāṭra vantiṭuvāyi
kāla minnum vantillayō karuṇaimiku vaṭivēlā

Aren't You hearing my song sung with devotion? Without giving me this suffering of separation, can't You come near me? I am calling out, "Kanda, Kanda". Has the time not yet arrived to protect me, O merciful Vadivela (the one with a spear)!

Mayilmītu bavani varum azhaku tanai kaṇṭuviṭṭāl
mayaṅkātam anamuṇṭō mutta mizhvaṭi vēlavā
Pāṭukaḷai tīrttiṭuvāy pārvatiyāḷ bālakanē
śīrmēvum śēvaṭiyil śēntukolvay śarava ṇanē

Whose heart will not be enchanted to see Your beautiful ride on the peacock? O Lord of the Tamil language (songs, prose, and play), Son of Parvati, remove my difficulties and let me merge in Your Lotus Feet!

Kanda nukku vēl vēl kaṭamba nukku vēl vēl
Muruka nukku vēl vēl kumara nukku vēl vēl

Victory to Kanda! Victory to Katamba! Victory to Kumara!

SIRMĒ MAYŪR MUKUṬA DHARĒ

Sirmē mayūr mukuta dharē
karmēm mōhan muraliliyē
vanmēm yamunā taṭ mēm śyām
rāga manōhar jōḍa rahē

He is wearing a peacock feather on His head, his hand holds a beautiful flute, He stands in the forest by the Yamuna river playing melodious tunes.

Sun muralīrav gōkul mēm
vraj lalanāyēm vyākul hō
Saja dhaj cal nikalīm jaldi
sabamil rās racānē kō

Hearing the sweet tunes from the flute, the people of Vraja become restless. They quickly congregate to dance the rasa dance.

Nabhamem cāndini udit huyī
bhūpar candan gandh bhari
Nandan kāḷindi taṭ mēm
sundar rās racānē kō

The moon rises and the beautiful fragrance from the sandalwood trees permeates everywhere. Krishna ecstatically dances the rasa on the banks of the Kalindi river.

Sur muni sab vṛndāvan kē
madhumaya nāc nihār rahē
Sab jag cañcalatā taj kē
sahaj samādhi mēm līn huyē

The gods and sages are enraptured by this joyous dance in Vrindavan. Forgetting the other activities of the world, they enter into a state of natural samadhi.

SITA RĀM RĀDHE ŚYAM

Sita rām sita rām sita rām rāma rām
Rādhe śyām rādhe śyām rādhe śyām śyām śyām
Jai raghu nandana sita rām
Jai yadu nandana rādhe śyām

Praise Sita Ram, born in the Raghu dynasty.
Praise Radhe Syam, born in the clan of Yadu.

Daśaratha nandana raja rām
Vasudeva nandana rādhe śyām

Son of Dasharatha, king Ram Son of Vasudeva, Radhe Syam

Sita rām rādhe śyām
Sita rām rādhe śyām
Śrī rāma jai rāma jai jai rāma

Praise Sita Ram, victory to Sri Rama.

ŚIVA NANDANĀ SUNDARA

Śiva nandanā sundara vadanā
kēka vāhana mōhana caritā
Raṇa mārdita tāraka danujā
sura nāyaka vīra kumārā (Śiva)

Gaṇanātha sahōdara sumukhā
girijā sukha varddhana murukā
Guru rūpa guṇākara kumarā
guha kumkuma varṇṇa varēṇyā

Muni mānasa rājita ramaṇā
chaturānana pūjita mahitā

Jita dānava sainya surēśā
viditākhila vēda vihārā (Śiva)

Amarā dhipa dhīr udārā
vara dāyaka valli manālā
Vēlāyudha vēda svarūpā
dīnāvana dēva dayālā

Sura vandita pāda sarōjā
duritā maya mōhana hṛdayā
Karuṇā maya kāmita varadā
pari pāvana nātha namastē (Śiva)

śiva nandana	O son of Siva (Lord Subrahmania)
sundara vadana	With a handsome face
keka vāhana	Whose mount is a peacock
mohana caritā	With an enchanting life history
rana mardrita tāraka danujā	Who beat the demon Taraka in battle
suranāyaka	Leader of the army of gods
vīra	Hero
kumarā	A name of Lord Subrahmania
gananātha sahodara	Brother of Ganesha
sumukha	Handsome one
girija sukha varddhana	One who increases the joy of his mother Parvati
guru rūpa	One who takes Guru's form
guṇākara	Ocean of good qualities
guha	A name of Lord Subrahmania
kunkuma varṇṇa	with saffron color
vareṇyā	Most distinguished
muni mānasa rājita	Who shines in the minds of the sages

ramanā	One who is charming
chaturānana pūjita	Worshipped by Brahma
mahitā	Revered one
jita dānava sainya	Who has beaten the armies of the demons
sureśā	Leader of the Gods
viditākhila veda vihārā	The abode of all known Vedas
amarādhipa	Leader of the Gods
dhīr udārā	Brave and generous
vara dāyaka	Giver of boons
valli manālā	Valli's husband
velāyudha	Who has a spear for a weapon
veda svarūpa	The embodiment of Vedas
dīnāvana deva dayālā	The compassionate deity of the downtrodden
suravandita pāda sarojā	Whose lotus feet are worshipped by the Gods
duritāmaya mochana hṛdayā	Who liberates from ills, sorrows, etc.
karuṇāmaya	Compassionate
kāmita varadā	Who grants desired boons
pari pāvana	Who is very sacred
nātha namaste	Salutations to the Lord

ŚIVA ŚIVA ŚIVA ŚIVA SADĀ ŚIVA

Śiva śiva śiva śiva sadā śiva
hara hara hara hara mahā dēva
Ōm śiva śiva śiva śiva sadā śiva
Ōm hara hara hara hara mahā dēva
Ōm namō namō namaḥ śivāya (4x)

Brahmā viṣṇu surachittaya
ōm namō namō namah śivāya
Uma ganeśa saravana sevita
ōm namō namō namaḥ śivāya
Ōm namō namō namaḥ śivāya

O auspicious and eternal One, destroyer, salutations! Worshipped by Brahma and Vishnu, served by Uma, Ganesha and Saravana (Muruga).

ŚŌKAM ITENTINU SANDHYĒ

Śōkam itentinu sandhyē nīyum
ōrmmatan tīrattil alayukayō?
Sindūra varṇṇattil kuḷiccu nilkkum nin
uḷḷilum śōkāgni eriyunnuṇṭō?

O Twilight, why are you sad? Are you also wandering on the shores of past memories? O dusk, bathed in reddish hue, is the fire of sorrow burning within you too?

Uṇṭō ninakkum oramma yituppōl atō
kaṇṭō nīyumā snēha candrikayē
Kaṇṭāl nī collumō śōkattāl
miṇṭān vayyātto rente sandēśam

O Twilight, have you a Mother like mine? Or have you seen my Mother who radiates the beauty and the coolness of purity like the full moon? O Dusk, should you see Her, please convey the message of this helpless son who cannot speak, weighed down with deep sorrow caused by the pain of separation.

Nalkumōyī puṣpa daḷaṅgaḷ sandhyē
collumō ennuṭe vandanaṅgaḷ

Pōyvarumbōḷ collām ennuṭe
pōya vasantattin nalkkathakaḷ

O Twilight, will you not offer these petals at Her Feet? Will you not convey my words? When You return, I shall relate to You the sweet stories of my bygone spring.

ŚRĪ HARI VARUMĪ

Śrī hari varumī vazhiyarukil niṅgaḷ
verute kaḷiciriarutē
kanakāmbarā bhayil mizhi yaṇaykkū snigddha
madhuramāy ōmkāra śruti yuṇarttū

Lord Hari is coming this way; be not engaged in fun and frolic. Behold the dazzling splendour of the golden dress. Awaken the melody of Pranava (Aum) with all the Love and sweetness.

Hṛdaya mandāraṅgaḷ irutteṭukkān kṛṣṇan
varuminnī vṛndāvanattil
kaḷa vēṇu nisvanam kātōrkkuvin neñcam
nirayaṭṭe ghana śyāma varṇṇan

Lord Krishna will come today to this Vrindavan, to pluck the Mandara flowers (flowers of the hearts). Listen to the sweet melody of the flute. May the dark complexioned One fill your heart.

Utsāha ttaḷḷalin āndōḷa naṅgaḷāl
utsavāhḷādattil līnayāyi
ātma harṣattāl pulakitayāy rādha
tūvunnu tōrāte harṣabāṣpam

Swaying in the waves of enthusiasm, Radha is immersed deeply in the joy of celebration. Reveling in the deep bliss within, She sheds endless tears of joy.

Vana mālayum varṇṇa mayil pīliyum
mazhamukil kāntiyum kaṇṭu koti tīrumō?
vraja bhūmiyil snēha latayāy kaṇṇā
ninnil paṭarān enne mōham taḷircūṭunnu

Adorned with the garland of wild flowers and sporting the peacock plume, having the hue of the rain cloud, O Lord, feasting my eyes on Your divine form, will I ever be content? A desire blooms in my heart to entwine You, becoming a creeper of Love in the land of Vraja.

ŚRĪ LALITĀMBIKĒ SARVAŚAKTĒ

Śrī lalitāmbikē sarvaśaktē
śrī lalitāmbikē sarvaśaktē)
śrī lalitāmbikē sarvaśaktē
śrī pādam ñānitā kumbiṭunnēn

O Sri Lalitambika, You are the All-powerful. I humbly prostrate to Your Divine feet.

Vaśamilla dhyāna rūpaṅgaḷ onnum
niśayil uzhalvatu kāṇmatillē
ima ilavum piriyāte yen hṛt-
kamalattil vāzhanam ambikē nī

I do not know how to meditate and on which form; don't You see me struggling in the dark? Dwell in the lotus of my heart, never leaving me even for a moment.

Taraṇam enikku guṇaṅgal sarvam
śaraṇam gamiccoru duḥkhitan ñān

teru terevīṇu vaṇaṅ gīṭuvān
oru poṭi kāruṇyam ēkīṭēṇē

Please bestow all the divine virtues for I am the miserable one, who has taken refuge in You. Please grant me a little of Your compassion so that I may always prostrate at Your feet again and again.

Tava kaṭa kaṇṇināl onnu nōkki
mama khēdamokke ozhikka dēvī
aviṭutte dāsane kakkukillē
alivezhān entini ceytīṭēṇam?

Casting a side glance at me, dispel all my sorrows. Please take care of this servant of Yours. What can I do to melt Your heart?

Arut arut ammē tyajicciṭollē
śaraṇam aṭiyanu nalkiyālum
gamanattil amma nayicciṭēṇam
gati vēreyillā śaraṇam ammē

Oh no, do not reject me! O Mother. Please give me refuge! Please guide me on every step of my journey. Other than You, there is no hope for me.

Akhila kāmaṅgalum nalkumammē
karuṇa yērīṭum mahēśī bhadre
mananam ceytīṭānāy śakti nalkū
manatāril nityavum nṛttamāṭu

O Mother, who fulfills all desires, O Maheshi (the Great Goddess), the auspicious One, full of compassion, please grant me the strength to meditate on You. Dance eternally in the lotus of my heart.

**Akhilāṇḍa jyōtissē divya mūrttē
agati yācikkunnu bhakti pūrvam
akhilarum enne veṭiññālum nī
abhayam ēkīṭēṇē lōkamātē**

O Light of the universe, embodiment of divinity, this helpless child begs with devotion. O Mother, even if all forsake me, You must give me refuge!

**Oru nūru janmam kazhiññat āvām
ittaruṇattil martyanāy tīrnnatākām
viralamāy tannī janmamaṅgē -
padamalar kumbilil nalkiṭaṭṭe**

Maybe a hundred births of mine have passed, and I have attained a human birth only now. This rare birth that You have granted me, let me dedicate at Your lotus feet.

**Pizhakal adhikamāy ceytirikkām
tanayaril ñān nindyan āyirikkām
jananī nīyellām kṣamiccivante
mana tāpamokke akattiṭēṇam**

I might have committed countless errors, I may be the most despicable of Your sons, O Mother, please pardon all my faults and dispel the sorrows of my heart.

**Jñānamō śāstramō yōgamō nī
ēkiyi ṭillennat ōrmma vēṇam
oru karmavum tiriyāttor enne
calana peṭuttunna tentināṇu**

Please remember You have not bestowed on me wisdom, knowledge of the Scriptures, of yoga, why upset me, who is unskilled in any work?

Oru kṛtya niṣṭha yeṭuttu dhyāna-
niratanāy mēvān tuniññi ṭumbōl
atu bata vannu muṭakkiṭunna-
tuchitamō nin kali paitalōṭo?

As I try to follow a regular routine, and immerse myself in meditation, is it right to hinder it? Am I not your child?

Mama mātāvum pitāvum guruvum
manavṛkṣa puṣpa phalavum amma
ninavukal okkeyum ninnilākān
kanivu nalkīṭuvān kaitozhunnēn

You are my Mother, Father, and Guru. You are the flower and the fruit of the tree of my mind. I join my palms in salutation. O Mother, shower Your grace on me so that all my thoughts are centered on You.

Akhilāṇḍa dīpamē ādiśakti
sakalādhi nāyikē viśva mātē
prēm āvatāramē mātṛrūpē
hṛdaya muruki ñān kēṇiṭunnēn

Light of the universe, O primordial power, empress of all, Mother of the universe, love incarnate, motherhood personified, I cry with a melting heart.

Oruvarum illillī mūvulakil
tava guṇa kīrttanam tīrttu pāṭān
anavadya sundaram aprameyam
vāṅmanō buddhi kalkappuram nī

There is nobody in the three worlds who can enumerate all Thy glories. You are beauty perfect, immeasurable, beyond words, mind and intellect.

Sāgaram nin gītam pāṭiṭunnū
ōmkāra mantram muzhakki ṭunnu
ōrō tirakalum nira nirayāy
praṇava dhvanikkottu tulliṭunnu

The ocean sings Thy song. It reverberates the mantra "OM." Each wave, one by one, dances to the tune of "OM."

Kulirtennal nin nāmam mūliṭunnu
kuyil nādam nin nādam ūttiṭunnu
malarmaṇam nin maṇam āliṭunnu
ī viśvam ākenin nam śamennāy

The cool breeze hums Thy name. The song of the birds echoes Thy voice. The flowers waft Thy fragrance. This whole universe is only a fraction of Thy glory!

Veṇṇilāv etti nin puñciriyāy
kālkoṇṭal etti nin kurunirayāy
sūrya candranmār nin kātilōla
ārunin vaibhavam kaṇṭu bhadrē

The bright moonshine has come as Thy smile. The dark clouds have come as Thy curls. The sun and moon are Thy earrings. Who knows Thy glory, O gracious One?

Nī nivarnn onnaṅgu ninna nēram
nin kēśam ākavē vyōmamāyi
vyōmakēśi paramēśi dēvī
nin muṭi pūkkalāy tārakaṅgal

When You stood up, Thy hair became the dark sky. O Parvati, Supreme Goddess, the stars are the flowers in Thy hair!

Nī nivarnnonnu garjji ciṭumbōl
pralayāndhya sandhyakal poṭṭiyārkkum

kaṭukoṭum kāttukal cuṭu cuṭunna
paṭu kūttan jvālakalk ottiṭunnu

When You let out your roar, the dusks of final dissolution arrive. Cataclysmic cyclones blow and huge blazing flames dance!

Sarva lōkaṅgaḷkkum kīzhileṅgō
nin pādam ammē marañña rippū
eṅgane nin pādam kumbiṭum ñān
eṅgane nin mukham kaṇṭiṭum ñān

Somewhere below all of the worlds, O Mother, Thy feet are hidden. How will I prostrate to Thee? How will I see Thy face?

Dikkukal kokkeyum appuram nin
tṛkkaikal nīṇṭu maraññi ṭunnu
eṅgane akkaikal kaṇṇil cērkkum
entoratyat bhutam ninte rūpam

Beyond all the horizons Thy blessed hands stretch wide. How will I touch those hands to my eyes? How magnificent is Thy form!

Eṅgane nin pūja ceytiṭum ñān
eṅgane nin nāmam pāṭiṭum ñān
eṅgane nin kṛpā lēśamillā-
tambikē ninne ariññiṭum ñan

How will I worship Thee? How will I sing Thy Name? How without Thy grace can I know Thee, O Mother?

Sarva vēdaṅgaḷum nin mahatvam
pāṭi talarnnu mayaṅgi ṭunnu
sarva śastraṅgaḷum nin niyamam
kutti varaccu valaññi ṭunnu

All the Vedas have tired out trying to sing Thy glory. All the scriptures tried to write down Thy codes of law, but in vain.

Ellāmāy onnum allāteyāyi
nī ninte līla tuṭarnni ṭumbōl
karalu takarnnu karaññiṭāne
kazhivillā paitaṅgalk āvatullu

As You became the All, and then the nothing, and as You continue Your play, these children can only cry with crushed hearts, for we are hapless.

Śāśvata dharma vidhāyikē nī
sadguru brahma sanātanam tān
nī vēdam nī guru premavum nī
prāṇante prāṇanum lakṣyavum nī

You are the eternal maker of dharma. You are the perfect master, eternal Brahman. You are the Vedas, the Guru, and pure love. Life of my life, You are the goal.

Nīyallāt illārum eṅgalkkammē
nī tanne śvāsa niśvāsa mennum
ninne piriññū kazhiññi-ṭānō
ñaṅgaḷ koralppavum vayya tāyē

Save You, we have nobody else, Mother. You alone are our very breath. Without You, we cannot live even for a moment!

Nī pintiriññu naṭannu ennāl
poṭṭi takarnniṭum ñaṅgaḷ ammē
ninne piriññor arakṣa ṇavum
ñaṅgal sahiccīṭuk illa tāyē

If You abandon us we will be shattered. We cannot be apart from You for even a second.

Ninne piriññoru nēram ammē
vayya vayyoṭṭum kazhiññi ṭuvān
nī maraññaṅgane ninniṭukil
ninne tiraññu ñān mattanākum

These moments in separation are agonizing. I will go crazy searching for You if You go on hiding like this.

Ōrō kaṭalkkara tōrum ammē
ninne tiraññu karaññiṭum ñān
ōro maṇalttari yōṭum ammē
ninne kuriccu tirakkiṭum ñān

I will look for You on every seashore and will enquire about You from every particle of sand.

Kēra vṛkṣaṅgale vallikale
niṅgaḷ endemmaye kaṇṭatuṇṭō
pon tārakaṅgale niṅgaḷeṅgān
endamma pōyatu kaṇṭatuṇṭō

O coconut trees, climbers, did you catch a glimpse of my Mother? O golden stars, did you see my Mother on Her way?

Rākkili kūṭṭamē niṅgaḷeṅgān
entamma tan vazhi kaṇṭatuṇṭō
hē niśāgandhi nī kaṇṭuvō chol
endammayī vazhi pōyatuṇṭō

O nightingales, have your eyes seen my Mother anywhere? O night blooms, tell me, did my Mother pass this way?

Minnā minuṅgē prakāśa muttē
rāvin veliccamē nillu nill
amma tan dūti nī yennu tōnnum
nīyeṅgān ennamme kaṇṭatuṇṭō

O fireflies, lights of the night, you look like messengers from my Mother. Have you not seen Her?

Māzhkiṭumambala prāvukale
ennammayī vazhi vannu kaṇṭō
ambalattinn uḷḷil pāttukāṇum
ambala dīpamē collu collu

O wailing temple birds, did you see my Mother go this way? Is She hiding in the temple?

Vayya vayyammaye kaṇṭiṭāte
nīri nīrittanne nīṅgiṭuvān
amma tan mārggam paraññi ṭuvān
ārārum illayō collu collu

I cannot go on living without Mother and I have none to show me the way to Her.

Yuga yugān taṅgaḷāy ñānalaññū
yuga yugān taṅgaḷāy nī maraññū
karuṇāmayi ninakkentu patti
karuṇa kāṭṭīṭān amāntamentē

I have wandered for ages and You have stayed away for ages, O merciful One. What happened to You? Why are You delaying in bestowing Your grace?

Prēma mūrttē ninakkentu patti
nin kṛpā sindhu varaṇṭu pōyō
ninne piriññu ñānetra kālam
iniyum alayaṇam colka tāyē

O love incarnate, has Your ocean of mercy run dry? How long will I have to wander without You?

Nin viralttumbil karaṅ giṭunnū
aṇḍha kaṭāhaṅgaḷ nūru kōṭi
ā viral tumbināl enneyiṭṭu
vaṭṭam karakkuvat entu ñāyam

Hundreds of billions of universes spin on Thy finger tips. Is it fair to spin me around with those finger tips?

Tōttu ñān, vīṇu ñān, satyamūrttē
ninn icca tanney inn endeyicca
nīyenney eṅgane tullikkumō
aṅgane tanne ṇān tullum ammē

Beaten I am, fallen I am, O form of Truth,Your will is my will. Mother, as You pull my strings, so I will act.

Ninde kāruṇyam labhicci ṭuvān
ñānentu vēlayum ceyyum ammē
ninne labhicciṭum vēla tanne
vēlayenna muni śyēṣṭhrarōti

Mother, to win Thy grace I will do anything! The sages of ancient times declared that true work is that which begets Thee.

Entu ninakku santōṣa māṇō
innatu ceytiṭāmende tāyē
onnonnu mātram inn endeyicca
nin maṭittaṭṭilī kuññirikkum

Whatever pleases You I will do. My only desire is to be on Your lap.

Ninne labhicciṭum cinta cinta
ninne labhicciṭum karmam karmam
ninne labhicciṭum dharmam dharmam
ninne labhicciṭum dhyānam dhyānam

Thoughts to gain You are the only real thoughts; actions to gain You are the only real actions; duty to gain You, is the only real dharma; meditation to attain You is the only real meditation.

Cintakal okkeyum ninde cinta
karmmaṅgaḷ okkeyum ninde pūja
nin nāmam colluvān cuṇṭanaṅgum
nīmātram ammē enikku sarvam

All my thoughts are about You, all my actions are worship offered at Your feet; my lips move only to chant Your divine name; I have only You as my All in all.

Nīyende munnil innetti ṭēṇam
ṣrī pādam kaṇṇīril mukkiṭēṇam
nin prēma bhaktiyenn ātma nādam
mattonnum entammē vēṇṭa vēṇṭa

Please come to me so I can wash Your blessed feet with my tears. I do not want anything except loving devotion to You.

Nīyenne viṭṭiṭṭ innō ṭiṭēṇṭā
ninne yuruṭṭi piṭiccitum ṇān
nāmam japicche riññinnu ninne
ñānende kayyil kurukkum ammē

You won't be able to leave me anymore. I am holding tightly onto You by chanting Your Divine Name.

Itrayum nālenne viḍhḍhiyākki
innini yappaṇi vēṇṭa durgē
nīyende śvāsamāy tīrnnu pōyi
nīyende prāṇande prāṇanāyi

O Durga, do not play Your tricks and abandon me again. You are my very breath, You are my life itself.

Ende hṛt spandanam ninnilallō
en cintayellām ninnullilallō
ṇān tanne ninde maṭiyilallō
tārāṭṭu pāṭān maranniṭolle

My heart beats within You and my thoughts are within You. I am in Your lap; please do not forget to sing me a lullaby.

Śrī rāma candrante pāṭṭu pāṭū
vṛndāvana ttinte pāṭṭu pāṭū
mīra tan rādha tan pāṭṭu pāṭū
nin pāṭṭu kēṭṭū mayaṅgiṭām ñān

Please sing about Ramakrishna and about Vrindavan, about Mira and Radha. Let me lull myself to sleep, in your song.

Ā pāṭṭil muṅgi mayaṅgiṭam ñān
saccidānandam nukarnneṇīkkām
ennēkkumen nidra tīrnniṭaṭṭe
endammayil ṇān uṇarnniṭaṭṭe!

I will wake up forever. My sleep will be over forever and I will be enlightened in my Mother.

ŚRĪ RĀMA JAYA RĀMA

Rāmāya rāma bhadrāya
rāma candrāya vēdasē
raghu nāthāya nāthāya
sītāyā patayē namaḥ

Śrī rāma jaya rāma jaya jaya rāma
Ō rāmā, ō rāmā, ōmkāra rāma
Śrī rāma jaya rāma jaya jaya rāma
Rāma rāma rāma rāma

Śrī rāma jaya rāma jaya jaya rāma

Pralamba bāhuvikramam prabhō pramēya vaibhāvam
niṣam gacāpa sāyakam kharam trilōka nāyakam
dinēśa vamśa vandanam mahēśa cāpa khaṇḍanam
munīndra santa rañjanam surādi vṛndavan danam (2x)

I worship the Lord who is valorous, whose glory is incomprehensible, who wields the bow and arrows, who is the king of the three worlds. I worship the Lord who is the joy of Surya Vamsha, who broke the bow of Lord Shiva, who gives happiness to saints and sages, who is adored by the devas.

Manōjñavairi khaṇḍitam ajāti dēva sēvitam
viśuddha bōdha vigraham samasta dūṣatāpaham
namāmi indirāpatim sukhā daram satām gatim
bhajēsa śakti sānujam śachīpatim prayānukam (2x)

I worship the Lord who is adored by Lord Shiva, the enemy of Kama, who is served by Brahma and others, who is the manifestation of pure consciousness, who is the remover of all evils. I prostrate to Him who is the Lord of Lakshmi, the One with nectarine lips, who is the support of saints, who is accompanied by his wife and brothers.

Namāmi bhakta vatsalam kṛpālu śīla kōmaḷam
bhajāmitē padāṁbujam nikāma bhakti dēhimē rāma śrī rāma
namāmi bhakta vatsalam kṛpālu śīla kōmaḷam
bhajāmitē padāṁbujam nikāma bhakti dēhimē
nikāśa śyāma sundaram bhavāmbu nātha mandiram

praphulla kañja lōcanam madādi dōṣa mōcanam (2x)

I worship the Lotus Feet of the Lord, who is affectionate towards His devotees. O Lord, grant me selfless devotion. I worship the Lord who has a dark-blue complexion, whose eyes are like a fully bloomed lotus, who removes all bad tendencies like pride, etc.

ŚRĪ RĀMA RAGHU RĀMA

Śrī rāma raghu rāma sītā patē rāma
sakalārtti nāśanā sujanārccitā
Sumanōhar ānanā mṛdu hāsa śōbhanā
manuj āvatāra hari nārāyaṇa

Sākēta puravāsa rājīva sama nētra
sītāpatē nātha sukha dāyakā
Dīnāvanā varada dēvādhi dēva jaya
hē jānakī ramaṇa raghu nāyakā

Muni mānasēśvara mṛti janma mōcanā
bhavaśoka tāraṇā śiva dāyakā
Raghu vamśa dīpakā daśakaṇṭha nāśanā
daśaratha sunandanā danujāntakā)

Ghana śyāma kōmalā śara cāpa samyutā
śaraṇāgat āśrayā bharatāgrajā
Kamanīya vigrahā karuṇā rasārṇṇavā
varadāyakā dēva kalayām yaham

raghu rāma	Rama of the dynasty of Raghu
sītāpate	husband of Sita
sakalārtināśana	Remover of sorrows

sujanārccitā	One who is worshipped by the virtuous
sumanoharānanā	One with a beautiful face
mridu hāsa ṣobhana	One who has a radiant soft smile
manujāvatāra	One who has incarnated in human form
saketapuravāsa	Inhabitant of Ayodhya
rājīva sama netra	One whose eyes are like lotus petals
nātha	Master
sukhadāyakā	One who gives happiness
devadhi deva	Lord of all gods
jānakī ramaṇa	Beloved of Sita
raghu nāyaka	Lord of the house of Raghu
muni manaseśvara	Lord of the minds of sages
mṛtijanma mochanā	Who liberates souls from the cycle of birth and death
bhavaśoka tāraṇā	Who guides us across the sorrow of worldly existence
siva dāyakā	One who bestows auspiciousness
raghu vamsa dīpakā	Beacon of the House of Raghu
daśakanta nāśanā	Slayer of Ravana
daśaratha sunandanā	noble son of Dasaratha
danujāntakā	Destroyer of demons
ghana śyama komalā	Cloud-colored handsome one
śara capa samyutā	Equipped with bow and arrows
śaraṇāgatāśraya	Shelter of those who seek refuge
bharatāgrajā	Elder brother of Bharata

karuṇā rasārṇṇavā	Ocean of Compassion
kamanīya vigrahā	One with an enchanting form
varadāyakā	Bestower of boons
kalayāmyaham	I hold in my mind

ŚUBHA VIDHĀYAKA

Śubha vidhāyaka śiva manōhara
śaśidharā hara śaṅkarā
bhaya vināśaka bhava vimōcaka
bhasma bhūṣana bhāsurā

Amara vandita varada mangala
girisutā hṛdayēśvarā
Tripura bhañjana bhuvana rañjana
hari viriñca supūjitā

Uraga bhūṣana vṛṣabhavāhana
sakala vandya padāmbujā
Ḍamaru vādana naṭana mōhana
suranadī dhara sundarā

Yama vināśana yati janārccita
viracitōjjvala tāṇḍava
Praḷaya kāraṇa sujana pālaka
pārvatī paramēśvarā

Madana sūdanā nigama varṇita
dēva dēva sadāśivā
Pramatha nāyakā himagirīśvara
mṛḍa mahēśa naṭēśvara

subha vidhāyaka	Who creates prosperity or auspiciousness
manohara	Enchanting
śaśidhara	Who wears the crescent moon as an ornament
hara	Shiva
śankara	Who bestows happiness or prosperity
bhaya vinśaka	Destroyer of fear
bhava vimocaka	Who liberates from worldly bondage
bhasma bhuṣaṇa bhasura	Who wears sacred ash, shining, resplendent
amara vandita	Who is worshipped by the gods
varada	Giver of boons
mangala	Auspicious
giri suta hṛdayeśvarā	The beloved of Parvati
tripura bhañjana	Destroyer of the three cities
bhuvana rañjana	Who pleases the whole world
harivirinca supūjitā	Who is worshipped by Vishnu and Brahma
uraga bhuṣana	Who wears a serpent as an ornament
vṛṣabhavāhana	Who has a bull as his mount
sakala vandya padāmbujā	Whose lotus feet are worshipped by all
ḍamaru vādana	Who plays the 'damaru'
naṭana mohana	Who dances a captivating dance
surandī dhara	Bearer of the Ganga
sundarā	Handsome
yama vināśana	Killer of Yama
yatijanārcita	Who is worshipped by the sages
virachitojjvala tāṇḍava	Who performs a brilliant wild dance

pralaya kāraṇa	Who causes the final dissolution of the universe
sujana pālaka	Protector of the virtuous
parvati parameśvarā	The Lord of Parvati
madana sūdanā	The killer of Kama, the god of Love
nigama varṇita	Who is extolled by the Vedas
deva deva	God of gods
pramatha nāyakā	Lord of the Pramathas
himagiriśvara	Lord of the Himalaya mountains
mṛḍa maheśa	Great God
naṭeśvara	God of dance

ŚYĀM GŌPĀLĀ MĀJHĀ

śyām gōpālā mājhā kṛṣṇa gōpālā
yē mājhā puḍe he nandā cyā bāḷā
Lapun nakko rāhus malā sōḍun nakko jhāvus
Raḍavu nakkōre malā giridhar bālā

O Shyama Gopala, my Krishna Gopala, please come before me, O son of Nanda. Don't hide from me, never part away from me. Do not make me cry. O Giridhara Gopala.

Āvaḍicā khāvu tulā mi dēyīn
āvaḍice khēḷu tujhe mi paṇ kheḷī
Thak lās tar tulā jhōpi lāvīl
Gāvūn amgāyi he giridhar bāḷā
Kṛṣṇa gōvinda harē kṛṣṇa gōpāla harē

I shall give You to eat all the delicacies You like. I shall also play with You, your favorite games. If You get tired, I shall put You to sleep, singing lullabies, O Giridhara Gopala.

Śōdhu kuṭhe mi vāṭ pāhu tujhī mī
de darśan malā naṭkaṭ bāḷā
Tujhā vinā kāhi malā āvaṭat nāhī
Ye re laukar mājhā giridhar bāḷā
Kṛṣṇa gōvinda harē kṛṣṇa gōpāla harē

Where shall I search You ? I am waiting for You. Give me your darshan, O naughty One. Without You, I have no interest in anything. Come quickly, O Giridhara Gopala.

SUNLĒ PUKĀR

Sunlē pukār dil kī sunlē pukār
Sunlē pukār dil kī sunlē pukār mayyā (repeat previous line first)

Listen to the call of my heart. O Mother

Cāyā hē ghōr andhērā
rāh dikhē nā mayyā
Kaisē dēkhūmē tujhkō
Kaisē dēkhūmē tujhkō mā
O mā sunlē mā mērī mā sunlē mā

Darkness has spread all around, the path is not visible to me. O Mother! How shall I search for You? How shall I see You? O Mother listen to me!

Nanhā hē bālak tērā
kaisē jīyē akēlā
kōn sambhālē abh isē
Kōn sambhālē abh isē mā
O mā sun lē mā mērī mā sun lē mā

This child of Yours is just a toddler. How can he live alone, without his Mother? Who will take care of him? Who will nourish him with love? O Mother. Listen to me!

SVĀMĪ ŚARANAM AYAPPA

Svāmī śaranam ayappa śaranam śaranam ayappa (2x)
You are my refuge, my sole refuge, O Lord Ayappa!
Hari hara tanaya svāmī cira sukha nilaya
giri varavāsa svāmī ghana sukha rūpa

O Lord, son of Hari Hara (Lord Shiva and Lord Vishnu), abode of eternal happiness, who resides in the mountains (Sabarimala), who is of the form of saturated bliss.

Adi malar ābhayam adiyanu śubha nila pūkān
atulita kīrttē arulaṇam avirata śānti
Hari hara tanaya svāmī cira sukha nilaya
giri varavāsa svāmī ghana sukha rūpa

O Lord of unparalleled glory, Your Lotus Feet are the refuge for this humble one; bestow on me everlasting peace for the attainment of the most auspicious state.

Tiru muṭi rūpam svāmī jani mṛti bhāram
palavuru pēri vēṇdē iniyoru janmam
Hari hara tanaya svāmī cira sukha nilaya
giri varavāsa svāmī ghana sukha rūpa

O Lord of auspicious form, I have borne the burden of life and death many times. No, no more do I wish for another birth again.

Tava tiru meyyil svāmī malar abhiṣēkam
attiloru malarāy tīrnnāl avikala saukhyam
Hari hara tanaya svāmī cira sukha nilaya
giri varavāsa svāmī ghana sukha rūpa

O Lord, on Your auspicious form I shower flowers, and if I become one among those flowers, that would grant me immaculate bliss.

TALARNN URANGUKAYŌ

Talarnn urangukayō? iniyum
viṣāda mūkatayo?
manuja kotikal viṣaya garalam
nukarnn urangukayō! tammil
marannu rangukayō?

Still sleeping the deep sleep of oblivion? Millions of human beings are asleep, drunken with the pleasures of the world, totally unaware of their true nature.

Kalattin kaiviral tumbāl virica
cāyā citraṅgalō manuṣyan
Uyartiya taḷakal! tazhtiya taḷakal
viralunna vilarunna mukhaṅgaḷ! engum
maravicu maruvunna manuṣyan!

Images painted by the fingers of time, some with raised heads, some with lowered heads, pale faces, grouchy faces, frozen and timid faces; are these men?

Niṅgaḷkku kanikānān niṅgaḷe kanikānān
innī jagattil manuṣyar untō?

Untenkil oru tāmara malar mottupōl
mizhiyatac uraṅgunnat ente hṛdayam
ital vitarttī dāttatentē?

Are there any real human beings in this day and age that one can perceive? If there are, why are they sleeping like unopened lotus buds? Why don't those hearts blossom?

TĀRĀPATHAṄGAḶĒ

Tārā pathaṅgaḷē tāzhōṭṭu pōrumō
tārāṭṭu pāṭuvān ammayuṇṭu
Tīrātta snēhattin nīrurav āṇavaḷ
tēṭum manassinu taṇal āṇavaḷ

O stars, can't you please come down? Mother is here to sing a lullaby to you. She is the stream of never-ending Love and She is the shade-giving tree for seeking minds.

Mauna rāgaṅgaḷum mūḷiyī rātriyil
mandamāy vīśivarunn oru tennalē
Sāndra madhuramāy mantriccat entu nī
mādhuryam ūṛumen ammatan kathakaḷō

O cool, gentle breeze, who comes slowly humming silent songs in the night, what did you whisper sweetly in my ears? Is it the sweet stories of my Mother?

Sūryanum candranum udiccasta mikkunna
nīla mēghaṅgaḷ ilūṭe melle
Niṅgaḷkku divyamām ī prabhayēkiya
amma yekkāṇān kotiyillayō

The sun and moon slowly rise and set in the blue sky every-day (above the dark clouds). Don't you have the desire to see my Mother who has given this divine splendour to You?

TĀTAN AVIṬUNNU ÑAṄGAḶ MAKKAḶ

Tātan aviṭunnu ñaṅgaḷ makkaḷ
pārinte maṇṇil piranna pūkkaḷ
pārile pūzhiyāl kaṇkal mūṭi
paitaṅgaḷāy ñaṅgaḷ kēḷiyāṭi
deva deva deva

You are our Father, we Your children. We are the flowers born on the soil of this earth. Blinded by the dust of the world, we children have played for long.

Śaraṇam aśaraṇarkkē kiṭuvōn
taraṇam aṭiyaṅgaḷkka abhayam ennum
Ariyātoru pizha ceytupōyāl
arivezhum tātan porukkukillē
deva deva deva

O granter of refuge to the destitute, always bestow protection on these humble children. Even if unknowingly we commit any mistake, will not the Omniscient Father forgive His children?

paitangaḷ ñaṅgaḷ kāliṭaṛum
tātapādaṅgaḷil āññu vīzhum
ñaṅgaḷuṭe nērē ī raudrabhāvam
entinu kāṭṭunnu nityavum nī

We children are bound to make mistakes. We fall at Father's Feet. Why do You show every day this angry mood to us?

Ñaṅgaḷe viṭṭu dayāparan nī
aṅgu dūrēykku gamikka yāṇō ?
Eṅkil inimēlil illa ñaṅgaḷ
mannil ennum kiṭannu pōkum
deva deva deva

O compassionate One, are You going far away, leaving us behind? If so, in the future we will be lost, being ever bound to this earth.

TĒNMAZHAYĀKA UNTAN

Tēnmazhayāka untan punnakaiyai
entan mītu pozhivāy
uḷḷattil māsakatti idayatril
entrenṭrum vītriṭuvāy

My fondest Mother, smile Your divine smile, pour your unearthly love into my barren heart, dispel all the gloom that grows thick, stay ever in me, Mother, never leave.

Allum pakalum ammā unnai eṇṇi
neñcam nekizhkiratu
īṭatta inpam tarum ambikayai
uttavarkku tavaḷē

In my heart's holy shrine all my musings, meditations ever centre on You; my little life is one long, soulful adoration unto You, my Mother of eternal charm.

Uḷḷakōvi linuḷḷē pukuntiṭa
uḷḷam tirantu vayttēn
ēkkam taṇintiṭavē amarntaṅku
taṇṇoḷi pāycciṭuvāy

My heart is hushed, awed, alert, I am rapt in prayer, ever expecting Your Grace, my beloved Mother, my all, my sole refuge, steal in and illumine my sombre soul.

Anpine tēṭittēṭi
kaḷayttu nān uḷḷam uṭayntu viṭṭēn
eṭṭātolay vilellām tēṭittēṭi
kaṇṇīr viṭṭu kaḷaittēn

I have been seeking, pining for love, I am alone, forlorn, dejected; I have wandered far chasing a vague vision,and have wept long and am tired.

Kaṇkaḷil kaṇṇīr illai
azhutiṭa tenpum illai uṭalil
tunnpakkanalil entan idayamō
ventu nīrākiratu

My parched heart is crushed to pieces, it is burning, burning in wordless agony. Won't You lift Your veil at least for once, revealing Yourself, Your divine form?

Īṭilla unkaruṇai pozhintu nī
tollaikaḷ pōkkiṭuvāy
aruḷmazhayil entrum idayatte
tiruttala mākkiṭuvāy

Drive away, Mother, the dark clouds weighing on my sinking heart; flood it with Your nectarine love, baptise it, make it a worthy offering at Your altar.

Viṇṇavar sukham vēṇṭā vēṇṭām tāyē
vāzhvin perum sukhamum
āzhnta nal bhakti vēṇṭum vēṇṭuvat
jñānavum muktiyumē

I do not ask for celestial joys, nor for earth's choicest gifts; all I seek is the all-devouring devotion which liberates me for ever from samsara's age-old delusion.

Vāy untan nāmam solla mahēśvari
kātuntan nādam kēṭṭkka
kaṇṇil ānanda kaṇṇīr perukiṭa
tōntiṭuvāy manatil

Let my tongue ever chant Your holy mantra, let my ears ever hear Your Divine voice, let my eyes be ever brimful with tears of love, let my heart ever revel in the vision of Your Divine form.

TĒṬI UNNAI ṢARAṆAṬAINTŌM

(MUTTUMARI)

Tēṭi unnai ṣaraṇa ṭaintōm deśa muttumārī
[amṛtamāyi tāye]
tēṭi unnai ṣaraṇa ṭaintōm eṅkal muttumārī
[amṛtamāyi tāye]
Muttumārī amma muttumāri (2x)
[Amṛitēśvari ammā amṛtēśvari (2x)]

We searched and found refuge in You, O dear Muttumari.

Allalkalai tīrttiṭuvāy
arulinai tantiṭuvāy
Anpuṭane manamiraṅgi
anparkalai kāttiṭuvāy

You remove suffering and bestow boons. With love and compassion, You protect Your devotees.

Nilayaṭra vaiyyakattil
nilayinni tavittiṭum
Eṅgalukku nalam ceyya
iṅguṭanē vanti ṭuvāy

In this impermanent world we suffer without any protection. Please come immediately and bless us.

Aṭaikkalam nīyēyentru
aṭipaṇin tīṭuvōm
Azhivillā nilai tantu
piraviyin payan alippāy

We come to Your Lotus Feet knowing that You are our sole refuge. Please give us the eternal state which is the fruit of the human birth.

TUYARANG KAḶAI KŪRUM

tuyarang kaḷai kūrum murai teriyāmal
kaḷaittu viṭṭēn inta vāzhvil
parivuṭan kaṭai kaṇ pārttāl pōtum
pukaliṭam ini vēr etarkku

Not knowing how to communicate my grief, heart-broken I remain. If Thine all-seeing eye falls on me with compassion, that shall be my refuge.

Vēṇṭuvat anaittum tarum aruḷ pārvaiyai
entrum pozhintiṭu povaḷē
śiritoru pārvai ivanatu uṭalai
varuṭi cellātō tāyē

Thy twin eyes radiate countless rays of auspiciousness. Mother, will not a tiny wave from among them caress my body?

Mati kulai kiratu manam alaikiratu
uṭalum sōrvaṭai kiratu
unataruḷ tavira gati enakkillai
enpatai nī ariyāyō

Bewildered, my mind is restless, the body is collapsing. O Mother! I see nothing else for support but Thy grace

Nī purakkaṇittāl vāzhvē vīṇ entrum
nanrē ninaivil koḷvāyē
unataṭi paṇiyum enakkitu pōtum
enpatuvō un eṇṇam

Mother, remember if You forsake me, my life shall be in vain. Am I not worthy to seek refuge at Thy lotus feet?

UḶḶAM URUKUTAYYĀ MURUKĀ

uḷḷam urukutayyā murukā
unnadi kānkayile
alli anaittidave
enakkul āsai perukutappā murukā

O Muruga (Kartikeya), my heart melts at the very sight of You. The desire to come and hug You increases with each passing day.

pādi para vasamāyi unnaiye
pārttida tonutaiyyā
ādum mayileri murukā
ōṭi varuvāyappā

I sing about You, I become ecstatic. All I want to do is to spend all my time looking at You. Will You come running, O Muruga, will You come mounted on Your peacock?

pāsam akantra taiyyā
bandha pāsam akantra taiyyā
untan mel nesam valantra taiyyā
īśan tiruma kane
entan īnam marainta tappā

The bonds are going away, bonds and birth-ties. My love for You is taking their place. O Son of Lord Shiva, my afflictions are disappearing.

āru tiru mukhavum arulai
vāri vazhan kutaiyyā
vīramikum tolum kadambum
vettri muzhan kutappā

All Your six effulgent faces radiate divine grace. Your divine weapons proclaim victory (to all those who come to You).

kan kanda daivam ayyā
nī inta kaliyuga varadan ayyā
pāvi yendrikalāmal
enakkum padamalar taru vāyappa

You are God incarnate, standing right before us in this dark age. Please don't reject me as unworthy, but grant me also Your divine grace.

UḶḶIL TUḶUMBUNNA MANTRA

Uḷḷil tuḷumbunna mantram - ātma
dharmam teḷikkunna mantram
"Amṛtēśvaryai namaḥ" mantram - ātma
nirvṛti dāyāka mantram!

The mantra "Amriteshwaryai Namah" wells up within me; it's like a beacon that sheds light on the path of righteousness; it's the mantra that liberates the soul.

Tāriḷam kayyāl talōṭi - amma
kāruṇya tīrtham pozhikkē
Mayūnnu mōhāndha kāram - manam
mēyunnor ekānta tīram!

When Mother caresses me with Her petal soft hands and lets the holy stream of Her compassion flow towards me, the darkness of delusion fades and my mind grazes in a pasture of solitude.

Tēṅgalum viṅgalum tīrum - tīrā -
vyādhikaḷ vērattu mārum
Ammay onnāśīrva dikkē - janma
janmāntar āndhyam naśikkum!

Then my throbbing pain and sorrows come to an end, and even incurable diseases are cured without a trace. Mother's blessing annihilates even the vestiges of spiritual ignorance existing within me.

Snēhāmṛtam ārituki - jīva
cētassuṇar tunna nēram
Ātmā vilātmā vuṇarum - sacci -
dānanda bōdham teḷiyum!

When Mother rains Her nectar of love on me, and awakens my inner consciousness, the awareness of Existence-Consciousness-Bliss finally dawns on me.

VANDANAM NITYA VANDANAM

Vandanam nitya vandanam — nin
padataḷiril ozhuki ṭunna vandanam;
bandhanam duḥkha bandhanam — ata
azhiyuv atinn anudinam en vandanam

My humble prostrations at Your lotus feet. I worship You to be free from the bondage of sorrow.

Karuṇa yuḷḷa manama tinnu vandanam — ente
duritam ākeya kaluvān āyu vandanam
Nanma cērnnaveṇ matiykku vandanam — ente
tinma viṭṭu pōvatinnu vandanam

I pray for a mind filled with compassion and to get rid of my sins due to past karmas. Let me have a pure mind, devoid of all imperfections.

Satyamonnu tirayu vōrkku vandanam — ata
nityamenu karutu vōrkku vandanam;
Hṛttilamba vāzhu vōrkku vandanam— ente
hṛttilamba vazhvatinnum vandanam

My humble respects to those wise people who have understood the Truth that is eternal. My respects to them who constantly see the presence of Divinity in their hearts.

VANDĒ VĒDA MĀTARAM

Vandē vēda mātaram
vandē dēha mātaram
vandē dēśa mātaram
vandē viśva mātaram

I prostrate to the Mother of the Vedas, to the Mother who gave birth to this body, to the Mother of this nation, to the Mother of the Universe.

Jaya jaya bhārata mātā jaya jaya
mātā amṛtānandamayī
Mangaḷa kāriṇi mañjuḷa hāriṇi
mātā amṛtānandamayī

Victory to Mother India! Victory to Mother Amritanandamayi, the Source of auspiciousness! O Beautiful One, Stealer of hearts, Amritanandamayi!

Jayatu samasta carācara bandhu
bhavatu sadāhṛdi sēvana sindhu
Manasica vāci sadā mama santu
madhurita cinta vāṅmadhu gandhā

Victory to the Friend of all creatures, to the One who in willingness to serve others is like a vast ocean. Please, constantly abide in my mind; dwell always in my mind as sweet thoughts, and dwell in my words like the sweetness of honey.

Mākuru mē hṛdi dōṣa vicaram
pūraya mē hṛdi dharma vicāram
Pālayamām akhilā padatōmē
dēhi sadā śubha kuśala mudāram

Let there not be any evil thoughts in my mind. Fill my heart with righteous thoughts. Protect me from all dangers. O Mother, bestow upon me a cheerful and solicitous attitude.

VĀṆĪMAṆĪ MĀTĒ

Vāṇīmaṇī mātē vīṇā dhṛtahastē
Gānāmṛtalōlē vāgīśvari vandē
Jai jagadambē jai jagadambē
jai jagadambē jai jai mā (4x)

Mother Saraswati, holding the veena in her amrs, the graceful One from whom flows the nectar of music, I prostrate to Thee, Mother of speech!

Nīlōlpala nētrē śōbhā paripūrṇṇē
Rāsēśvari rādhē rājēśvari vandē (Jai)

O blue-lotus eyed Mother, full of radiance, Thou art also Radha, the Goddess of the rasa dance. I prostrate to the supreme ruler of all rulers!

Śyāmē śubha rūpē śōkā mayahīnē
Kāḷīka ruṇārdrē kāmēśvari vandē (Jai)

O dark-hued One of auspicious form! There is no place for sorrows in You. O Kali, tenderly compassionate, prostrations to the ruler of desires!

Ōmkāra śarīrē pāśāṅkūśa pāṇē
Kālānta kajāyē kāḷīśvari vandē (Jai)

O Mother! embodied in the Om, who bears the noose and the goad in her arms, Consort of the dispeller of death (Shiva), I prostrate to Thee!

Līlā dhṛta mūrttē mōhāpaha kīrttē
Dīnēṣuda yārdrē sarvēśvari vandē (Jai)

Assuming a form merely as a play, renowned for dispelling delusion, who is tenderly merciful toward the destitute, I prostrate to You, Ruler of All!

Ādyanta vihītē ānanda suśīlē
Ēkānta vilōlē lōkēśvari vandē (Jai)

O Mother! who has no beginning or end, who is blissfully charming, who revels in solitude, I prostrate to Thee, Sustainer of the Universe!

VĀZHIYA ENṬRUM VĀZHIYAVĒ

Vāzhiya enṭrum vāzhiyavē
amṛtā dēvī vāzhiyavē
Untan punnakai kaṇṭālē
eṅkaḷ kavalai tīrntiṭumē

May Amrita Devi live long and forever. If we keep seeing Your smiling face, we will get rid of our worries.

Makkaḷ nāṅkaḷ seykinta
pāpaṅkaḷ anaittum tīrntiṭavē
Puṇṇiya bhūmiyil pirantāyē
amṛtā dēvī vaṭivi nilē

You were born in this sacred land as Amrita Devi to counteract all the sinful deeds of people like us.

Untan kaṭaikkaṇ pārvvayilē
eṅkaḷ janmam kazhintiṭavē
Nāṅkaḷum kāttu nirkinṭrōm
ammā nīyum kārppāyō

O Amma, won't You please look at us? We are ever waiting, yearning for Your sidelong glances.

Ariyā piḷḷaiykaḷ nāṅkaḷumē
unnai tuṭarntu naṭantiṭavē
Pātai onṭru vakuttu tantu
nalvazhi kāṭṭum dēvī ammā

We, Your ignorant children, have been following You. O Mother, please carve out a path for us to tread.

VERUM ORU PULKKOṬI

Verum oru pulkkoṭi ñan ammē, nin
kṛpa illennal ñan illa,
Kanaka mayī nin kāruṇyāmṛta —
Rasam ennuḷḷil coriyēṇam

I am just a blade of grass, Mother. I will not exist without Your benevolence. O Golden Mother, let the nectar of Your compassion rain on me!

Ñānenna bhāvavum mōhā vēśavum
kūṭi kalarnnoru rūpam ñan
Pāpaṅgaḷ pōkkiyen hṛdaya talattil
nī vasiccīṭa ṇamammē

I am just a bundle of ego and delusions mixed together. Please rid my heart of its sins and stay there forever, O my Mother.

VIHARATI YAMUNĀ TAṬMĒ

Viharati yamunā taṭmē hari sadā
viharati yamunā taṭmē

Hari (Lord Krishna) roams around on the banks of the Yamuna, He roams around all the time.

Madhuram gāyati nṛtyati laḷitam
praviśati saghana nikuñje
Mandam mandam calati vane'yam
sundar mañju padōm sē

He sings sweetly, dances enchantingly and stealthily enters the dense bower. He moves about slowly in the forest with His tender feet prancing about here and there.

Rādhā vadana vidhūkī śōbhā
pibatimudā nayanōm sē
Yugaḷ manōhar rūpī mādhav
madhu varṣati gōkul mē

Radha drinks in the radiance of that moon-like face with intoxicated eyes. Madhava, so attractive to all, drenches the village of Gokul with nectar-like sweetness.

Yamunā taṭinī tīr manōhar
puḷakitu hari narttan sē
Hari svaraśanko vyākul laharēm
nāch uṭhīm svāgat mēm

Even the banks of the Yamuna are overjoyed when Hari chooses that as the site for His dance.The waves of the Yamuna respond eagerly to Hari's presence, and rise up in a joyous welcoming dance.

VINATI HAMĀRI TŪNE SUNI

Vinati hamāri tūne suni nahi kānhā
Kasūr hamāra kyā he kucc to batāna

O Lord, You turned a deaf ear to our fervent requests. Please tell us, what wrong did we do?

Gōpiyōm ke duḥkh ko tūne nahi jāna
Vraj ko kanaya tum bhūl na jāna

You do not know the grief of the gopis. O Krishna, please do not forget the land of Vraja (Vrindavan).

Śyām ḍale phir bhi āye nahi kānhā
Kōyī nahī jāne kab lōṭṭēṅkē kānhā

Though it is past evening, Krishna has not come. Nobody knows when he is going to arrive.

Ik kṣaṇ ko to ā jāo kanhā
Jīnā nahī dēkhē binā, tujhkō kānhā

O Krishna, please do return at least for a moment. We do not wish to live without seeing You.

Āvō śyām mērē śyām mērē pyārē ghanaśyām

Please come, O Krishna, my darling Kanha.

VINATI SUNO VINATI SUNO

Vinati suno vinati suno
vinati suno mā vinati suno
Sankata hariṇi santoṣi mā
sādhu jana priya dēvī mā
Sadā ānandamayī mā
sadāśiva priya dēvī mā

O Mother, please listen to this prayer. Mother, You are the One who eradicates all sorrow, one who is easily pleased, one who loves Her devotees. You are forever blissful, the beloved of Sadashiva.

VIṢĀDAMĀKAVĒ

Viṣādam ākavē vazhi māri nilkkum
manuṣyan manassine aṛiññāl
iruḷinte curulukal akale poy marayum
udayārkka bimbam teḷiyum - hṛttil
uṇarvvinte kiraṇaṅgaḷ pozhiyum!

All melancholy shall give way if man knows his mind illumining the heart swaddled with darkness. One day the morning sun shall rise showering the heart with the rays of awakening!

Paraspara vairuddhyam kaṭaṅkatha yākum
aniścita gati māri māyum
Parajana sukham svanta sukham ennu tōnnum
hṛdayam hṛdayam ōṭiṇaṅgum - ellām
orumayil theli varnu viḷaṅgum

Conflict shall prove to be a fairy tale, uncertainty shall vanish, the well-being of others will become one's own well-being, heart shall befriend heart, and everything will shine in harmony.

Sarga sahiti kalkku varavēlpu nalkum
samatva viśālānta rangam
Snēha vaikharī nādam amṛtamāy ozhukum
avaniye avirāmam tazhukum ullam
asulabha nirvṛti nukarum

The expansive heart established in equality shall offer welcome to creative expression. The voice of Love shall flow as divine nectar and ceaselessly caress the earth. The inner Self shall enjoy a rare beatitude.

VIŚVA MĀNAVA

Viśva mānava vaśya snēhamē
śuddha vātsalya dhāmamē
hṛdyamām tava satccari tramī
martya jīvita darśanam

O abode of pure affection, pure love that charmed the entire humanity, Thy blessed life is the message for the people.

Kāvya nirbhara lōla mānasa
vīṇa mīṭṭiya pallavi
mauna sāndra vilīnamāy tava
padapāmsu tīrtthaṅgaḷil

The melodies that the veena of my mind hummed soulfully, have become silent as they merged in the sacred waters washing Thy feet.

Vēdasāra viśāradātma
sukhālaya maṇi dīpamē
prāṇanil svaratāḷamē ī
rāga nirjhariyāy varū

O effulgent light of consciousness that shines as the essence of the Vedas, Thou art the rhythm of my life's throbs, please come to me as a stream of melody.

Nin dayā vayvaipil immahī talam
nanma pūviṭṭu ṇaravē
tingum ādaravōṭ anāratam
ninne vāzhttiṭunn ēvarum

This planet basks in Thy compassion and goodness blooms everywhere, all of creation hails Thee ever with hearts full of reverence.

VIṬARĀTTA TĀMARA

Viṭarātta tāmara malarmoṭṭu ñān ammē
mizhi aṭaccinnum tapas irippū
prabhayākum jagadamba arikatt aṇāyunpōḷ
prabhayēttu viṭarān koticc irippū

O Amma, I am an unblossomed lotus bud ever sitting and meditating with closed eyes. O Effulgent Mother of the world, I long to blossom in the ray of Your radiance when You come close to me.

Iruḷārnnorī van taṭākattil jyōtissāy
jananiye neṭunāḷāy kāttirippū
Mizhi nīr ozhukki koṇṭ anūdinam aviṭutte
tiru darśana tināy kēṇiṭunnu

In this huge lake of darkness, I have been waiting long for You, O Mother, the embodiment of light. Shedding tears everyday I long for Your Divine vision.

Viṭarāte kozhiyān nī karutallē lōkēśi
vīṇṭum ñānī bhūvil aṇaññi ṭende
Arutammē ōrkkumbōl talarunnu taṇṭukal
tavapādam ammē ñān kumbiṭunnu (2x)

O Goddess of the Universe, don't let me wither away without blooming, else I may have to be born again. Oh no! Mother, I shudder to think of it. I bow at Your Feet, O Mother, I bow at Your Feet.

VIṬHALĀ HARI VIṬHALĀ

Viṭhalā hari viṭhalā (2x)
Paṇḍuraṅga viṭhalē hari nārāyaṇa
Purandara viṭhalē lakṣmi nārāyaṇa
Hari nārāyaṇa lakṣmi nārāyaṇa
Śrī nārāyaṇa satya nārāyaṇa

Viṭhalā	Lord at Pandarpur
Hari	Lord Vishnu
Paḍuraṅga	of white hue

Hari Nārāyaṇa	Vishnu, reliever of distress, resting on the Causal Ocean.
Lakṣmi	Goddess of prosperity ; consort of Vishnu.
Satya	Truth

VRAJAVANA KUÑJAVIHĀRĪ

Vrajavana kuñjavihārī jai jai
yadukula nātha murārī
Navaghana nīla śarīri jai jai
jayatu sadā danujārī
Hari hari bol jai hari hari bol jai

Victory to the One who moves freely in the huts of Vraja's forest, the leader of the Yadava clan. O dark blue bodied One, always eternal praises to You, destroyer of wicked people!

Gōvārddhana giridhārī jai jai
kāḷiya mada samhārī
Mṛdu pītāmbara dhārī jai jai
jayatu sudarśana dhāri
Jai jai jayatu sudarśana dhāri

Victory to You, who lifted Govardhana hill, who killed the ego of the serpent Kaliya, who wears soft yellow robes, who has the Sudarshana (weapon)!

Nirupama karuṇā śālī jai jai
surabhila suma vanamālī
Nikhila carācara rūpi jai jai
jayatu varābhaya pāṇī
Jai jai jayatu varābhaya pāṇī

Victory to You, who is incomparably merciful by nature, garlanded with fragrant forest flowers, formed as whole moving and unmoving, may Your hands bestow boons and protection!

Āsura dharma virōdhī jai jai
śāśvata dharmōdhārī
Pāṇḍava ratha sañjārī jai jai
jayatu jaganmaya śaurī
Jai jai jayatu jaganmaya śaurī

Victory to You, who is against demonic acts, the upholder of everlasting dharma, the driver of the Pandava's chariots, the powerful One dwelling in this whole world!

VṚNDĀVANA KUÑJĀŚRITA

vṛndāvana kuñjāśrita kṛṣṇa
mandāra sumālamkṛta kṛṣṇa
indī varada lōcana kṛṣṇa
kāḷindītaṭa narttana kṛṣṇa

Krishna, who resides in the Vrindavana gardens, adorned beautifully by lotus flowers, with the eyes resembling the blue lotus petals, who dances on the shore of the river Kalindi.

kṛṣṇa kṛṣṇa mana mōhana kṛṣṇa
kṛṣṇa kṛṣṇa madhu sūdana kṛṣṇa
kṛṣṇa kṛṣṇa muraḷī dhara kṛṣṇa

Krishna, facinator of the mind, who slayed the demon Madhu, Krishna, who holds the divine flute.

nanda yaśōda nandana kṛṣṇa
manda gamana mana mōhana kṛṣṇa
cintita mangaḷa dāyaka kṛṣṇa
santāpāntaka sundara kṛṣṇa

Krishna, son of Nanda and Yashoda, who moves slowly, infatuating the mind, giver of auspiciousness to those who contemplate Him Eliminator of sorrow, handsome Krishna.

jaya jaya dēva jaganmaya kṛṣṇa
jagada bhirāma kaḷēbara kṛṣṇa
jaya karuṇā maya kēśava kṛṣṇa
jaya muraḷī dhara mādhava kṛṣṇa

Victory to Krishna, the shining One who pervades the whole world, whose form makes the world very happy, the compassionate One. Praises to the one who holds the divine flute, the controller of the senses.

VṚNDĀVANA RĀJI PŪTTU

Vṛndāvana rāji pūttu maṇam tūki
vraja gōpika māra ṇaññuṣassu pōle
mōhana muraḷi madhugāna lahariyil
mati marannava rōrō naṭanamāṭi

The trees of Vrindavan have bloomed and sweet fragrance is wafting along. The milkmaids have arrived, like the rosy dawn. Losing themselves in the sweet melodies of the flute, they dance ecstatically.

Paninīr malar pōle pari śōbha yārnnuḷḷil
maruvunnu madhusmitam tūki kaṇṇan
Uḷḷatte yuṇarvvētti nalliḷam tennal pōl
mellavē tazhukunnu kara valliyāl

Radiant, like the rose blossoms, Kanna smiles sweetly from within. Enlivening like the fresh breeze, He caresses with His gentle hands.

Pativupōl rādha yanna ravinda nayanante
tirumāril talachāyccu mayaṅgi ninnu
Uṇarnnappōḷ manamāke maraviccu maṇi varṇṇan
maraññat ōrttariyāte karaññu pōyi

That day, as usual, Radha lay her head on the lotus-eyed One's august chest; Radha stood dreamily. When She woke up, her mind staggered. She burst in tears for the dark-hued One had vanished.

Yamunayil ōḷaṅgaḷ nērma yilinnu mā-
muraḷī ninādam muriññiṭāte
Mūḷunnu vērpaṭil vyatha puṇṭa rādhatan
cutumizhi nīrum viyarppu māki

Even today, the waves of the Yamuna, truly hum the notes of that flute, unbroken. The tears and sweat of Radha, pining for Krishna, have also commingled with the melancholic strain of the Yamuna.

VṚNDĀVANATTILE SAKHIMĀRE

Vṛndāvanattile sakhimāre
niṅgaḷ eṇṭe kaṇṇane kaṇṭuvō ?

O mates of Vrindavan, have you seen my Kannan?

Nanda nandanā nitya sundarā
śyāmaḷa kōmaḷa bālā
Kaṇṇā kaṇṇā

Pīli tirumuṭi aramaṇi kiṅgiṇi
chārttiya muraḷī lōlā
Āṭi cāñcāṭi cariññāṭi koṇṭōṭi vā

The son of Nanda, eternally beautiful One the dark handsome boy, the tender flute-player who wears a crown of peacock feathers and a garland of pearls, come dancing, swaying, and running!

Gōpa kumārā gōpi vallabhā
nīlāmbara mukha dhārā
Kaṇṇā kaṇṇā
Anudinam ennuṭe sirakaḷil ozhukān
nāda brahmamāy vā
Āṭi cāñcāṭi cariññāṭi koṇṭōṭi vā

O Cowherd boy, Lord of the Gopis, whose face is like the blue sky! Come as the primordial rhythm/sound to flow in my veins everyday! Come dancing, swaying and running!

Kāḷiya mardana kamala vilōcana
tālappolikaḷ uṇarttu
Kaṇṇā kaṇṇā
Vākaccārtti pīli viṭarttiya
mōhana darśana mēkū
Āṭi cāñcāṭi cariññāṭi koṇṭōṭi vā

O Tamer of Kaliya, lotus-eyed One, light the lamps, grant me the darshan of Your resplendent form adorned with various costumes, Come dancing, swaying, and running!

YATHA YARIYIYKKĀN

Vyatha yariyiykkān vazhi yaṛiyātivan
avaśam vāzhuka yāṇē
viśada vilōcāna yalivōṭe yivanil
patiyukil atutān abhayam

Not knowing how to communicate my grief, heart-broken, I remain. If Thine all-seeing eye falls on me with compassion, that shall be my refuge.

Śubhaśata vīcikaḷ anavaratam tava-
mizhiyiṇa tūkuvatillē
Atilōru kuññala yivanuṭe tanuvē
tazhukuka yillē tāyē (2x)

Thy twin eyes radiate countless rays of auspiciousness,Will not a tiny wave from among them caress my body, O Mother?

Mati yuzhalunnu manam alayunnu
tanuvum taḷaruka yāṇē
Tirukṛpa yozhike tuṇa yini yonnum
jananī kāṇmatum illē (2x)

Bewildered, my mind is restless, The body is collapsing, But for Thy Grace, O Mother, I see nothing else for support.

Veṭiyukil ennuṭe jīvitam ammē
verutē yāyiṭu mōrkkū
tava tiruvaṭiyil śaraṇam aṭaññava-
nucitam itennō bhāvam (2x)

Remember if you forsake me, My life shall be in vain, Mother. Am I not worthy to seek refuge at Thy Lotus Feet?

VYATHAYURAÑÑU

Vyatha yuraññu vikalamāya vīthiyil carikkavē
viṣaya dāhamagni pōle nāḷamuḷḷil nīṭṭavē
śama damaṅgaḷ kaiviṭunna śiśuvine tuṇaykuvān
śiva samīpam eppozhum vasikkum amba kaniyaṇē

My steps trod along a path, laden with sorrow. The flames of carnal craving blaze within me. My Mother, who abides in the Supreme, protect this child who forsakes observances of mind and sense control.

Tanu taḷarnnu tapam oralpavum tara peṭillini
manam alaññulaññu pōyi mantra japa vumāyiṭā
Manam aliññu nīyivaṇṭe nēreyonnu nōkkumō
tuṇa yivannu nin kaṭākṣam onnu mātram ambikē

My body is exhausted, unable am I for austerities any more. My wayward mind is tired and even chanting the mantra has become impossible. Will You turn Your loving gaze towards me? O Mother, Your compassionate glance alone is my refuge.

Arivum illa balavum illa sādhanā diyum na mē
stutikaḷ pāṭuvān vicitra vākpaṭutvam illamē
Kadana bhāramēkuvān orittu kaṇṇunīrumē
kaṭhinamī hṛdantam aṅgozhukki ṭunnum illahō

Neither knowledge nor power do I have, nor practice of sadhana. To sing Your glories, I do not have the gift of words This stubborn heart of mine is refusing to shed. even a teardrop, so that I may surrender my sorrows.

Paraka ninnil ettiṭān ivannu sādhyam ākumō
karuṇa hētu venniye coriññiṭaykil nīyumē

Atinikṛṣṭa dīna hīnan oruvan eṅkilum śivē
tava kaṭākṣa vīkṣaṇam labhikkilō avan śivan!

O Mother,do tell me, can I ever reach Thee, if You never shower Your causeless mercy upon me, though I be the worst helpless sinner? He upon whom Thy glance falls, becomes Shiva!

YAMUNĀ TĪRA VIHĀRĪ

Yamunā tīra vihārī
vṛndāvana sañcārī
gōvarddhanō dhārī
gōpāla kṛṣṇa murārī

The One who sports on the banks of the Yamuna river, who roams in Vrindavan, who lifted the Govardhana mountain.

Māyā mānuṣaveṣā ivane
māyārṇṇa vamatil āzhtarutē
Mānasa mōhana malaritaḷil
māyādhīśa vilasuka nī

O Lord, You appear as a man veiling Your divinity by illusion (maya). Please do not drown us in the ocean of maya. Please shine in my heart, O Lord of maya.

Satyattiṇṭe mukham darśippān
śānti manasssil kaḷiyaṭān
Tirupāda malaraṭi aṇayānāy
anumatiyēkū jagadīśā

Let me have the vision of Truth; let peace dwell in my heart; let me merge in Your lotus feet, O Lord, please grant these desires.

English bhajans

AMMA CAN YOU HEAR ME?

(AMMA NIN RŪPAM)

Amma, can You hear me?
Through tears I'm calling out Your Name.
Let me see You now, clearly in my mind.
Amma have mercy, answer my prayer.

Truth is hidden behind all we see.
I'm fooled believing Thy play.
Tortured and weary, my mind is on fire
with a burning desire for peace.
Set me free from this cruel illusion.
Show me what is real.
Wake me from this dream, purify my mind.
Amma, I'm waiting. Show me the way.

Hearing this prayer, do You not feel my pain?
Do these tears not melt Your heart?
Lonely and frightened, I've no one to turn to.
Mother please don't abandon Your child.
Like a river always seeks the ocean,
I am seeking Thee.
Lead me to the goal. Never let me fall.
Amma! Please help me merge into Thee.

OH MY DIVINE MOTHER

(AMME YI JIVENDE)

Oh my divine Mother, there is no one other
than You to dry these tears and set this soul free.
Oh Mother divine, at Your sweet Feet sublime,
this wayward soul finds its divinity.

Alas! This mind now wallows in deep sorrow,
lost in illusion, not finding its goal.
Mother, please bless me that I may embrace Thee
tightly forever with pure devotion.

In this fearsome ocean of living and dying,
the only refuge is Your Lotus Feet.
To cool the fire of fear and desire,
please sprinkle me with the nectar of Your love.

This little infant spends every moment
by meditating upon Your Form.
Don't keep me waiting! Draw me close to You and
bestow tranquility on this poor soul.

AMRITANANDAMAYI, HOLY MOTHER

(AMṚTĀNANDAMAYI JAI JAI)

Amritanandamayi, Holy Mother,
Saviour, Guru Divine.
She is a river of Grace
carrying us all to the ocean of Love.

Radiantly clothed all in white,
She illumines the world with Her light.
In Her beauty lives perfection,
in Her heart only truth.

Melting each heart with Her smile,
gently showing that all are but one.
Goddess Shakti, ever-blissful,
how divine Her grace.
Blessing the many that come,
She is taking their pain as Her own.
Guiding every soul to freedom
in Her sweet embrace.

Pure is the joy that She gives
in Her wisdom supreme and divine.
She reveals the goal of life to those who look within.

PLEASE GIVE ME REFUGE

(DEVI SHARANAM)

Please give me refuge oh Mother Divine.
Do not forsake me, most cherished One of mine.
The gods declare Thee the energy supreme.
Sing praises to Thee, the heavenly Queen.

Oh Universal Mother, Embodiment of Truth,
Thou art the light and darkness,
Thou art both age and youth.
The world's duality is unified within Thee.
Thine is the only form I can see.

**I pray the pure and radiant form of Thine,
will live inside my heart and there forever shine.
Please bless me with the taste not of fortune or
fame,
But the bliss of always repeating Thy name.**

**Please let me see Thy light ever before my eyes.
Consider me Thy servant and remain in my mind.
While Thou art omniscient, I am ignorant still.
Hou can this helpless one follow Thy will ?**

**How many universes have been created by Thee ?
Millions of living beings are but waves in Thy sea.
The wondrous mystery of this perfect creation,
allows all beings to someday be free.**

**When each one realizes that life is naught but
Thee,
detachment from the world will come so easily.
Like actors in a play when the last curtain closes,
they'll end the masquerade and merge into Thee.**

**Remover of illusion, I take refuge in Thee.
Attachment and aversion just lead to misery.
Protect me from sorrow, my Divine Mother Devi.
Oh Ruler of the World I bow at Thy feet.**

THERE IS NO NEED TO SPEAK

(ELLAM ARIYUNNA)

**There is no need to speak in words
to the Divine Mother.**

Forever Mother will be walking beside us,
always seeing, and understanding.

All thoughts that dwell within the innermost self,
are not a secret from the Supreme One.

In truth all things that we do or say
are an expression of the Divine Self.

The Supreme power dwells in all,
and all are dwelling in Her.

May we remember to worship with joy,
the Divine Embodiment of Awareness and Truth.

FAITH BE MY COMPANION

Faith be my companion,
stay beside me all through the night.
Never let me be without You.
Be my guiding light.

Truth reveal Your beauty.
You're the essence of all I see.
Fill my mind with perfect wisdom.
Teach me to be free.

Grace, You bring salvation,
pure compassion in every form.
Melt away my sorrows like the sun after a storm.

Peace, You are my refuge.
Like a gentle rain, You cool my mind.
Let me rest within the silence I have longed to find.

**Love, You're like a fragrance,
giving sweetness to everything.
You're the reason for rejoicing,
You're the reason I sing.**

**Faith be my companion,
stay beside me all through the night.
Never let me be without You.
Be my guiding light.
Be my guiding light, Amma, be my guiding light.**

**Truth, reveal Your beauty.
You are the essence of all I see.
Fill my mind with perfect wisdom.
Teach me to be free.
Teach me to be free, Amma, teach me to be free.**

**Grace, You bring salvation,
pure compassion is Your Form.
Melt away my sorrows like the sun after a storm,
Sun after a storm, Amma, sun after a storm.**

**Peace, you are my refuge.
Like rain, you cool my mind.
Let me rest within the silence I have longed to find.
I have longed to find, Amma, I have longed to find.**

**Love, the sweetest fragrance,
you give me everything.
You're the reason for rejoicing,
you're the reason I sing.
You're the reason I sing.
Amma, you're the reason I sing.**

Be my guiding light. Teach me to be free.
You're the reason I sing.

HOW CAN I EXPRESS MY LOVE?

How can I express my love for You,
Mother of the universe?
What words can I offer You
when You know my every thought?
Amma, I love You so much.
I yearn to feel Your touch in my heart, in my heart.

How can I express my gratitude, Mother of the universe?
What can I offer You that's not already Yours?
Amma, thank You so much for giving me
Your touch in my life, in my life.

Help me dedicate to You, Mother of the universe,
everything I think or say or do,
every moment of my life.
Amma, I need You so much.
May I always remember Your your touch
in my heart, in my heart,
Holy Mother of the Universe.

MOTHER, YOUR WILL IS THE SOURCE

(ICHAMAYI)

Mother, Your will is the source of the universe,
All that occurs is Your Divine play.

We foolish ones think we act on our own, Amma
You are the power behind all we do.

You are the One who creates and destroys again,
She who forms maya then sweeps it away.

Only with Grace can we carry these burdens,
Filled with Your love we abandon all fear.

Mother You serve us the fruits of our actions,
Sweet they may be, or so bitter and hard.

I am the carriage, You are the Driver,
I am the house, Amma, You dwell within.

Mother, I pray to surrender my life to You,
laying my will at Your holy feet.

A FRAGRANCE IN THE DARK

(IRUL TINGI)

In my heart I look for You, a fragrance in the dark.
O have I lost the honey; the sweetness of your love?
And the blossom that You placed so deep inside of me, Amma, weeps in silence for your grace to warm me in your light.

Was I born to cry out for You,
Mother of my soul, Amma?
I am yearning for true meaning
and a path that's clear.
I wonder if it's fate that brings me close to You?
Yes, I can rest and be content
that You are guiding me.

How do I know where to send my prayer
to reach your door, Amma?
If I whisper through my tears,
will you be there to hear?
But can I trust and open to receive your care?
Still, through the fire of devotion,
I'll reach out to You.

Is it true that there is peace and bliss
within your arms, Amma?
I have seen the comfort in the eyes of those You hold.
Please help me to surrender all my misery.
Even that which I have hidden from my deepest memory.

WONDROUS GODDESS

(ISHWARI JAGADISHWARI)

Wondrous Goddess, precious Goddess,
giver of the gift of Grace,
lighting fires of liberation,
please rid me of these many sorrows.

With its pleasures and its troubles,
I have seen this wordly life.
Must I suffer like the moths,
who blindly fly into the fire's glow?

Trying to reach the destination, tragically
I am standing still. Anchored by the fear of death,
I am battered by the winds of desire.

I am pleading for Thy Grace to hold me firmly
on the path. Mother who destroys all misery,
please remove this burden of sorrow.

What the eyes can see today,
by tomorrow will not be there.
Clouded by illusion's veil,
what is real quietly remains.

Humbly I ask in prayer to know the fruit
of human birth. Merciful and radiant Goddess,
I will lovingly bow at Thy Feet.

O MIND, BECOME SURRENDERED

(MANASE NĪN SVANTAMAYI)

O mind, become surrendered,
allow only truth to be your friend.
Nobody belongs just to you, no one is your own.

Round and round this world you wander,
not seeing the reason why you're here.
By doing such meaningless actions,
you cannot escape.

As you listen to the praises of those who admire all you do, remember life passes quickly like leaves on a stream.
After being celebrated, this body that carries you from birth will be an abandoned dwelling, forsaken by life.

On and on you struggle bravely,

fulfilling desires of those you love.
You sacrifice everything for them, in
cluding your life.

Even those who love you dearly cannot stay beside you after death. Your body they found so attractive now scares them away.

Captured in the snare of maya,
you're traveling a road that has no end.
Remember the Divine Mother,
repeating Her Name.

Leaving behind all desires,
join in the eternal dance of bliss,
by singing to Mother Kali, Kali Mata.

MOTHER OF ALL

Mother of All, Mother of All,
Amma, Mother of All.
I am your child, You have answered my call.

Caught by desire, often I fall,
yet You've never forsaken me, Mother of All.
No, You have never forsaken me, Mother of All.

Round this wheel of illusion,
through each trial that I face,
I feel You protecting me, keeping me safe.
I feel You protecting me, keeping me safe.

MOTHER OF LOVE

(ANPIYANNAMBA)

Mother of love pouring out Your smile
like a sweet rain of honey on me,
please take my darkness away,
come into my heart, Amma stay inside me.

You are the one in my mind, Oh Mother—
I'm constantly thinking of You,
eternal bliss and compassion
and beauty embodied, I'm bowing to You.

Opening up my heart wide,
as always I'm waiting inside there for You.
Bring Your light into my heart,
O bright-shining Goddess, with eyes lotus-blue.

Forever searching for love,
Amma—I was yearning for You to appear,
searching so far and so wide;
at last I became weak, and cried in despair.

No tears are left in my eyes,
for I am unable to cry anymore.
Mother I feel all my sins,
they're buring me deep down to my very core.

Please take this bondage and pain,
O Amma—please fill me with love nectar sweet.
Mother of Love, take this heart;
and make it a footrest for Thy Holy Feet.

COME CHILDREN, LEAVE ALL YOUR SORROW

(OMKARA DIVYA PORULE II)

**Come children, leave all your sorrow.
Find the truth that is dwelling within you.
Om is the essence of all you are searching for,
Om is you own true nature. Om. Om. Om. Om.**

**Sacred are words of the Mother,
in Her voice there is wisdom so tender.
She knows that you are the essence of love divine,
She has forever been with you.**

**Weary of feeling so lonely,
seek your refuge in oneness of spirit.
When you remember the many are really one,
darkness will vanish forever.**

**Always remember the teachings
that your Mother Divine has provided.
Bravely you'll face all the struggles that life can bring,
reaching the goal that you cherish.
Know that your mind is a burden,
it will steal your faith with its reason.
Treasure a heart that is pure and is innocent,
there you will see truth is shining.**

**Sharing your love and your kindness,
you can heal the wounds of the lonely.
Carry the lantern of peace for the world to see,**

lighting the path of freedom.

Be not deceived by the wonders
that this world of illusion will offer.
Joy turns to sadness and pleasure will turn to pain,
only the truth is unchanging.

Slowly your Mother will free you
from this prision of thoughts and of ego.
Leading the way through the fire of worldliness,
holding your hand She will guide you.

OPEN MY HEART

Help me to open my heart to You,
losing myself I will melt into your arms.
Allow me to feel the peace of surrender,
filled with the joy of your love.

I feel such emptiness when You are far away.
Sadly I sit like a bird that cannot fly.
If I could behold your sweet form right inside me,
I'd never be lonely again.

Searching for happiness I've traveled many roads,
some have been joyful and some were full of pain.
Only when You hold me can I start believing
pure love can never go away.

Living in illusion I don't know what to feel.
If this is dreaming, why is the pain so real?
When will You give me a glimpse of the freedom
I've waited so long to see?

I am a prisioner of doubt and of fear,
bound like a slave on a boat I cannot steer.
How long must I sail on this sea of confusion
before You will carry me ashore ?

Mother, only You know the secrets of my heart,
only your eyes see the yearning in my soul.
Only to your ears can I tell all my sorrows,
knowing that you will always hear

IN THIS NIGHT FILLED WITH BLUE MOONLIGHT

(PRANESHWARA)

In this night filled with blue moonlight
In this night, with all my tears I made you a garland
and I am eagerly awaiting to adorn you.
Giridhari, I am awaiting you, Vanamali O.

In the silent quarter of the night,
the goddess presiding over night is sleeping
Am I the only one intently waiting
to hear the jingling of the anklets on your feet?
Giridhari, I am awaiting you, Vanamali O.

YOU ARE CREATION

(SRISHTIYUM NIYE)

You are creation, You are creator,
You are the breath of life in all nature.

Devi, this universe begins and ends in You.
Yours is the power supreme, the highest truth.

You are within my heart, You are in all names and forms.
You are the rhythm of life, the ocean of bliss.
Divine, Divine, Mother Divine.

TEACH ME THE LANGUAGE

Teach me the language of Your heart
Only Your love will bring peace inside me.

Teach me the language of Your smile
Looking at you all my sorrows vanish.

Teach me language of Your voice
Help me to speak only words of kindness.

Teach me the language of Your eyes
Deep in Your gaze is the Truth I long for.

Teach me the language of Your light
Feeling Your strength I will fear no darkness.

Teach me the language of Your touch
Please let me stay in Your arms forever.

Teach me the language of Your heart
Only Your love will bring peace inside me.

Promise me that You will always guide me,
I need to know You are right beside me.
Teach me the language of Your heart.

YOU MEAN EVERYTHING TO ME

**As a child needs a mother,
as a seed grows beside the tree,
deep inside I long to tell You,
You mean everything to me.**

**From the rainfall comes the river,
from the river comes the sea,
all I need is to look upon You,
You mean everything to me.**

**As the valley has the mountain
watching over it silently,
I am grateful for Your presence,
You mean everything to me.**

**When the wind is full of sorrow,
there are souls longing to be free,
like the moon shining through the darkness,
You mean everything to me.**

**In the thunder lies a warning,
now awaken from the dream,
You're the fire of my yearning,
You mean everything to me.**

**In my heart I hear You calling,
You are holding my destiny,
on the path to eternal freedom,
You mean everything to me.**

Ślokas and mantras

AMṚTEŚVARI MANGALAM

amṛteśvari mangalam
praṇamatām muktiprade maṅgalam
bhuvaneśvari mangalam
sukṛtinām ekāśraye mangalam
hṛdayeśvari mangalam
hṛdilasa tejo mayi mangalam
mṛdu bhāṣiṇi mangalam
vijayatām prema kṛtē mangalam (3x)

O Amriteshwari, may there be auspiciousness, O bestower of Liberation of those who surrender to You, may there be auspiciousness. O Goddess of the universe, may there be auspiciousness. O Mother, the sole refute of the noble hearted, may there be auspiciousness.

O Goddess of the Heart, may there be auspiciousness. O Effulgent One who shines in the heart, may there be auspiciousness. O Mother who speaks softly, may there be auspiciousness. Victory unto you, the embodiment of Love; may there be auspiciousness.

ANANTA SAMSĀRA

ananta samsāra samūdra tāra-
naukāyi tābhyām guru āktidābhyam
vairāgya sāmrājya dapūja nābhyām
namo namaḥ śrī guru pādukābhyām

My prostrations to Sri Guru's Sandals (Padukam), which serve s the boat to cross this endless ocean of samsara, which endow one with devotion to the Guru, and which grace one with the valuable kingdom of renunciation.

kavitva vārāśi niśāka rābhyām
daurbhāgya dāvām buda mālikābhyām
durikṛtā-namra vipattati-bhyām
namo namaḥ śrī guru pādukābhyām

My prostrations to Sri Guru's Sandals, which serve as the down pour of water to put out the fire of misfortunes, which remove the groups of distresses of those who prostrate to them.

natā yāyoḥ śrī patitām samīyūḥ
kadāci-dapyāśu daridra varyāḥ
mūkāśca vācas-patitām hitābhyām
namo namaḥ śrī guru pādukābhyām

My prostrations to Sri Guru's Sandals, adoring which the worst poverty stricken, have turned out to be great possessors of wealth, and even the mutes have turned out to be great masters of speech.

nālīka nīkāśa padā hṛtābhyām
nānā vimohādyi nivāri-kābhyām
namajjanā-bhiṣṭatati pradābhyām
namo namaḥ śrī guru pādukābhyām

My prostrations to Sri Guru's Sandals, which remove all kinds of ignorant desires, and which fulfill in plenty, the desires of those who bow their heads tot hem.

nṛpāli mauli vrajaratna kānti-
saridvi-rājajjha-ṣakanya-kābhyam
nṛpā-tvadābhyām natalo-kapamṅkte-
namo namaḥ śrī guru pādukābhyām

My prostrations to Sri Guru's Sandals, which shine like the precious stones that adorn the crown of kings, by bowing to which one drowned in worldliness will be lifted up to the great rank of sovereignty.

pāpānda-kārārkka-paranpar-ābhyām
tāpa-trayā-hīndra khageśvar-ābhyām
jāḍhyābdhi samśoṣa-nabādav-ābhyām
namo namaḥ śrī guru pādukābhyām

My prostrations to Sri Guru's Sandals, which serve as the sun smashing all the illusions of sins, which are like garuda birds in front of the serpents of the three pains of samsara, and which are like the terrific fire that dries away the ocean of Jadatha or insentience.

samā-diṣaṭka prada vaibhavābhyam
samādi dānavra-tadīkṣi tābhyām
modavāmghri sthira bhakti tābhyām
namo namaḥ śrī guru pādukābhyām

My prostrations to Sri Guru's Sandals, which endows one with the six attributes which can bless with permanent devotion at the feet of the Lord Rama and which is initiated with the vow of charity and self-settledness.

svārccā-parāṇāma dhileṣṭa dābhyām
svāhāsa hāyākṣa duranda rābhyām
svāntā-ccabhāva pradapūja-nābhyām
namo namaḥ śrī guru pādukābhyām

My prostrations to Sri Guru's Sandals, which bestows all the wishes of those who are absorbed in the Self, and which grace with one's own hidden real nature.

kāmādi arppavra-jagāru dābhyām
vileka vairāgya nidhi pradābhyām
bodha pradābhyam druta mokṣa dābhyām
namo namaḥ śrī guru pādukābhyām

My prostrations to Sri Guru's Sandals, which are like garudas to all the serpents of desires, and which bless with the valuable treasure of discrimination and renunciation, which enlighten wit bodha – true knowledge, and bless with instant liberation form the shackles of the world.

namo namaḥ śrī guru pādukābhyām

LOKAḤ SAMASTAḤ SUKHINO

lokaḥ samastaḥ sukhino bhavantū
lokaḥ samastaḥ sukhino bhavantū
lokaḥ samastaḥ sukhino bhavantū
om śanti śanti śantiḥ
oṁ śrī gurubhyo namaḥ hariḥ oṁ

Let the whole world be happy. (3x). Om peace, peace, peace. Om salutations to Sri Guru.

NA KARMAṆĀ NA PRAJAYĀ

Na karmaṇā na prajayā dhanena
tyāgenaike amṛta tvamānaśuḥ
pareṇa nākam nihitam guhāyām
vibhrājate yadyatayo viśanti

Neither by actions, nor by (acquiring) progeny and wealth, but by renunciation alone is immortality attained. (That Supreme State) is far beyond the highest heaven, and the sages perceive it, hidden in the cave of the heart, shining brilliantly therein.

vedānta vijñāna suniścitārthāḥ
samnyāsa yogadyataya śuddha sattvāḥ
te brahma lokeṣu parānta kāle
parāmṛtāh parimucyanti sarve

(Those) sages, who have a clear understanding of the principles of Vedanta, who have purified themselves by means of the yoga of renunciation, and who are (thus) established in the state of supreme beatitude, are totally liberated in Brahman at the time of dissolution of the body.

dharam vipāpam parameśma bhūtam
yad pundarīkam puramadhya sagastham
tatrāpi dahram gaganam viśokam
tasmin ya dantastatu pāsidavyam

Located in the center of the city of the body is the subtle lotus of the heart, pure and untainted, which is the abode of the Supreme. Meditate on the Supreme Being residing in that inner expanse, which is subtle and free from sorrow.

yo vedādau svara proktah vedānte ca pratīṣtitaha
tasya prakṛti līnasya yah paraḥssa maheśvaraḥ

That which is described as the Primal Sound (OM) in the beginning of the Vedas, has been fully established as the Supreme Truth at the end of the Vedas (the Upanishads). The One who realizes that Supreme Principle is beyond the pale of those totally immersed in physical realities. Indeed, He is none other than the Supreme Lord!

na tatra suryo bhāti na candra tārakam
nemā vidyuto bhānti kutoyam agniḥ
tameva bhāntam anubhāti sarvam
tasya bhāsa sarvam idam vibhāti

There the sun does not shine, nor do the moon and the stars. These streaks of lighting do not shine there either, (so) what to speak of this fire? That, shining, makes all other shine. By virtue of its luminosity, all these (manifestations) are illuminated.

YĀ DEVĪ SARVA BHŪTEṢU

yā devī sarva bhūteṣu
viśṇu māyeti śabditā
namastasyai namastasyai
namastasyai namo namaḥ

Salutations again and again to the Goddess who in all beings is called Vishnumaya.

yā devī sarva bhūteṣu
cetanetya-bhidhīyate
namastesyai namastesyai
namastesyai namo namaḥ

We prostrate before Her who is at once exceedingly gentle and exceedingly terrible; we salute Her again and again. Salutations to Her who is the support of the world. Salutations to the Goddess who is the form of volition.

yā devī sarva bhūteṣu
buddhi rūpena samsthitā
namastesyai namastesyai
namastesyai namo namaḥ

Salutations to the Goddess who resides in all beings as intelligence.

nidrā (sleep)
kṣudhā (hunger)
chāyā (reflection)
śakti (power)
tṛṣna (thirst)
kśanti (patience)
jāti (birth)
lajjā (modesty)
śanti (peace)
ṣraddha (faith)
kānti (loveliness)
lakṣmī (good fortune)
vṛtti (activity)
smṛti (memory)
dayā (compassion)
tuṣṭi (contentment)
mātṛ (mother)
bhrānti (error)

indriyanā madhiṣṭhatrī
bhūtānām cakhileṣu yā
bhūteṣu satatam tasyai
vyāptidevyai namo namaḥ

Salutations to the Goddess who constantly presides over the senses of all beings and governs all the elements.

Index of Bhajans Volume 3

Adharam madhuram III-8
Ādi divya jyōti mahā III-10
Ādimūla param jyōti III-10
Ādyamāy amma darśanam III-12
Ajam nirvikalpam III-13
Akatāril arivinte III-14
Akhila māṇamma III-15
Ālaya maṇiōsai kēkkudammā III-16
Amba bhavāni nin ambhōja III-17
Ambāṭi kaṇṇā III-18
Ambē mā jagadambē mā III-20
Ambikē jagadīśvarī III-21
Ammāvai pārkka pōkalām III-22
Ammayē kaṇḍu ñān III-23
Ammē agādhamāy III-24
Ammē ammē amṛtānandamayī III-25
Amme amritānandamayī III-26
Amṛta padattil anaykkuka III-28
Amṛta rūpiṇi III-29
Amṛtamayī ānandamayi III-30
Amṛtānandamayi sadguru mama janani III-31
Amṛtēśi diśatu saukhyam III-32
Amṛteśvari ammē sukṛteśvari III-33
Amṛtēśvari jagadīśvari III-34
Amṛtēśvari mā amṛtēśvari III-36
Amṛtēśvari susmita III-37
Amṛtēśvari vandanam III-38
Ānanda rūpiṇi ammē enikku III-40
Anārā vinārā III-41
Annaikku nīrāṭṭa vēṇṭum III-42
Anpiyannamba III-44

Anpum aruḷum	III-46
Anutāpam vaḷarunnu	III-47
Arivukkum arivāna	III-48
Arivum abhayavum	III-49
Ārōtu collitum	III-50
Āṭiṭuvōm nāmum āṭiṭuvōm	III-51
Āvō mērē nandalāl	III-52
Bahut tarasā	III-53
Bhajō rē bhajō	III-54
Brahma murari	III-55
Cinna cinna	III-57
Darśanam ambikē mōhanam	III-59
Dē darśan mā dēvī	III-60
Dēvī mātē	III-61
Dēvī ninne kaṇi kaṇṭiṭṭu	III-62
Dīnatāriṇi durita vāriṇi	III-62
Ēkāsrayamām amma	III-64
Ellam ariyunnar amme	III-65
Entinu śōkam manassē	III-66
Gajamukha gajamukha	III-67
Gam gaṇapatayē namō namaḥ	III-67
Ganēśa namaḥ ōm	III-69
Girijāsuta ṣaṇmukha	III-69
Gōpa bālaka gōkulēśvara	III-71
Gōpāla kṛṣṇā giridhāri	III-72
Gōpī gōpāla vēṇu gōpāla	III-73
Govinda damodara	III-74
Gōvindam gōpāla	III-74
Guru caraṇam sadguru	III-74
Guru dēva	III-75
Gurukṛpā añjan pāyō	III-76
Guruvaṭivānavaḷē	III-77
Guruvāyūr appā tuṇa nīyē	III-78
Har har mahādēv śiva śiva	III-79

Harāya jaya III-80
Harē kṛṣṇa kṛṣṇā III-81
Hari om namo nārāyaṇaya III-82
Hē gōvind hē gōpāl uddhara III-82
He prabhū tū ānanda dātā III-83
Hṛdaya mandākini III-84
Īśvara līla yitellām III-85
Jai jagadambē durgē mā III-86
jai mā ambe jai mā ambe III-87
Jai mā jai jai mā III-88
Jananī tava pada malarukalil III-90
Japa japa ammā ammā III-91
Jaya jagadambē jaya jaya mā III-92
Jaya jaya bhaya bhañjini III-93
Jaya jaya dēvī dayāla hari III-94
Jaya muralīdhara mādhavā III-95
Jaya paramēśvari jagadambē III-96
Jayatu jayatu sadguru III-98
Jhilam jhilam III-99
Jis hāl mē III-101
Jyōtir māyi mā III-102
Kahā hō kanhā III-102
Kāḷi mā jai jai mā III-103
Kāḷikē dēvī amṛteśvari III-104
Kāḷikē śyāma candrikē III-105
Kalyāna kṛṣṇa kaminīya III-106
Kamalē karuṇārdra mānasē III-106
Kanḍrukal mēytiṭa vantāy III-108
Kanivin kaṭākṣam III-109
Kanivuṭayōn kaṇṇan III-110
Kañjalōcanē III-111
Kaṇṇā tāmara kaṇṇā III-112
Kaṇṇunīr vārnnu III-113
Kartturāñjayā prāpy III-114

Karuna sindho bhairavi	III-115
Karuṇāmayī hṛdayeśvarī	III-117
Karuṇāmayī kanivu tūkaṇē	III-118
Kāruṇya dhāmamē ammē	III-119
Kārvarṇṇane karuṇāmayane	III-121
Kaṭalōram tavam	III-122
Kattīṭukammē ī kōmaḷa	III-122
Kēḷkkātta bhāvam	III-124
Kṣaṇam ennu vanniṭum	III-124
Kūriruḷ pōle	III-126
Mā nām bōlē dil sē	III-127
Mā oh meri mā	III-129
Māheśvarī rāja rājēśvarī	III-130
Manamōhana kṛṣṇa	III-132
Mānasa malaril	III-132
Mandahāsa vadanē	III-133
Māṇikkyacilaiyē	III-134
Mātā māheśvari	III-135
Mātṛ vātsalya	III-136
Maunattil iruntu	III-138
Mayilontru āṭutu	III-140
Mōhana muraḷi mōhitamen	III-142
Mṛdula nīla kaḷēbarā	III-143
Mṛtyuñjayāya namaḥ ōm	III-144
Mujhē darśan dō bhagavān	III-145
Namō bhūtanāthā namō	III-145
Namō namastē mātaḥ sarasvatī	III-146
Ñān śollum mantiram	III-147
Nanda nandanā	III-148
Nanda nandanā harē	III-149
Ninne piriyunna	III-151
Nizhalinte pinnāle	III-152
Ōm amṛteśvariyai namaḥ	III-154
Ōm bhadra kāḷi	III-155

Ōm jagad jananī dēvī mātā	III-155
Ōmkāra divya porūle viii	III-156
Ōmkāra divya porūle x	III-167
Ōmkāra divya porūle xi	III-178
Onnu tiriññiṅgu nōkkaṇē	III-189
Oru koccu kuññinte	III-190
Oru koccu pulnāmbin	III-191
Oru maṇal taripōlum	III-193
Oru nimiṣam eṅkilum	III-194
Oru piṭi dḥukhattin	III-195
Oru piṭi snēham tiraññū	III-196
Pāhimurarē pāvana caritā	III-197
Pālana parāyaṇi amṛtēśvari	III-198
Paṅkilamām en manassu	III-199
Pannaga bhūṣaṇa parama	III-200
Parama pāvana vadanē	III-201
Pariśuddha snēhatte	III-202
Pāṭīṭum ammē āṭīṭum	III-203
Pāṭupeṭṭēre ñān	III-204
Pāśāṅkuśa dhara	III-205
Praneśvara giridhāri	III-206
Prapañcattin okkeyum	III-207
Rādhā mādhava gōpāla	III-208
Rādhaye tōzhare	III-208
Rādhe kṛṣṇa	III-210
Rādhē rādhē gōvinda	III-211
Rādhe śyām	III-212
Rādhē śyām rādhē śyām	III-213
Rādhikēśa yadunātha	III-214
Rāma rāma jaya rāma	III-215
Rāmacandra mahā prabhō	III-215
Rāmakṛṣṇa harē	III-216
Rāvēre nīṇṭupōy	III-217
Sādaram bhajicciṭunnu	III-218

Sadguruvāy vantutitta	III-219
Sakalāgama samstutē	III-220
Sanātanī sangīta	III-221
Santāpa śāntikkāy	III-222
Sapta svara rūpiṇi	III-223
Śaraṇam kāḷi śaraṇam	III-223
Śarīram surūpam	III-224
Sarva carācara jananīm	III-227
Sarva mangaḷe	III-229
Siṅkāra kāvaṭiyil	III-231
Sirmē mayūr mukuṭa dharē	III-232
Sita rām rādhe śyam	III-233
Śiva nandanā sundara	III-233
Śiva śiva śiva śiva sadā śiva	III-235
Śōkam itentinu sandhyē	III-236
Śrī hari varumī	III-237
Śrī lalitāmbikē sarvaśaktē	III-238
Śrī rāma jaya rāma	III-249
Śrī rāma raghu rāma	III-251
Śubha vidhāyaka	III-253
Śyām gōpālā mājhā	III-255
Sunlē pukār	III-256
Svāmī śaranam ayappa	III-257
Talarnn urangukayō	III-258
Tārāpathaṅgaḷē	III-259
Tātan aviṭunnu ñaṅgaḷ makkaḷ	III-260
Tēnmazhayāka untan	III-261
Tēṭi unnai ṣaraṇaṭaintōm	III-263
Tuyarang kaḷai kūrum	III-264
Uḷḷam urukutayyā murukā	III-265
Uḷḷil tuḷumbunna mantra	III-266
Vandanam nitya vandanam	III-267
Vandē vēda mātaram	III-268
Vāṇīmaṇī mātē	III-269

Vāzhiya enṭrum vāzhiyavē	III-271
Verum oru pulkkoṭi	III-272
Viharati yamunā taṭmē	III-272
Vinati hamāri tūne suni	III-273
Vinati suno vinati suno	III-274
Viṣādamākavē	III-274
Viśva mānava	III-275
Viṭarātta tāmara	III-276
Viṭhalā hari viṭhalā	III-277
Vrajavana kuñjavihārī	III-278
Vṛndāvana kuñjāśrita	III-279
Vṛndāvana rāji pūttu	III-280
Vṛndāvanattile sakhimāre	III-281
Yatha yariyiykkān	III-283
Vyathayuraññu	III-284
Yamunā tīra vihārī	III-285
Amma can you hear me?	III-286
Oh my divine mother	III-287
Amritanandamayi, Holy Mother	III-287
Please give me refuge	III-288
There is no need to speak	III-289
Faith be my companion	III-290
How can I express my love?	III-292
Mother, Your will is the source	III-292
A fragrance in the dark	III-293
Wondrous goddess	III-294
O mind, become surrendered	III-295
Mother of all	III-296
Mother of love	III-297
Come children, leave all your sorrow	III-298
Open my heart	III-299
In this night filled with blue moonlight	III-300
You are creation	III-300
Teach me the language	III-301

You mean everything to me III-302
Amṛteśvari mangalam III-303
Ananta samsāra III-303
Lokaḥ samastaḥ sukhino III-306
Na karmaṇā na prajayā III-306
Yā devī sarva bhūteṣu III-308

www.ingramcontent.com/pod-product-compliance
Lightning Source LLC
Chambersburg PA
CBHW070137100426
42743CB00013B/2733
* 9 7 8 1 6 8 0 3 7 0 2 3 2 *